PHILOSOPHY
AS
DIPLOMACY

PHILOSOPHY AS DIPLOMACY:

ESSAYS IN ETHICS AND POLICY-MAKING

A. Pablo Iannone

HUMANITIES PRESS
New Jersey

First published 1994 by Humanities Press International, Inc.,
Atlantic Highlands, New Jersey 07716.

© 1994 by A. Pablo Iannone

Library of Congress Cataloging-in-Publication Data

Iannone, A. Pablo.
　　Philosophy as diplomacy : essays in ethics and policy making / A.
Pablo Iannone.
　　　　p.　　cm.
　　Includes bibliographical references and index.
　　ISBN 0-391-03808-7
　　1. Policy sciences—Moral and ethical aspects.　I. Title.
H97.I16　1993
174′.932—dc20　　　　　　　　　92-39814
　　　　　　　　　　　　　　　　CIP

A catalog record for this book is available from the British Library.

Printed in the United States of America

To my wife, Mary Kay Garrow, whose wealth of policy-making experience provided an everyday touchstone for this book's ideas, and to our daughters, Alejandra Emilia and Catalina Patricia, whose joy of life and incipient love of learning provided an everyday touchstone for this book's aspirations.

Contents

So far as morals go, there probably has never been an age quite so perplexed and torn by discord as the present one, or so little disposed to be submissive to the admonition of the good and great; and the reason is that for large numbers of people the things valued in the past have lost their motive power, and no one seems to know just how to go to work to replace them.

—A. K. Rogers, *Ethics and Moral Tolerance*

Preface

It has been said that life is like a foreign language: Everyone mispronounces it. This book grew from the realization that the analogy tellingly applies to policy-making. It obviously applies when different societies or cultures are involved, but it also applies within comparatively homogeneous cultures or social groups, for example, within the United States or within Western Europe. That it does is evidenced by the lack of integration between the languages, concepts, methods, and practices of the branches of inquiry and the institutions relevant to policy-making. These include political science, sociology, economics, technology and business studies, and philosophy, as well as the academic institutions connected with them. The fragmentation, however, reaches outside academia, to the relations between the studies and academic institutions on the one hand and governmental institutions on the other. Indeed, partly because modern societies have become enormously complex and modern technology has become extremely esoteric, the fragmentation has reached an unprecedented degree in the relations between all of the said studies and institutions and the public at large.

Such fragmentation constitutes a significant obstacle to politically sound and morally sensitive policy-making. This book is designed to help correct the situation by attaining two objectives. The first is to achieve greater integration between the languages, concepts, and methods of the social sciences and technology and business studies and institutions, those of ethics and sociopolitical philosophy, and those of the policy-making community, in a manner reasonably accessible to the general public. The second objective is to outline an approach for dealing, in a politically sound and morally sensitive manner, with policy-making problems that arise in this fragmented situation. The book builds on work carried out in my previous *Contemporary Moral Controversies in Technology* (Oxford, 1987) and *Contemporary Moral Controversies in Business* (Oxford, 1989). These provided evidence for the said lack of integration and began to help correct the situation in the areas of business and technology. In doing so, they outlined a theoretical framework that combines rights, consequences, and pragmatic considerations. This framework is substantially developed in the present book.

In developing this framework, the book also develops a conception of philosophy as diplomacy. This conception has been rarely, if at all, discussed by philosophers. It applies primarily to ethics and sociopolitical philosophy, but it also has applications to other areas of philosophy. One reason this concept has such a wide scope of application is that there is no sharp line separating ethics and sociopolitical philosophy from other areas of philosophy such as epistemology and the philosophy of science. Another reason is that the conception of philosophy as diplomacy paradigmatically applies to policy- and decision-making in institutional contexts, and, in the twentieth century, such policy-making is involved in the practice of all or nearly all philosophy, regardless of school or tradition.

The notion of philosophy as diplomacy is discussed throughout the book, especially in Essay 6. However, since the term *diplomacy* has various senses, some of which have acquired derogatory implications, some indication of the sense in which I use *diplomacy* in this book is necessary. As I further explain in Essay 6, by diplomacy I do not mean, as cynics would have it, the activity of saying and doing the nastiest things in the nicest way. Rather, I mean the activity of dealing with relations between groups or individuals so that ill does not prevail. In this activity, social decision procedures are crucial. They range from those that primarily appeal to reason and involve meaningful dialogue, such as discussion of merits and negotiation, to others that are primarily confrontational, such as strikes and other pressure tactics. A concern with the policy-making role and justification of all these social decision procedures plays a central role in this book.

As indicated, the book is primarily concerned with policy-making, that is, with a characteristically forward-looking activity. It is not designed (though it may also be of use) to explain or pass judgment on social change, its history, or any of its stages. No doubt, these are intellectually valid enterprises, and their results are relevant to the present study. Precedents and recurrent circumstances are useful in establishing the feasibility of policy and decision options. However, in and of themselves, those studies are primarily backward-looking—not, like this book, aimed at the future.

In accordance with the book's integrative purpose, its primary (though not exclusive) method of research and presentation is one that has been used in both philosophy and social process studies. It consists in merging description and argument. That is, it describes a number of cases or observations to exemplify categories, classifications, and theories and then uses the same or similar cases or observations as evidence for the utility or accuracy of the categories, classifications, and theories. This method is current in social science. For example, Lewis Anthony Dexter has recently used and described it in his "Intra-Agency Politics: Conflict and Contravention in Administrative Entities."[1] It is also current in philosophy among philosophers who practice conceptual analysis but move beyond that method, in an attempt to connect the results of scientific research and the experiences of the general public with the theoretical aims of ethics and sociopolitical philosophy. A recent work that exemplifies this approach is David Bray-brooke's *Meeting Needs*.[2]

The methodological approach just described is justified on both philosophical and social science grounds. From a philosophical standpoint, a sound moral assessment of policies and decisions depends on the establishment of a morally sensitive characterization and classification of the problems the policies and decisions address. One might think that this is the type of study social scientists, not philosophers, would pursue because, as indicated, the method used here relies heavily on the discussion of cases and observations about how policymakers deal with them. However, the said impression is mistaken. Hypotheses and theories in moral philosophy, especially those about policy-making, are significantly confirmed or disconfirmed through their applications. Hence, a concern with cases and observations, and the taxonomy issuing from them, is philosophically crucial.

From a social science standpoint, the characterizations and classifications of cases developed in this book should prove useful. They contribute to structuring the enormous body of available case studies in a manner that is readily applicable to policy- and decision-making. This meets a policy-making as well as a scientific need, for without such characterizations and classifications, the results of these studies remain largely unstructured data—not a body of knowledge applicable to new policy and decision cases. And with inadequate categories and classifications, the applications to policy-making are questionable.

To be sure, taxonomies exist in both social science and philosophy. But their purpose has been geared primarily to the study of social change, its history, and stages, not the moral assessment of policies and decisions. In addition, when concerned with policy-making, various categories and classifications are incomplete and, at times, slanted toward a conflict (or, alternatively, a consensus) model of society. Hence, there is a need for the characterizations and classifications of cases that this book develops.

The book is of interest to the initiated and is reasonably accessible to the uninitiated. Philosophical language and categories are introduced by reference to concrete problems, and the language and categories used in discussions of cases are those used by policymakers and ordinary people. This helps meet the needs of those who are more familiar with the world of political, economic, and other everyday decisions than with that of philosophy. It also helps clarify the extent to which particular positions in moral philosophy have practical applications in the actual policy-making world.

The book is unique, or nearly unique, in that its treatment of theoretical and practical problems is guided by a concern crucial to the integrative approach it develops: a concern with the applicability of theories in ethics and social and political philosophy to actual policy-making practice. I know of few other books that do this with the degree of detail, comprehensiveness, and reliance on empirical information found in this book. First, most books being published in the area of philosophy and policy-making presuppose somewhat simplistic conceptions of policy-making. Second, most of them rely much less on empirical social studies. Third, most of them use primarily, if not exclusively, philosophical language and categories. Hence, they make it difficult, if not impossible, to establish the extent to which the particular positions they take in moral philosophy have practical applications in the actual policy-making world.

In addition, some books in the area have an advocative slant that is betrayed by their disregarding or misconstruing influential traditions in ethics. For example, some characterizations of utilitarianism currently invoked in the philosophy literature are largely preposterous straw men quite unrelated to classical utilitarianism as formulated by Bentham, Mill, and Sidgwick. That they are is no discovery. David Braybrooke mentioned it in his *Ethics in the World of Business*,[3] yet the matter is still to be corrected.

This book, in contrast, is sensitive to ethical traditions. It outlines a theory that is a partial synthesis of consequentialist, deontological, character-based, and pragmatic concerns. Also, the book is in no way an advocacy book though, of course, it is not neutral. In fact, it builds a case for a set of conditions, which are formulated in Essay 8's hypotheses, for dealing with policy-making problems in a politically sound and morally permissible manner.

In addition to this preface, the book consists of twelve essays, twelve short dialogues connecting the essays to each other, a selected bibliography, and an index. The essays are largely self-contained but, taken together, they carry out the book's two primary tasks. The first is largely taxonomical, involving the previously mentioned characterization and classification of cases in a manner that permits greater integration between the social sciences. It consists in describing crucial political, economic, and organizational conditions that constrain the applicability of moral theories to policy-making. Its upshot is one of the book's objectives: to achieve greater integration between the languages, concepts, and methods of the social sciences and technology and business studies and institutions, those of ethics and sociopolitical philosophy, and those of the policy-making community in a manner reasonably accessible to the general public.

The book's second task is primarily normative. It consists in using the said constraints, together with other moral concerns, to formulate hypotheses for dealing with policy-making problems in a politically sound and morally permissible manner. In the process, the book examines the applicability of various theories such as rational choice, decision, game, and social choice to policy-making problems. It also examines the role of various concepts such as objectivity, judgment, decision, moral rules, laws, principles, and social decision procedures as they apply to those problems.

The essays are wide ranging. Some examine traditional positions in moral philosophy as they apply to current policy-making problems. Others discuss recently developed theories and advance equally recent positions. But all are united by their focus on policy-making problems posed about matters of current concern.

Many of these matters are technology related. They include fetal research, new health care technologies and genetic engineering, environmental deterioration and its relation to energy and materials technologies, and high-tech weapons in the post–cold war international order. However, not all the policy problems addressed in the book's essays are prompted by technological developments. Some essays discuss policy-making problems related to such matters as objectivity in news reporting, civil rights, preferential treatment, and abortion.

As always, I accept responsibility for my mistakes, but there would have been many more had I not benefited from the many discussions about philosophy and policy and decision problems I had with teachers, friends, and colleagues for the past two decades. Among these, I owe the greatest thanks to Lewis A. Dexter and David Braybrooke for their encouragement and sound advice at crucial moments in the book's development. Thanks go also to the members of the Department of Philosophy at Dalhousie University, and the visitors present during my 1987 visit, for their comments on an early draft of what is now Essay 11. I also thank my colleagues and former colleagues at Central Connecticut State University, especially David Blitz, Lee Creer, Eleanor Godway, and Judith McBride, for their helpful comments on drafts of what eventually became sections of this book. Special thanks go to Mario Bunge for his encouragement and help and for providing office space and access to McGill University's resources during my 1990 visit. For the comments on topics related to my project that they made, at different times, during the past two decades, I am also grateful to Tom Auxter, Annette Baier, Kurt Baier, Robert J. Baum, Geoff Bryce, Claudia Card, Margaret Carter, Elizabeth Diaz Herrera, Tom Garrow, Patrick W. Hamlett, William Hay, Richard P. Haynes, John Jakovina, Don Kanel, John P. Kavanagh, Susan Levine, Robert B. Louden, María C. Lugones, Jon N. Moline, Tom Simon, Marcus G. Singer, Axel Stern, and Suzanne Stern-Gillet. For their extremely effective library support services, I also thank the staff at the Central Connecticut State University Elihu Burritt Library, especially Emily S. Chasse, Norma Chute, Marie A. Kascus, Barbara Sullivan Meagher, Faith A. Merriman, Joan G. Packer, and June Sapia Welwood. I should also mention and thank the Connecticut State University and the Connecticut Department of Higher Education for providing funds supporting the research that led to this book, the Central Connecticut State University

College of Arts and Sciences for granting reassigned time, the Yale University Libraries for granting the library privileges that gave me access to their priceless resources, and the Department of Philosophy and the Institute for Environmental Studies at the University of Wisconsin-Madison for providing the excellent academic conditions under which the project leading to this book took shape about one and a half decades ago. And I very much thank Keith M. Ashfield, president of Humanities Press, for his editorial sense and encouragement, the project reviewers for their invaluable and detailed comments, Humanities Press's Production Editor, Karen Napolitano Starks, for her patience and sound editorial advice, and all the Humanities Press staff members with whom I had the pleasure of working during the book's planning and production process.

What I owe my wife, Mary Kay Garrow, for her unfaltering encouragement, experienced policy-making comments, and sound editorial suggestions, as in my previous philosophy books, I cannot possibly repay. They were invaluable. As for our daughters, Alejandra Emilia and Catalina Patricia, they have played an essential part in all this by simply being with us, which has filled my life with happiness.

1 Issues and Issue-Overload: A Challenge to Moral Philosophy

There is hardly a matter of policy that is free from controversy today. The list ranges from nuclear energy and environmental deterioration; through genetic engineering, fetal research, and abortion; to preferential treatment in education and business and the international debt. Indeed, it keeps growing at an accelerating pace, prompting greater numbers of increasingly heated discussions, some highly confrontational.

These discussions constitute *issues*, which I define initially as sharp differences of opinions or conflicts of demands, together with what people do to uphold their opinions or satisfy their demands. They are certainly not cool and detached discussions about the matters of concern.[1] This conflictive nature of issues, together with their complexity and sheer multiplicity, poses policy and decision problems over and above those posed by any one issue in isolation. Among these is what I call *issue-overload*. This is a situation in which issues are so many, complex, or intractable that they exceed, or nearly exceed, what ordinary individuals can understand and ordinary societies can handle through the courts, legislation, or executive or other institutional channels as traditionally set up.

In this essay, I focus on issues and issue-overload. That is, I am not concerned with the matters at issue per se. Rather, I focus on the *social facts* of the issues and issue-overload and ask: What type of ethical theory is best suited for dealing with policy and decision problems posed by issues and the fact of issue-overload itself?

THE THESIS

I argue for one main thesis: The ethical theories best suited for dealing with such problems include social decision procedures that go beyond such primarily argumentative ones as discussion of merits and negotiation. These additional procedures range from those that primarily involve appeals to reason and reliance on meaningful dialogue, such as mediation and

1

arbitration, to those that primarily involve tactics, such as manipulation, outflanking, boycotts, and strikes, in which reason and meaningful dialogue are not predominant.[2] Of course, theories of this type do not exclude moral rules, laws, and principles from the process of dealing with problems morally, but these are not their only crucial components. Such theories have a pragmatic component as well.

To take the position just formulated is in no way to hold that the ethical theories best suited for dealing with policy and decision problems are strictly pragmatic. As I argue in this and later essays, they must combine consequentialist, deontological, and pragmatic considerations. This combination makes them sensitive to the various components of actual policy and decision problems, hence preferable to alternative, simplistic theories.

POINTS OF METHOD

In accordance with the book's primary method, I argue for the above thesis by merging description and argument. That is, I describe cases or observations to exemplify certain hypotheses and then use the same or similar cases or observations as evidence for the utility or accuracy of the said hypotheses.[3] In applying this method, I discuss and rely on observations from some notable contributions to the topic of discussion. First, I examine Daniel C. Dennett's "The Moral First Aid Manual."[4] I follow Dennett in holding that the type of theory needed should be sensitive to real time constraints. However, I argue that this should not involve the moral cost of Dennett's suggestion: the undermining of critical scrutiny in ethics.

Second, I discuss Marcus G. Singer's conception of a moral issue as it relates to policy-level shifts. I argue that, though it is a significant contribution to the subject, this conception has four limitations that make it too narrow and unclear for dealing with the entire range of moral problems related to policy- and decision-making about issues. Accordingly, I further refine the definition of *issues* presented at the outset, so that it is free from such limitations. The fact of social conflict, however confrontational it may be, is placed at the center of issues.

Finally, I discuss a central aspect of Habermas's theory: steering away from conflict and making consensus the touchstone of morally acceptable policies and decisions. This discussion involves a critical examination of modifications suggested by Jon Elster. Though largely in agreement with Elster's criticisms, I argue that his suggested alternative does not go far enough. Accordingly, I sketch a theory that is neither simply consequentialist nor simply deontological. It combines both types of considerations and is sensitive to pragmatic constraints. The main components of this theory are further developed in the remainder of the book.

SOME CAUTIONARY REMARKS

This essay's approach may cause impatience among both philosophers and social scientists. Philosophers, eager to reach the thick of philosophical argument, may find it conceptually too sketchy. Social scientists may grow impatient for more than one reason: Those eager to deal empirically and in great detail with particular cases may find the essay too theoretical; those primarily interested in social science discussions may feel that the essay covers ground already adequately covered by their own studies of policy-making's problems in general or of nonethical rational contributions to policy-making. In response, I can only ask for patience and offer a few reasons for the approach taken here.

First and foremost, in this essay, I am not primarily concerned with what is problematic about policy-making generally. Nor am I primarily concerned with nonethical rational contributions to policy-making. These matters are no doubt of interest in social science, and this essay has something to offer toward clarifying them, but their exhaustive elucidation falls outside its scope. The book, however, does address them to some extent in Essays 2 and 3 and, to a lesser extent, in Essays 6, 7, and 12.

Second, what does fall within the scope of this book and, in particular, of this essay, is an introductory discussion of politics and policy as these are relevant to applied ethics. Such a discussion may at times seem trivial to political scientists. I can only suggest that they skip the trivial sections. What I cannot do is omit them. Trivial matters of politics and policy-making need attention in moral philosophy, where *actual* politics and policy-making have often been significantly disregarded.

Throughout, this book emphasizes the fact that whether specific pieces of conduct or policies are permissible (or even required) when dealing with given problems depends on economic, political, and other pragmatic constraints. Such constraints are especially pressing when dealing with problems posed by issues or, as in issue-overload, by their combination. A more detailed examination of the complex case of issue-overload indicates the nature and significance of these constraints and sets the stage for assessing specific moral theories.

ISSUE-OVERLOAD AS MANIFESTED IN COURT-CASE OVERLOAD IN THE UNITED STATES

Issue-overload can manifest itself in a variety of settings, for example, in a judicial or legislative setting. Depending on the setting, issue-overload has some different sources and effects and calls for different remedies. Yet in each setting, certain general features of issue-overload are involved. Here, though I focus on court-case overload, I am concerned with these general features.

In the United States, issue-overload has often—though not exclusively—manifested itself in court-case overload. Evidence and an interpretation of this development were provided by Eugene Kennedy at the end of the 1970s in the *New York Times Magazine*:

> Many social critics have noted with alarm the tendency to use the courts excessively, with judges now running prisons, hospitals and school systems; their decisions replace those of physicians in assaying diagnosis and treatment, they signal if the ball game may be played, if the strike can be held, if the child may receive a certain medical treatment. Then, hundreds of other issues became the courts' business as the nation lost faith in other forms of negotiation and gave the courts power they did not seek, without any guarantee that they could exercise it prudently or effectively over a long period of time.
>
> The 70's were the setting for bringing down on the nation the old Mexican curse, "May your life be filled with lawyers."[5]

One might object that this description provides evidence of litigiousness, imprudence, and burdens on judges and litigants, but no evidence of excessive strain on the U.S. court system, let alone the society. However, there is evidence that such strain has resulted from excessive or misplaced litigiousness. David L. Bazelon, a federal judge who dealt with many issue-related cases over more than three decades, has described how the shift toward litigiousness destabilizes the society in politically and economically significantly ways.[6] Indeed, his views have been echoed by the U.S. Justice Department, the American Bar Association, and business. In mid-1980, they supported a bill encouraging Federal agencies to settle their disputes through mediation rather than litigation. Its purpose was to avoid overload caused by issues such as the eighteen-year court battle between the Food and Drug Administration and peanut butter makers about the percentage of peanuts their product should have, and conflicts concerning the cleanup of hazardous wastes sites and the savings and loan crisis.

THE CHALLENGE TO MORAL PHILOSOPHY

As the preceding discussion makes plain, issue-overload results not only from the number of issues or the speed with which new ones develop but also from addressing the issues through inadequate and costly institutional channels. In democracies, where public accountability is crucial, it may also result from addressing them through institutional channels that make little if any room for this accountability. In general, frequent mismatches between issues and the procedures used for addressing the policy and decision problems they pose are indicators of issue-overload. When, as a consequence of these mismatches, a crucial social institution or sector—or an entire society—is politically undermined (e.g., through loss of public acquiescence) or economically destabilized (e.g., by runaway inflation or by an enormous national debt), issue-overload is present.

Once this situation develops, the overloading factors become pragmatic constraints. That is, they limit the social decision procedures that are politically sound and morally permissible for dealing with the situation. No doubt, in overload situations, available information suggesting how to cut the inflation rate or rebuild public trust is both politically and morally crucial. But it is equally crucial for this information to be put to policy-making use. And this is accomplished by communicating, evaluating, and contributing to settle the information's practical import through the ongoing policy-making dialogue found in every political system. Static moral theories that ignore, or treat as a mere political externality, the ongoing nature of political discourse are inadequate. And those theories that undermine critical scrutiny in this dialogue are equally inadequate.

One aspect of policy and decision problems that has special significance concerning issues and issue-overload is time constraints. In "The Moral First Aid Manual," Daniel C. Dennett argues that philosophical practice and traditional ethical theories are inadequate in this regard:

> For the most part philosophers are content to ignore the practical problems of real-time decision-making, regarding the brute fact that we are all finite and forgetful, and have to rush to judgment, as a real but irrelevant element of friction in the machinery whose blueprint they are describing. It is as if there might be two disciplines—ethics proper, which undertakes the task of calculating the principles of what the ideal agent ought to do under all circumstances—and then the less interesting "merely practical" discipline of *Moral First Aid*, or *What to Do Until the Doctor of Philosophy Arrives*, which tells, in rough-and-ready terms, how to make "on line" decisions under time pressure.
>
> *In practice*, philosophers acknowledge, we overlook important considerations—considerations that we shouldn't overlook—and we bias our thinking in a hundred idiosyncratic—and morally indefensible—ways; but *in principle*, what we ought to do is what the ideal theory (one ideal theory or another) says we ought to do.[7]

Dennett wisely acknowledges that in philosophy or, for that matter, in science, to theorize is to simplify, hence to develop idealizations of reality. The problem is determining which idealizations help deal with ethical problems and issues and which, as he says, "will just land us with diverting fairy tales."[8]

This is sound doctrine. What about Dennett's suggested solution, the first aid manual? At one point, Dennett describes it as "the book the ideally rational agent would write as his own vade mecum, written in the light of his perfect self-knowledge about his many limitations."[9] This description, however, is a bit too simple, for the manual has varied purposes. For example, Dennett imagines it "to be framed as advice to a rational, heeding audience," but also as rendering agents "impervious to the invasions of hyperrationality." Given this latter purpose, the manual "can also be viewed as not having achieved its end unless it has the effect of changing the "operating system"—not merely the "data," not merely the contents of belief or acceptance—of the agents it addresses."[10] As Dennett acknowledges, "For it to succeed in such a special task, it will have to address its target audiences with pinpoint accuracy."[11] Hence, as Dennett infers, "There might, then, be several different *Moral First Aid Manuals* each effective for a different type of audience."[12]

This notion of several moral first aid manuals, each giving on-line moral advice to a different audience, has significant shortcomings. I mention three here.

First, the moral first aid manuals' emphasis on ready answers undermines a central feature of ethics: critical scrutiny. It simply aims at fulfilling the all too common desire to be told what to do, no questions asked. This amounts to putting authority in the place of reason—too high an ethical cost to pay for acting effectively under pressure.

No doubt, there are people who would be more likely to act rightly were they simply to follow such ready advice instead of thinking about what to do. And in very special cases, a bit of moral first aid may be unavoidable. However, right behavior is not the only or main thing to secure in ethics. The openness of ethical discourse and unsurrendered freedom of thought are equally if not more significant. The question is how not to preclude or undermine them while taking into account, as one must, time and other constraints on policy- and decision-making.

Second, the task of writing the manuals raises a cluster of questions: Who could write such a book? Under what conditions would such a person have written it? Dennett's answer, like the sort of theory he criticizes, falls prey to the excesses of idealization. He states that the first aid manual would be "the book the ideally rational agent would write as his own vade mecum, written in the light of his perfect self-knowledge about his many limitations."[13] Why appeal to an ideally rather than ordinarily rational agent, and perfect self-knowledge (we may lack the time to attain it) rather than adequate knowledge for the task at hand?

In contrast with Dennett's vision and with the approaches he criticizes, it appears that the guidelines to be sought should be developed by *ordinarily rational agents with adequate, though by no means perfect, knowledge for developing them*. These agents would have a general knowledge of the world's workings: an awareness of relevant findings in the sciences, an adequate sense of the various ethical concerns relevant to the guidelines, some policy-making or related practical experience. Also, the process for developing the guidelines sometimes needs to involve limited interactions with alternative solutions. And it needs to involve ongoing interactions and discussions among those affected by the problems and those involved in making policy about the problems (who are often different people).[14]

This leads to the third shortcoming of Dennett's approach. It undermines the discussions just mentioned because it presupposes acquiescence to authority as a rule. Hence, it cannot help but undermine the political system by making it unresponsive to the outcome of these social decision procedures of interaction and public discussion.

TASKS FOR MORAL PHILOSOPHY

In the approach I am proposing, the guidelines' purpose is something other than to tell people what to do. If morality is to make room for reason among ordinary people, then it should not lead to something like a platoon where the commander issues moral orders. Nor is the guidelines' purpose to tell people what they ought to do, though this is not generally objectionable. Rather, it is to guide policy-making, which involves giving directions for three activities: (1) identifying issues; (2) focusing on the types of social conflicts they involve—from mere controversies to the sharpest confrontations; and (3) deciding what social decision procedures may be used to deal with the policy and decision problems the issues pose individually or, as in issue-overload, in combination with others. Here, it is crucial that the guidelines help ask sensible questions rather than find answers to questions that misconstrue political or moral realities.[15]

Given this purpose, a taxonomy of issues that is reasonably accessible to ordinary policymakers is needed. Such a taxonomy, and the questions formulated with the taxonomy's help, will not use excessively technical language. For if the sought guidelines are to guide ordinary policymakers, as intended, their language should not sacrifice clarity to technicality or precision.

To say this in no way implies that studies formulated in more technical language are of no use. On the contrary. Dennett himself envisions systematic empirical studies in psychology and formal analyses of task domains and the useful heuristics for them, of the sort sometimes produced by people studying artificial intelligence.[16] No doubt, this would fit the approach I am suggesting. In addition, empirical studies by sociologists and political scientists should complete the picture.[17]

At any rate, a taxonomy of policy and decision problems would help distinguish the different levels at which questions need to be asked. For example, in discussing issues concerning abortion policy, one needs to address the higher-level question: Is the policy question what abortion policies should we have, given that there is controversy and even confrontation about it and that this economically and politically destabilizes large social sectors or society itself? or rather, what abortion policies should we have, given abstract principles of right and wrong and regardless of the controversy, the confrontation, and their destabilizing consequences? This shifts the issue to the policy level. I consider this type of shift next. The needed taxonomy is outlined in Essay 7.

LEVELS OF POLICY AND DECISION PROBLEMS

Marcus G. Singer has discussed questions that arise about issues at a policy level other than that predominantly presupposed by the exchanges among those involved in the issues. In "Moral Issues and Social Problems: The Moral Relevance of Moral Philosophy," he says:

> Where there exist strong differences of opinion on opposing sides of some moral matter we have a moral *issue*, as I shall call it, rather than a moral *problem*, for there is something *at issue*. The discussions that are resorted to as means of settling them often turn into disputes, controversies, or conflicts, some of which, owing to the failure of other mutually agreed-on means of resolving them, may be resolved only by threats, intimidation, terrorism, or warfare—at least this is what the parties may resort to. . . . For every issue on which opinion is inflamed, in which the controversy gets worse and degenerates into conflict . . . the *society* has a problem, the problem of how best to resolve the issue. Thus every serious, strongly felt, and long-standing moral issue in a society constitutes a *social* problem, which in turn is itself a moral problem—a second order moral problem— of how best and most effectively to settle the issue.[18]

This characterization constitutes a significant contribution to social ethics. However, it has at least four limitations that make it inadequate for dealing with problems posed by issues in all their variety.

First, Singer's characterization of issues restricts them to differences of opinion. It excludes conflicts—especially highly confrontational situations—that appear to be dominantly, though not merely, conflicts of demands. Think of labor disputes in which moral opinions are voiced, but they turn out to be largely a front for sheer demands on the part of management or labor. Think of organized crime or drug-cartel wars. Conflicts such as these sometimes pose a second-order policy problem for society, even though they amount to conflicts of demands, with opinions and reasons being used merely as persuasive tools for satisfying the demands. Any approach and guidelines like the ones needed to deal with issues and their collective consequences on large social sectors or entire societies should apply to these cases too. Singer's characterization of issues is too narrow to help in this respect.

In defense of Singer's characterization, one might point out that it is not intended to cover the cases just mentioned, because its purpose is to characterize *moral* issues. And, given the motivations in the above-mentioned disputes, one might argue that the issues are not moral. This position, if sound, merely justifies Singer's characterization. It does not make it any less limited. The second-order policy problems for society are still not covered by it.

Second, Singer's conception is also too narrow to cover moral problems. Although in the above cases there is largely something at stake but nothing at issue, and those opposing each other are not themselves moved by moral considerations, the second-order policy problems posed by such conflicts of demands are nonetheless moral problems. Society and individual lives are disrupted by such conflicts, and there are viable (however imperfect) policy-making opinions for dealing with them. Singer's characterization of second-order moral problems falls short of covering not just the whole range of second-order policy problems but, as a result, the whole range of second-order moral problems as well.

Third, this characterization does not cover third-order questions, which sometimes become the core of issues themselves. Their general form is: Should the question be asked at the first-order level (e.g., What, if any, abortions are morally permissible and what abortion policies are accordingly justified, regardless of any controversy or confrontation there may be about it?) or second-order level (e.g., What abortion policies are justified, given that there is a societally disruptive controversy and even confrontation about it?)?

Finally, Singer's characterization is not sufficiently clear about the relation of disputes, controversies, or conflicts to moral issues. At the beginning of the paragraph quoted above, he says, "Where there exist strong differences of opinion on opposing sides of some moral matter we have a moral issue."[19] Here, an issue would appear to be simply the strong differences of opinion on opposing sides of some moral matter. A bit later, however, a controversy and its degeneration into conflict are said to occur *in* an issue. Are they then part and parcel of issues or merely a political externality?

Since the guidelines needed should cover all levels of moral issues and moral policy and decision problems *posed by issues*, the wider notion of an issue should be adopted. Accordingly, the position I am taking is that social conflicts, however heated, are part and parcel—indeed, are at the very core—of issues. Further, since some of these conflicts are irreducible during the time available for dealing with the issues, ethical guidelines must make ethically acceptable room for compromise, voting, bargaining, negotiation, and other procedures for dealing with opposing demands or opinions. What the appropriate procedure is will depend on the type of issue being faced. I should add, however, that this position does not rule out the search for consensus in dealing with issues of certain types. But this is best discussed by reference to recent discussions in the ongoing consensus-conflict debate.

CONSENSUS, CONFLICT, AND ETHICAL THEORIES

What constraints do social conflicts create on ethical theories meant to help guide policy and decisions about issues and issue-overload? None according to some theories. Jürgen Habermas's theory, for example, rules out any procedure for dealing with conflict except discussion of merits. According to this theory, the goal of politics should be rational agreement attained through "a cooperative search for truth in which only the force of the better argument prevails."[20] As Jon Elster sees Habermas's theory, "the decisive act is that of engaging in public debate with a view to the emergence of consensus."[21]

Elster is largely in sympathy with this theory, yet fears "that it might be dismissed as Utopian, both in the sense of ignoring the problem of getting from here to there, and in the sense of neglecting some elementary facts of human psychology."[22] Accordingly, his objections focus largely on how difficult it is to reach a consensus and how questionable it is to seek it or even approach it, let alone to require that everyone be involved in the task.[23] Elster describes his own position about the place of consensus in policy- and decision-making in a manner reminiscent of Dennett's views:

> It is the concern with substantive decisions that lends the urgency to political debates. The ever-present constraint of time creates a need for focus and concentration. . . . Yet within these constraints arguments form the core of the political process.[24]

This sensitivity to time constraints is a move in the right direction but, I believe, a somewhat simplistic doctrine. As previously indicated, the constraints on argument in politics go far beyond matters of time. The discussion in preceding sections indicates that some policy and decision problems are intractable because of the type of social conflict (e.g., the confrontation) that poses the problem, or because of other social circumstances (e.g., the existence of issue-overload). Even if time were not of the essence (which it often is), seeking consensus might be an irrelevant way of dealing with the problem. It might be as irrelevant as trying to give reasons for being rational to those who are set on not listening to reason at all. I next sketch a theory of the type needed to soundly deal with the variety of policy and decision problems.

POLICY-MAKING, MEANINGFUL DIALOGUE, AND MORAL PHILOSOPHY

The type of theory needed for soundly addressing policy and decision problems should be sensitive to the variety of policy-making problems in which reason and meaningful dialogue are not the only components. The ones I have emphasized in this essay are problems about issues. Concerning them, the type of theory needed should focus on two questions that are crucial for ethically and politically sound policy- and decision-making: What is the type of conflict involved in the issue or combination of issues posing the policy and decision problem? And, given time pressures and other pragmatic constraints (e.g., the unsettled nature of some of the concerns involved), what are the likely social implications of the conflict or combination of conflicts and of various viable social decision procedures for dealing with it? Focusing on these questions provides evidence that, from the standpoint of the type of theory suggested, the variety of policy and decision problems is taken seriously, as is the variety of social decision procedures for dealing with these matters.[25]

The theory I am suggesting combines deontological and consequentialist considerations with the pragmatic constraints of time, social attitudes, political institutions, economic realities, technological feasibility, and the often unknown or even unsettled nature of data about these things. It is guided by two overall hypotheses. One concerns ethics. It is the *range hypothesis.* According to it, there is a range of ethical problems with the following characteristics: At one extreme, individual rights carry much more weight than any other consideration in dealing with problems because, for example, natural rights are significantly and unequivocally at stake in those problems. At the other extreme, consequences carry the most weight because, for example, the very existence and well-being of a reasonably good society are at stake. In between, rights and consequences have less decisive weight, though, fortunately, they often reinforce each other. Sometimes, however, they appear to conflict with each other, constituting hard cases to deal with. All along the range of problems, pragmatic considerations set limits to alternatives that would otherwise have served to address the problems.[26]

This hypothesis finds support in the cases and observations made throughout the previous discussion. So does the second: the *balance hypothesis.* According to it, there is a range of policy and decision problems with the following characteristics: At one extreme, the search for feasible and effective policies and decisions through a reliance on meaningful dialogue and the use of reason carries much more weight than any other consideration; time and other constraints make the search possible. At the other extreme, the need to deal with the social facts posing policy and decision problems (e.g., with the conflicts central to the abortion issue, or with public acquiescence to socially disastrous environmental practices) carries more weight than any other consideration. Meaningful dialogue and the use of reason are not dominant in these circumstances, which involve a clear and immediate threat to the very existence and well-being of one or more reasonably good societies. In between, the search for policies and decisions through reliance on reason and meaningful dialogue, and the pressing need to deal with the problems, have less decisive weight, though, fortunately, they often reinforce each other. Sometimes, however, they appear to conflict with each other, constituting hard cases to deal with. All along, pragmatic considerations set limits on (1) the extent to which the cases can be emphasized, and (2) the procedures suited for realistically attending to them.

The theory just sketched is outlined in more detail in the book's remainder. It treats a variety of social decision procedures—from bargaining, voting, and compromise to lottery, arbitration, policy insulation, and manipulation—as no less morally crucial than discussion of merits and no less politically crucial than confrontational procedures such as striking and combat. This is how things should be. Depending on the circumstances, each one of these procedures constitutes a politically viable and morally preferable alternative to seeking to rely only on reason and dialogue and invariably opting for nonrational, often confrontational, procedures. Exaggerating the role of reason and unreason can only undermine morality and paralyze politics. As the preceding discussion suggests, the approach this book adopts is best suited for avoiding these consequences. If systematically pursued, it offers a chance of cementing society along morally acceptable lines. It will certainly not eliminate the fact that most currently significant policy and decision problems involve social conflict. But dealing with this fact from this book's standpoint involves a less wide-eyed and less divisive process.

Dialogue

— You are jumping to conclusions! Suppose that Habermas's theory has the shortcomings you suggest. This does not in any way mean that all moral theories do. To be sure, Dennett argues that utilitarian as well as Kantian theories fail to provide advice in very concrete situations, when time is of the essence. But why accept his arguments so readily?

— You are right in thinking that more arguments than Dennett provides are needed to establish that both utilitarian and Kantian theories are unable to provide advice in such situations. Indeed, I will give some in later essays. There is, however, no good reason why I should not indicate my position in the book's first essay. I agree with Dennett's assessment of the theories, although I disagree with his suggested solutions. Besides, in this essay, my main purpose was not to discuss the theories. Rather, it was to characterize issues and issue-overload and argue for some features that theories need to have if they are to be of help in dealing with issues and issue-overload.

— OK. But putting that matter aside, why argue in the manner you do? First, you point out that there are certain realities about the world of policy. Then you argue that if we take them into account, we should end up with the type of moral theory capable of helping address those realities. It is not a very startling discovery that a theory that incorporates pragmatic considerations is sensitive to pragmatic constraints.

— I grant you that this is an almost tautological point to make; but, given the disregard that traditional moral theories display for the facts of politics, it is necessary to make it. However, this point is not my argument. Instead, I argue that the ethical theories best suited for dealing with issues and issue-overload must include not just

13

abstract moral rules, laws, and principles but also social decision procedures (from mediation to strikes) that go beyond primarily argumentative ones. This is something that traditional moral theories do not do.

— In any case, even if traditional moral theories have the shortcomings you and Dennett suggest, why should new ones, developed along the lines of rational choice theory and its offspring (decision, game, and social choice theory), have the same shortcomings? These are theories you have not discussed, and Dennett says little, if anything, about them. Yet they are widely touted as theories capable of helping us deal with the situations in which issues and issue-overload trap us.

— You seem to be reading my mind. I entirely agree that the theories you just mentioned need discussion, though I am not sure that they are as different in approach from some traditional moral theories as you seem to imply. Indeed, I will discuss them in the essays coming up, after outlining a taxonomy of the social traps you mention. Be patient, and you may find that apparently trivial starting points have not so trivial consequences for both moral and political theories.

2 Social Traps: High-Tech Weapons, Rarefied Theories, and the World of Politics

Dealing with international conflicts, economic difficulties, and environmental decay often leads to social traps. These are situations in which, individually or in groups, people are stuck behaving in a manner they perceive as favorable to their aims when, in fact, it is contrary to them.[1] This essay is about social traps in policy-making. It asks: Can rational choice, decision, and game theory help deal with social traps? How? What, if any, are these theories' shortcomings? Do any other theories appear more plausible? I argue that rational choice, decision, and game theory are of little help in dealing with social traps in policy-making, whether as theories or merely as heuristic devices. Establishing this thesis prepares the groundwork for establishing Essay 3's thesis that "satisficing" theories are better suited for dealing with social traps.

The ensuing discussion emphasizes problems posed by high-tech weapons escalation and proliferation and examines actual constraints on addressing these problems. Its results, however, should be relevant to the examination of how the said theories apply to policy and decision problems about environmental deterioration, economic instability, overpopulation, and a variety of other matters. Before proceeding, I sketch a typology of social traps, which should help examine the applicability of rational choice, decision, and game theories to the policy and decision problems posed by social traps.

TYPOLOGY OF SOCIAL TRAPS

Some social traps result from ignorance; others, from more knowledge than one can handle; still others from lack of cooperation; and others from

15

conflict. Ignorance leads to traps in various ways. In *time delay* traps, people misperceive the amount of damage their behavior does to their aims because the damage is delayed—as in deficit-building public spending. In *sliding reinforcer* traps, the damage is misperceived because it gradually increases over time—as in the use of agricultural methods that cause soil erosion. And there are *total ignorance* traps, in which the damage, present or future, is not known at all. An example is the 1941–1971 use of diethylstilbestrol (DES) in the United States to prevent miscarriages.

As stated, traps may result from things other than ignorance. In *overload* traps, the damage results from excessive information that the individual or group tries to process but cannot—as in the U.S. court overload. There are also *externality* traps, in which the actions of others or simply the external circumstances cause one's otherwise harmless behavior to damage one's aims. Some of these are *parameter* traps, in which others (e.g., hostage takers) or the circumstances (e.g., natural catastrophes) confront people with desperate choices. Others are *collective* traps, in which the actions of enough others cause one's otherwise harmless behavior to damage one's (and some-times also their) aims. Some of these are *noncooperation* traps, and others are *conflict* traps. Overpopulation, where the overall effects but not the indi-vidual decisions are interdependent, exemplifies a noncooperation trap. The arms race, where the decisions themselves are interdependent, exemplifies a conflict trap.[2] Of course, the traps just described, and others, can form hybrid types of social traps.

One of the questions I address is: Can rational choice, decision, and game theory help deal with social traps in policy-making? To establish this, let us first briefly characterize these theories and their intended applications in policy-making.

RATIONAL CHOICE THEORY, POLICY-MAKING DECISIONISM, AND STRATEGIC GAMES

The standard version of rational choice theory purports to tell us what to do in order to achieve our aims, but not what these aims should be. It has four main components: (1) the set of feasible courses of action, that is, the courses of action that satisfy (or are rationally believed to satisfy) various logical, physical, and social constraints; (2) the causal connections (or the set of beliefs about the causal connections) that determine which courses of action lead to which outcomes; (3) a subjective ranking of the feasible courses of action, typically on the basis of the outcomes they are expected to have; and (4) the notion that to choose rationally is to choose the highest ranked among these courses of action.[3]

The application of rational choice theory to policy analysis is decision theory. It was initially applied to the study of military operations, logistics, and tactics during World War II. In the early 1950s, it was formalized at the Rand Corporation and other policy-oriented institutions. From then until the 1960s, it was widely used in microeconomics—primarily in the context of market transactions—management science, and military strategy.[4] The structure of decisions was thought to be the same for all cases. In *The Economics of Defense in the Nuclear Age*, for example, Hitch and McKean say: "How choices should be made—the whole problem of allocating scarce resources among competing ends—is the stuff of economics and the subject of this book."[5] Indeed, this methodology came to be called *decisionism*.[6] In accordance with rational choice theory, the decisionist approach requires rational policymakers to specify their aims; specify the feasible courses of action to attain these aims; rank them, typically by appeal to the outcomes they are expected to have; and choose that which ranks the highest. In addition, it envisions a unitary, consistent policymaker or a group acting consistently and as a unit.[7]

In the 1970s and 1980s, rational choice theory's offspring, game theory, attracted the attention of sociobiologists, philosophers, and even more po-litical scientists. This is the theory of rational choice as it applies to conflicts. Most conspicuously, it applies to conflicts involved in those externality traps that involve strategic decisions, that is, decisions that are interdependent. Its main component is the payoff matrix. In the simplest case of a two-parties game, the payoff matrix is that shown on page 18.

In accordance with rational choice theory, game theory assumes that to be rational is always to act to maximize one's expected utility. It also assumes that there is a utility function that can be precisely calculated for everyone and everything.[8]

I next address the questions: Can rational choice, decision, and game theory help deal with social traps in policy-making? What, if any, are their shortcomings? My treatment is not exhaustive. It focuses on a collective type of trap—or presumed trap—involving conflict: high-tech weapons escala-tion and proliferation. Within this framework, I describe some crucial moral and political considerations that such theories, and any modifications that preserve them, cannot take into account. In other words, I formulate reasons for abandoning these theories. At the same time, I set the stage for a consideration of alternative, satisficing theories in dealing with social traps and related policy-making situations.

THE CASE OF HIGH-TECH WEAPONS: ESCALATION AND PROLIFERATION

Since the cold war ended sometime in 1990, the arms race between the superpowers has slowed down, though it has not ended. But the catch-up race involving other countries has reached new speeds. This is no minor

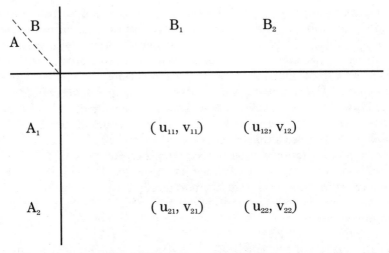

In this matrix, u_{12} is the expected utility of player A, and v_{12} is the expected utility of player B, when player A chooses strategy A_1 and player B chooses strategy B_2. In more complex cases, u_{ij} is the expected utility of player A, and v_{ij} is the expected utility of player B, when player A chooses strategy A_i and player B chooses strategy B_j. In accordance with common practice, i and j are variables for natural numbers.

matter. Consider nuclear weapons: To be sure, two countries are in possession of by far the largest nuclear arsenals—the United States and Russia. However, they are not the only ones currently capable of using nuclear weapons. China, France, and the United Kingdom can use them too. Nor are these five countries the only ones with nuclear weapons capability. Argentina, Brazil, India, Israel, Pakistan, and South Africa are known to be capable of producing them. Indeed, there have been concerns that some of them are doing precisely that.[9]

In addition, all these countries have been involved in at least one international war during the twentieth century; some have been under military or quasi-military dictatorships; and some of the latter have shown little restraint on war matters.[10] Add to this the fact that other nonnuclear countries involved in recent international confrontations have other high-tech weapons. For example, about two months after Iraq's August 2, 1990, invasion and annexation of Kuwait, intelligence reports indicated that Iraq had more than its well-known chemical weapons capability. It also had a sizable stockpile of biological weapons and was expected to have a militarily significant biological weapons program by early 1991. The ex-Soviet Union, Israel, Syria, and other nations are also known to have done extensive research into this type of weapon. To complicate matters, the use of these weapons can easily proliferate, and their production sites can be identified only with great difficulty, because they can be produced in almost any pharmaceutical laboratory. In addition, the size of the stockpiles increases the chance of theft, and the wide dispersion of these weapons makes breaks in the chain of control more likely.[11]

Such a situation suggests that a high-tech weapons confrontation could start in a number of places, setting up a chain of retaliatory measures sufficient to destroy human, if not all, life in large regions or even on the entire planet. The risk that these weapons will be used and lead to escalation grows as they become smaller and more accurate, because these modifications foster visions of so-called surgical strikes and graduated uses of these weapons, especially nuclear weapons, in battle. Under what constraints is this all happening? I turn to this question next, beginning with the most commonly recognized variables in the situation. For the purposes of this discussion, I describe them in the manner typical of rational choice, decision, and game theories.

VARIABLES OF THE HIGH-TECH WEAPONS RACE

As the preceding discussion indicates, a variety of states could use high-tech weapons, as could a variety of terrorist groups.[12] This is a significant *epistemological* variable of the high-tech weapons race. To be sure, a few states have far greater knowledge of and technological ability to produce and use the weapons, but a great and growing number of additional states and other groups have enough relevant knowledge and ability to use them.

There is also the *behavioral* variable. Though different states and other groups are led into the arms race by a variety of reasons, they share significant tendencies whose aims constitute the national interest of each country. Each tends to (1) try to increase its security; (2) decrease its members' anxiety, if possible; and (3) behave so as to preserve ideas, values, or principles predominant among its members.

These ideas, values, and principles may sometimes be upheld by a country's public officials merely as a way of defending a public image or saving face at the international level. Other times, they may go deeper than that.[13] Sometimes, they may be somewhat forgotten.[14] In any case, these ideas, values, and principles do not generally rule out some form of cooperation. Such cooperation may be understood as peace—the notion predominantly used in cold war Soviet Union official statements. Or it may be understood as fairness or equitability—a notion frequently used in U.S. official statements. In any case, cooperation cannot be inconsistent with the aims of increasing security and decreasing anxiety.

Next, significant among the variables of the high-tech weapons race are *resources*. They set constraints on the way in which the various aims or motivations involved in the behavioral variable can and should be balanced against one another. The resources are those that a state (or group) has at its disposal to keep up with the race.

Finally, the situation just described points to a fourth variable of the arms race, the *liberty* variable: Each participant is at liberty to introduce a new device or weapon whenever and however it pleases, so long as its resources permit, its knowledge makes it possible, its motivation does not falter, and existing treaties (whose force, at any rate, is often questionable) do not rule it out.

Given these variables alone, countries often appear to be stuck generating high-tech weapons escalation and proliferation. That is, they appear caught in a social trap. Let us next see how it is supposed to work.

THE ESCALATION AND PROLIFERATION PROCESS

Given the above variables alone, four main steps lead to escalation and proliferation. First, at each juncture, the countries involved are expected to develop their high-tech weapons arsenals for the sake of their national interest. For example, even now that the cold war is over, the United States and the ex-Soviet Union are expected to develop weapons usable in regional confrontations such as that prompted by Iraq's August 1990 invasion and annexation of Kuwait.[15] Second, this expectation is perceived as a threat to other countries involved—for one, to Iraq. Third, it is taken for granted that each country should act for the sake of its own national interest. Hence, fourth, those behind in the race try to catch up—for instance, Iraq tries to develop biological and nuclear weapons.[16] Those ahead try to stay ahead. And those in the middle try to keep up with one another and, in some cases, surpass the others. As a consequence, the number of weapons escalates. Partly as a result of this, the weapons become much easier to obtain by those countries that still lack them.

Whenever a country makes a decision to escalate, insecurity and anxiety may decrease, but this is a short-lived development that lasts only until the other side's escalation takes place. At decision time, however, the short-term benefits of minimizing insecurity and anxiety outweigh the later and greater dangers of continued escalation. After all, those greater dangers are later dangers; those dangers posed by failure to escalate are perceived as clear and present and, quite arguably, are so.[17] Hence, the race is not blatantly a result of misjudgment or ignorance of likely risks. Indeed, all policymakers in charge can be said to be fully aware of the situation. And they are generally guided by the same overall motivation: avoiding the destructive consequences of the arms race.

A HIGH-TECH WEAPONS TRAP?

If the preceding account were all there is to the societal problem posed by the high-tech weapons race conflict, the viable options for dealing with the problem would, no doubt, be quite restricted. Some would argue that the situation is a social trap. If it is, its nature is hybrid, involving elements of at least collective conflict, time delay, and sliding reinforcer traps.

There are a variety of reasons to consider it a social trap. First, changing the underlying motivations would not, by itself, do much to change the problem. Some of these motivations do not even conflict: All states involved are determined to avoid nuclear holocaust and comparable catastrophic consequences of the race. And when the underlying motivations do conflict, they are unlikely to change readily. Each state is committed to increase its security and decrease the anxiety among members of its population and will take actions to accomplish this.

A second reason for considering the situation a social trap is that actions taken are likely to be unilateral. Even when they are the result of talks between the states involved, the decision to rely on these talks and perform or omit actions on the basis of these talks is itself unilateral and may be secretive. Or, if there was an agreement, the states may manipulate the agreement's meaning. As was the case with the 1972 ABM treaty, they may even manipulate the meaning of agreed-upon interpretations.[18]

Only actions aimed at building trust between the states involved will tend to minimize such developments. However, such a process takes time, perhaps more time than those involved are prepared to wait in order to prevent a catastrophe. This is evidenced by the United States' slowness and relative reluctance to accept the Soviet Union's disarmament proposals shortly after the cold war ended. The expressed grounds were that the old order might return to power and reinstate the cold war at any time.[19] Hence, setting out to change motivations alone will not do.

Nor will it do to set out to enlighten those in charge about the likely eventual catastrophe the race will lead to. Except for a few public officials who were influential in the United States during the 1980s and appeared convinced that things would be fine so long as there were enough tables for everyone to crawl under, policymakers know the likely nightmarish outcome of the race.[20] Nor can the resources of the other powers involved be easily exhausted as a means of bringing the race to an end (though it appears to have been tried in the late 1980s). Finally and obviously, no appeal to a higher enforcing authority to stop the race and get rid of the weapons is possible. There is no such authority.

Does the situation then amount to a social trap? How—if at all—can rational choice, decision, and game theory help resolve this matter? Can other theories do better?

THE POVERTY OF RATIONAL CHOICE
THEORY AND ITS OFFSPRING

As stated, rational choice theory is applied to policy-making through decision theory and, specifically, to social conflict through game theory. The four variables in game theory—epistemological, behavioral, resources, and liberty—can be described in a variety of ways. For instance, the only aim game theory ascribes to the countries involved in the arms race is the maximization of their own individual interests. But this interest is open to interpretation. Some think that if a country aims at maximizing its national interest it also aims at maximizing the difference between its advantage and that of competing countries. In the high-tech weapons race, these thinkers tend to be hawks. They aim at attaining or, if already there, keeping and, if possible, increasing their technological edge. For them, cooperation with the enemy is unthinkable, and the enemy's gaining the advantage is worse than the risk of generalized destruction.

Others, however, think that a country's maximizing its national interest has nothing to do with increasing the gap between its own advantage and that of others. In the case of the high-tech weapons race, they are sometimes—quite inappropriately—called doves. For them, cooperation is thinkable, and generalized destruction is the worst possible fate. But they think that it is possible for one country to surpass others without bringing about generalized destruction. They prefer having a weapons advantage over the enemy rather than the other way around.

Still others argue that cooperation is the only way. First, generalized destruction is irrational. And second, in the real world, increasing the weapons gap over a competing country simply leads that country to escalate, thus making generalized destruction more likely.

Can rational choice, decision, and game theory help settle these differences? It cannot. By itself, it can simply help bring out the different interpretations of the utilities, and hence the expected utilities involved. As Mario Bunge puts it, "all the utilities (and probabilities) handled by decision theory and its offspring are assumed to be subjective."[21]

This poverty of game theory might be described as parsimoniousness by its partisans.[22] Yet its lack of content limits it to being at best a heuristic model for studying policy-making situations, not a theory for dealing with them. It cannot address the previously formulated question: Does the situation amount to a social trap? This is an empirical question, and game theory is merely a mathematical tool incapable of furnishing the data needed to answer it. Is game theory (or rational choice or decision theory) at least heuristically useful to find the needed data?

THE POLITICS OF HIGH-TECH WEAPONS

If used as a heuristic model, rational choice, decision, or game theory may help bring out the need to empirically investigate the previously discussed four variables of the high-tech weapons race. It may even tell us, given certain specified conditions, what situations to avoid. But it would be a misleading model if it left things at that, for those components are not the most significant ones. Another component is the *political* variable. One might think that this is covered by the behavioral variable, but it is not. It cannot be, because of the tunnel-vision aims and unilateral decisions characteristic of the behavioral variable when described, as above, within the constraints of rational choice, decision, and game theories.

The political variable concerns the place and policy-making limitations of modern states as they relate to public response under the above-described state of affairs. There is, no doubt, an authority relationship between states and their members who, at the international level and given the absence of world government, are subjects rather than citizens.[23] As Hannah Arendt suggested, however, this relationship between those who command and those who obey depends partly on "the hierarchy itself, whose rightness and legitimacy both recognize and where both have their predetermined stable place."[24]

One consequence of the arms race is to erode this hierarchy by eroding public recognition of state authority on matters of foreign policy. This is especially so when such matters are supposed to include conventional or nuclear war (as they traditionally do) as one of the options open to states in the pursuit of their interests.[25] Until recently, public response to high-tech wars as an extension of state foreign policy was, by and large, simple acquiescence. It appears to have resulted partly from a sense of policy-making powerlessness, partly from a belief that official policymakers are to be trusted and know better, partly from anxiety about the likely catastrophic consequences of the race, and partly from sheer psychological resistance to face it. But this has changed with the appearance of the peace and related nontraditional movements both in the West and, now more than ever before, in the East.[26]

This is not to say that these movements have clear aims or a well-worked-out strategy, nor that they are likely to succeed. Rather, they are evidence of a political variable not covered by the behavioral, epistemological, resources, or liberty variables typically considered in rational choice, decision, and game theory descriptions of the situation. The significance of politics has been known all along by political scientists, policymakers, and ordinary people. It needs to be mentioned here simply because it gets lost in theoretical approaches such as those previously described. It is also worth mentioning because it makes room for additional policymaking options that cast doubt on the notion that the high-tech weapons escalation and proliferation process is a social trap.

In fact, politics provides a crucial element for establishing the shortcomings of rational choice, decision, and game theories as theories and as heuristic models. These shortcomings concern the ongoing process of political and, indeed, moral evaluation in policy-making. In a rational choice, decision, or game theory approach, the choice must be made on the basis of utilities and probabilities as determined *at decision time*. That is, *the data must be all in*. But this rarely, if ever, happens. Aside from the problem of determining probabilities in an objective manner, there is no reason to believe that, at decision time, all expected consequences will have the same utilities as in the future.[27] So, for reasons of prudence, the parties involved may want to leave options open so that these are worked out through negotiation, bargaining, and other social decision procedures.

For example, the parties involved may want to engage in political dialogue, negotiation, and bargaining concerning arms reductions. This is not just a matter of gathering further evidence to make more accurate predictions or determine utilities more precisely, so that a sounder political judgment can be formed.[28] The utilities themselves are worked out in the process, because people's attitudes and judgments about the alternatives change with the process. It is high time to pursue a line of research that—like that pursued in the ensuing essays—makes room for this aspect of the policy-making process. The alternative is to remain caught in the rational choice, decision, and game theory trap.

Dialogue

— I grant you that rational choice and game theories simplify reality. But why shouldn't they? As Milton Friedman said in his *Essays in Positive Economics* in 1953 (p. 14), a theory is the more important the more its postulates are unrealistic.

— As for Friedman's dictum, let me just say that it would turn many a highly unscientific theory—say, astrology—into very important ones. But this would make them no less unscientific.

— The point of the dictum, however, is that important scientific theories are important because, against what we would realistically expect, they explain much with little. Simplicity, after all, is a scientific desideratum.

— Granted that, within limits, there is something to be said for simplicity of explanation. However, if things were as simple as you make them sound, one explanation—God's will—should suffice to explain everything, and even rational choice theory and its offspring would have to be discarded. The point is that, as Mario Bunge made plain in *The Myth of Simplicity* in 1963, there are many kinds of simplicities. The question is, which ones bring us closer to the truth. My position is that rational choice theory and its offspring are simple, but they attain their simplicity by being so abstract that they are incapable of approaching the truths of policy-making, hence, they have no sound application to it.

— At any rate, even if you had established that rational choice theory and game theory have shortcomings, there are no better alternatives to them. Hence, since some theory is better than none at all, you have not debunked them yet.

— First, it is not obvious that in policy-making some theory—however inadequate—is better than no theory at all. Second, as I will argue, there are better theories.

— There is something else you should do. You should show how your critique applies to social choice theory. So far, you have not discussed it.

— Right. Once again, you are reading my mind. This is precisely what I will do next.

3 Social Choice Theory: Formalism Infatuation and Policy-Making Realities

Social choice theory is a source of fascination for many scientists and philosophers concerned with social matters. This fascination results from the precision of the theory's mathematical formalism: Conditions are exactly formulated in axioms, which, together with valid rules of inference, help prove theorems. There is no doubt about these features of the theory. What is doubtful, however, is that the theory provides useful insight into the relations between individual preferences and social welfare or collective decisions. For one thing, how is the theory applicable to *actual* policy-making? This is the main question I address. In addressing it, I also ask: What are some of the features traditionally associated with social choice theory as a field of study? How do current approaches in social choice theory reflect these features? What features are crucial for an approach to belong in the social choice theory category? After answering these questions, I return to my main concern and ask: How, given these features, is social choice theory applicable to actual policy-making? And what, if any, alternative theories promise to do better?

I argue for seven theses. First, a crucial feature of social choice theory is the requirement that, in applying the theory to policy and decision problems, the social decision function be known at decision-making time. Second, in many significant policy-making situations, this requirement can be satisfied only by disregarding the social process of critical scrutiny and social interaction that helps work out many policy-making data. Third, social choice theory as a field of study must treat policy-making decisions as mere logical consequences of given data fixed at decision-making time. Fourth, this leaves room only for approaches—social choice theories—that are hopelessly static and disregard the interactive and ongoing nature of critical scrutiny and other social decision procedures involved in forming policy judgments and decisions. Fifth, primarily for this reason, the entire field of study—not just any particular social choice theory—is useless as a tool for sound policy-making. Sixth, because it is misleading, social choice theory as a field of study is also useless as a source of heuristic models for policy-making understanding and guidance. Seventh, satisficing theories are applicable and much more promising in this regard.

POINTS OF METHOD

Discussions of social choice theory are sometimes confused by the fact that those involved have different conceptions of the theory. Amartya Sen, for example, views it first as a field of study and then as a particular approach or collection of approaches typically used in this field of study.[1] Others appear to view it only in the latter, narrower sense.[2] This tends to confuse the discussions, because criticisms of particular approaches are sometimes presented as criticisms of the field of study. In fact, Amartya Sen defends social choice theory against some criticisms on the grounds that they deal merely with particular social choice approaches, not social choice theory as a field of study.[3]

Of course, in and of themselves, criticisms of particular social choice approaches are not criticisms of social choice theory as a field of study, but they may point out its shortcomings. Indeed, as I argue, this is precisely the situation concerning the applicability of social choice theory to policy-making. Given the features that any approach belonging in this field must have, no such approach can have significant application to actual policy-making.

This is not to say that social choice theory is inadequate as a field of study in general. I leave that matter open. My position concerns what has been thought to be its significant—indeed, predominant—area of application: policy-making. I argue that, in policy-making, the theory is inadequate because of its hopelessly static nature. Before proceeding, however, let us characterize the theory and the types of interpretations it can have.

ARROW'S UNINTERPRETED CONCEPTION

Arrow's conception of the main problem of social choice theory is uninterpreted. The problem is to try to arrive at a social preference ordering, R, from an n-tuple of individual preference orderings $(r_1 \ldots r_n)$, where for each person in a group of n people there is a corresponding ordering. The social welfare function $R = f(r_1 \ldots r_n)$ is supposed to arrive at this ordering. According to Arrow, this will happen given three conditions: (1) the function's domain is unrestricted—that is, f works for any n-tuple of individual preference orderings; (2) f is always Pareto optimal—that is, its orderings are such that not all the parties can be made better off in terms of utility in an alternative feasible ordering; and (3) f is independent of other alternatives— that is, the social ranking of any pair of alternatives (x, y) depends only on the n-tuple of individual rankings of that pair.

INTERPRETING SOCIAL RANKING

Various interpretations of social preference or ranking of alternatives can be adopted in using the theory. For example, with the *outcome evaluation* interpretation, the ranking is simply a matter of social welfare judgments. It amounts to the statement that, according to the individual preferences expressed, x is better than y. In contrast, with the *revealed preferences* interpretation, the ranking is a matter of preferred social decision proce- dures. It amounts to the statement that decision-making in society should be organized so that y is never chosen whenever x is feasible. Of course, other interpretations are also possible.[4] The fact remains, however, that one inter- pretation of social choice theory concerns social decision procedures. This interpretation is crucial for any policy-making application of the theory. Hence, I will use it in addressing this essay's main question: How is social choice theory applicable to actual policy-making? This does not mean, however, that my criticisms will be limited to it. As previously indicated, they will focus on central features of social choice theory as a field of study and on features that, as a consequence, any of its interpretations must have.

In order to discuss the features of social choice theory and those of its interpretations realistically, I next sketch the actual social context in which the theory has come into being and gained acceptance. That is, I sketch the theoretical and historical background of social choice theory through that of its ascendants: rational choice and decision theory.

SOCIAL CHOICE THEORY, RATIONAL CHOICE THEORY, AND DECISIONISM

Social choice theory can be interpreted as yielding injunctions about how social decision-making should be organized in society. Indeed, its applicabil- ity to policy-making depends on this interpretation. But based on this interpretation, social choice theory amounts to a straightforward application of rational choice theory.

As discussed in the previous essay, the standard version of rational choice theory purports to tell us what to do in order to achieve our aims, but not what these aims should be. It has four main components: (1) the set of feasible courses of action, that is, the courses of action that satisfy (or are rationally believed to satisfy) various logical, physical, and social con- straints; (2) the causal connections (or the set of beliefs about the causal

connections) that determine which courses of action lead to which outcomes; (3) a subjective ranking of the feasible courses of action, typically on
the basis of the outcomes they are expected to have; and (4) the notion that
to choose rationally is to choose the highest ranked among these courses of
action.[5] As for the connections between rational choice theory and social
choice theory, they concern decisionism—the application of rational choice
theory to policy analysis discussed in the previous essay[6] and summarized
below.

In accordance with rational choice theory, the decisionist approach requires rational policymakers to specify their aims; specify the feasible
courses of action to attain these aims; rank them, typically by appeal to the
outcomes they are expected to have; and choose that which ranks the
highest. In addition, it envisions a consistent policymaker or a group acting
consistently, if not as a unit.[7] When decision theory is applied in the context of
translating individual preferences into collective preferences concerning how
social decision-making should be organized, it yields an interpretation of social
choice theory that is crucial for its applicability to policy-making. Is the
theory, based on this interpretation, useful for policy-making purposes?

SOCIAL CHOICE THEORY AND POLICY-MAKING

Politics provides a crucial element for establishing the shortcomings of social
choice theory both as a theory and as a heuristic model. This shortcoming
concerns the ongoing process of political and, indeed, moral evaluation in
policy-making. With a social choice theory approach, the choice must be
made on the basis of utilities and probabilities as determined *at decision time*.
That is, *the data must be given as fixed*. But there is no reason to believe that,
at decision time, all expected consequences will have some utility, let alone
the same utilities they will have in the future.[8] Let us examine this objection
in some detail.

THE STATIC THEORY OBJECTION AND A CURRENT RESPONSE

Aanund Hylland presents the static theory objection as follows:

> Social choice theory is usually thought of as a static theory. The members
> of society are those currently living and belonging to it, and the prefer-
> ences considered are their present ones. But actions taken today often
> affect future generations, and people's preferences change over time.[9]

His response to this objection, however, does not address the objection's full
force. He simply says:

> Nothing in the formalism prevents us from including among the "indi-
> viduals" unborn persons and several time-instances of the same person,
> each with separate preferences.[10]

This response takes the objection to be simply that the future preferences of individuals cannot be included in the present set of preferences, even if we can predict them. It is not.

SOCIAL CHOICE THEORY AND UNSETTLED PREFERENCES

Sound policy-making is not attained by including unborn persons or several time-instances of the same person, each with separate preferences, in the calculations. Why include half-baked preferences that will be abandoned upon reflection and after interactive critical scrutiny with others involved in the policy-making process? Part of the static theory objection hinges on the fact that politically crucial preferences are often unsettled, and therefore cannot be taken into account. Hylland's suggested extension of the theory certainly cannot help take them into account.

One might respond that the objection applies to the outcome evaluations interpretation of social choice theory, but not to the revealed preferences interpretation. In the latter, social decision procedures, not outcomes, are supposed to be chosen. However, in actual policy-making, preferences for social decision procedures are often as settled as preferences for outcomes— if not more so. People are often taken by surprise by the policy-making choices they face and do not know whether they prefer to negotiate or strike; use quiet diplomacy or confrontational methods; politically insulate an issue or, instead, expand it. Hence, in either interpretation, crucial preferences are unpredictable at decision time. But a requirement of social choice theory—both as a field of study and as any approach in this field—is that the data be in the form of given preferences at decision time. Hence, social choice theory—both as a field of study and as an approach—must not just disregard the eventual content of preferences being formed. It must also disregard the politically crucial policy-making process through which they are formed. In other words, it is cut off from politics and, therefore, not soundly applicable to policy-making.

In this regard, the objection that social choice theory is static is not simply that we cannot predict certain preferences. Rather, the objection is that we cannot predict many preferences—sometimes crucial ones—because they are unsettled. This points to the fact that policy-making is dynamic. But it is dynamic in several ways, not merely, as Hylland appears to believe, because preferences change by being transformed. Some preferences are formed, not transformed. To be sure, they are normally formed on the basis of previous preferences, but these need not be preferences about the same things. For example, a preference for a quiet life might have led me to form a preference for negotiation rather than war in dealing with Iraq's 1990 invasion of Kuwait, when I previously had no preference about the matter.

Second, policy-making is dynamic because it is interactive. Indeed, the formation and transformation of preferences take place through this interaction. In this regard, policy-making centrally includes interactive critical scrutiny and other social procedures for reaching persuasion and mutual adaptations.[11] Social choice theory cannot make room for these at all. The problem is not with specific social choice theories or approaches; as I have argued and will further argue, it is a problem with social choice theory as a field of study. But first let us consider a case.

THE CASE OF THE AUTOMOBILE AT THE
BEGINNING OF THE TWENTIETH CENTURY

When automobiles were introduced in the United States at the beginning of the twentieth century, nobody could have predicted the carnage they were going to bring upon the population. This carnage was a significant result of the interstate highway system, whose construction was motivated by the cold war. And no data were then available to predict the cold war. Nor were any data available to predict the fact that the U.S. population was going to find the carnage tolerable enough not to outlaw the automobile or significantly restrict its use. This is not just a matter of unpredictability. A process involving various social decision procedures—most significantly, critical scrutiny and social interaction with the new technology and people affected by it—helps *work out* morally significant details such as these.

No doubt, from the start, the process involves reasons for morally assessing policies and decisions. For example, upon cool and careful reflection, people may prefer policy arrangements that do not preempt future corrections—for example, those that would permit corrections when the seriousness of smog and highway fatalities becomes evident.

In addition, the parties involved may want to leave options open, so that these are worked out through negotiation, bargaining, and other social decision procedures. For example, they may want to engage in political dialogue, negotiation, and bargaining concerning automobile use. This is not just a matter of gathering further evidence so that more accurate predictions can be made or utilities can be determined more precisely so that a sounder political judgment can be formed.[12] That is, the utilities themselves are worked out in the process, because people's attitudes and judgments about the alternatives are formed and transformed with the process. This process of critical scrutiny and social interaction leads to the settlement of reasons for assessing policies and decisions. For example, it leads to new attitudes and judgments about automobile use.

POLICY-MAKING AS AN ONGOING PROCESS

A partisan of social choice theory might argue that the preceding discussion applies to isolated policy-making cases or areas and does not establish that social choice theory is useless for all significant policy-making. But all policy-making is dynamic. First, it is an ongoing process. And second, in this process, a policy-making decision can, and often does, have the unpredicted and unpredictable effect of turning those who favored it or its overall outcome against both the decision and the outcome. Such situations develop for a variety of reasons. One reason is that undesirable aspects of the previously preferred overall outcome come to be seen as crucial, when they were not given much importance before the decision. This seems to be precisely the situation with a variety of policy-making decisions aimed at introducing a market economy in the Soviet Union around 1989. In less than one year, public opinion appeared to oppose both the decisions and the expected outcomes previously favored.[13] How can social choice theory be applied under such circumstances? In a cumbersome manner at best.

Suppose that, as Hylland suggests, both present and future preferences are taken into account when applying social choice theory to a policy-making situation. When predominant preferences in the near future will become the opposite of what they are now, including them all in the calculations would lead to a stalemate, not to a decision. The presently predominant preferences would balance out the future predominant preferences, and vice versa.

In contrast with social choice theory, actual policy-making has ways of working out what preferences to take into account, how much weight to give them, and the purpose of going along with a decision that reflects them at a given time. After all, it has always been known that policy decisions can have the function—and, for some, the use—of shaking up those who currently support or acquiesce to them. For example, some nationalist groups supporting Gorbachev's 1989 decisions in the Soviet Union seem to have been well aware of the likely backlash in public support Gorbachev would face in October 1990 and later.[14]

Based on these policy-making features, one might argue that social choice theory requires new applications of the theory to circumstances as they develop. Hence, the above problem would not arise, because only present preferences would be considered at any one time. However, this solution creates other equally damaging problems for social choice theory. First, such an application process would amount to a continuous shuttling back and forth between theory and practice. This would turn policymakers into something akin to decapitated chickens. As a rule, it is an unrealistic solution.

Second, and more significantly, when matters of policy—not simply decisions—are at stake, it is necessary to exercise a judicious, somewhat comprehensive, and long-range judgment. Such a judgment takes time to form and cannot be simply given up as soon as the political winds change.[15] Hence, the suggested application process would make social choice theory inapplicable to decisions about *policy*.

THE POVERTY OF SOCIAL CHOICE THEORY

As the preceding discussion indicates, social choice theory has nothing to say about the ongoing nature of policy-making. This shortcoming is a feature of not merely one or another social choice theory approach but of the entire field of study. According to social choice theory, one must decide at decision time for one of the formulated courses of action. Leaving matters open while one engages in negotiation, bargaining, and other social decision procedures where the participants' preferences are open is *not* one of the courses of action formulated in the feasible set. Yet it is crucial in policy-making.

This evidences the poverty of social choice theory—a poverty that makes it useless in policy-making. Its uselessness does not extend merely to the isolated case of policy-making concerning automobiles, but to most, if not all, significant policy-making. For example, it extends to policy-making about new technologies such as genetic engineering and the use of computers in everyday life. Beyond the very short term, the circumstances surrounding these technologies, and the implications of their use, are not predictable— may not even be imaginable. But they are capable of being worked out and have been worked out to some extent—no thanks to social choice theory.

These facts are reason enough to conclude that social choice theory, both as a field of inquiry and as particular approaches, is useless for understanding and assessing policy-making and for making policy-making decisions. But is social choice theory heuristically useful? No, it is useless as a heuristic model as well because, by excluding from consideration the options just discussed, it tends to steer people away from sound policy-making.

At this point, one might respond that, though social choice theory has the said shortcomings, there are no better alternatives to it. Hence, given that some theory is better than no theory at all, social choice theory has not been debunked either as a theory or as a heuristic model. I contend that it is not obvious that, in policy-making, some theory—however inadequate—is better than no theory at all. But I will not pursue this matter here. Instead, I ask whether there any alternative theories that help deal with policy-making problems better.

SATISFICING THEORIES

Satisficing theories, first developed by Herbert Simon, assert that people do not seek the best alternative in the feasible set, but limit themselves to what seems good enough.[16] This is especially significant concerning the information gathered for decision purposes; at some point, the information is considered good enough. Various objections have been raised against theories of this type.

THE UTILITY MAXIMIZATION OBJECTION

One might think that to engage in the process just described is to maximize utility while taking the cost of information into account. However, as Jon Elster states, to do this one would have to know the expected value of information.[17] But one generally does not, because it is not always—if ever—predictable. The specific value that further information will have is also open-ended, working itself out in the search and critical scrutiny process.

THE OPTIMAL RULES OF THUMB OBJECTION

Another objection is that optimal rules of thumb are used because, otherwise, those using them would be wiped out by competition.[18] But the rules simply minimize or avoid disaster; they do not maximize the interests of those who use them. Nor are the rules used as a result of a choice of the rational choice theory type.[19] It is simply contrary to fact that the rules of thumb used are optimal. They may seem good enough to their users, but often they are not, though they do not face their users with disaster.

THE AD HOCNESS OBJECTION

A stronger objection is that, in traditional satisficing theories, people's levels of satisfaction are entirely ad hoc. This points to the fact that satisficing theories need to join forces with psychology. The work leading to such interdisciplinary effort has already been significantly carried out. People's levels of satisfaction can begin to be explained by appeal to such psychological studies of moral development as those initiated by Piaget and continued by Kohlberg, Gilligan, and Moessinger.[20]

THE INCOMPLETENESS OBJECTION

A fourth objection might be that even such joining of forces between satisficing theories and developmental psychology falls short of the mark. It is still necessary to explain how people's level of satisfaction and their concomitant behavior relate to social norms. This, however, can begin to be explained by appeal to empirical studies of organizational behavior and norms. There is a plethora of such studies today.[21]

CONCLUDING REMARKS

There is no doubt that social choice theory is quite fashionable in policy-making about matters of aggregation and collective choice. Why is this so, given its significant shortcomings? A plausible hypothesis is that social choice theory owes its fame to its formal precision. Indeed, it is a mathematical theory. Unfortunately, as previously argued, when it comes to most, if not all, policy-making, its mathematical formalism is useless. In contrast, satisficing theories do not have the same shortcomings. No doubt they need further development and testing, but they have one crucial feature in their favor: They are applicable to actual policy-making and promise to be fruitful in offering policy-making understanding and guidance.

This is not to say that satisficing theories preclude mathematization. But whatever mathematization they permit (I believe it will have to use the theory of fractals and chaos theory because of how suitable they are to deal with complexities and change, which are characteristic of policy-making), its usefulness is likely, given the theories' focus on policy-making reality. It is high time to pursue this line of research. The alternative is to remain caught in the currently widespread infatuation with the intellectually and politically sterile formalism of social choice theory.

Dialogue

— You seem very satisfied with your defense of satisficing theories. Whatever your particular satisficing theory turns out to be, it will probably be a highly dynamic one emphasizing the ongoing nature of policy- and decision-making. Am I right about this?

— Yes. I think its dynamic character is a virtue of the theory. Don't you?

— Other things being equal, it might be. But I'm afraid other things are not equal. Indeed, they may serve to raise objections against the theory.

— I'm at a loss to figure out what they are.

— For one, since your theory is meant to be politically realistic, it will have to make room for the myriad interest groups involved in politics. Yet, I suppose that, at some point, the theory will lead to practical injunctions. The problem then arises: How could the injunctions be objective, or be reached through an objective process? They will simply be the reflection of some interest group's biases or some equilibrium point between the biases of various interest groups.

— Not so fast. Policy- and decision-making do not invariably involve fanatics pushing for their own interests. You assume that the theory makes no room for objectivity because it is true to the world of politics, which is a world of fanatics. Hence, objectivity has no place in it.

— I am not assuming any such thing, though I think it is plain that fanatics are common in politics. What I mean is that even those people who are not fanatics have their own biases. Therefore, whatever their role turns out to be in evaluating or making policy according to your theory, their biases will be reflected in the evaluations.

— I think your objection plays fast and loose with the notion of objectivity, and a clarification of this notion is accordingly in order.

— Maybe so. But given the realistic emphasis of your theory, you should discuss objectivity in the context of policy- and decision-making at its most heated. It will not do to use examples drawn from the detached conversations of tea-club members concerning how the pyramids of Egypt were built, or how the Mayas calculated the orbit of Venus.

— You are right. I should discuss the notion of objectivity and test its applicability to the world by reference to heated political events. If objectivity has any applicability in such cases, then it is also likely to be applicable to less heated ones.

— That is a hypothesis, but I am willing to go along with it for now. What cases will you use?

— I will focus on news reporting during electoral campaigns. You will grant me that it is then that foul play, exaggerations, and sheer lies tend to abound in politics, won't you?

— I will. Except for wars, political campaigns are among the most vicious political events.

— Your suggestion is well taken. I should also consider war-related matters, such as the reporting of the massacre of Israeli athletes during the 1972 Munich Olympic games. So, if objectivity makes sense and is applicable in news reporting of events such as these, won't you conclude that, in all likelihood, objectivity makes sense and is also applicable to policy- and decision-making concerning these and other matters?

— I might then be inclined to conclude such a thing. But doing so would in no way imply that I would be assenting to your theory. Even if objectivity is applicable to policy- and decision-making, your theory might not do a good job concerning such application.

— Fair enough. Whether the theory does a good job of dealing with objectivity, however, will have to be established after I have substantially formulated it. For the time being, let us concentrate on the relation between objectivity and policy- and decision-making using, as our examples, cases of the type we just discussed.

4 Informing the Public: Ethics, Policy-Making, and Objectivity in News Reporting

Newspaper reports claim that Will Rogers once said: "I hope we never live to see the day when a thing is as bad as some of our newspapers make it."[1] Slanted, exaggerated, or simply false reports, frequently emphasizing the bad, are commonplace and have led many to doubt that objectivity can play any role in news reporting. This is a source of uneasiness to some and elation to others. Some claim that objectivity is a myth and hail subjectivity as the road to freedom and rightness. Andrew Kopkind did so when he stated, "objectivity is the rationalization for moral disengagement, the classic cop-out from choice making."[2] This position is often echoed and extended to policy-making in general by various philosophers. For example, J. L. Mackie states, "there is an inescapable subjective ingredient, an element of choice or preference, in the reasoning that supports any policy decision."[3] Accordingly, there "is no merit in pretending that our choices are rationally constrained in ways that they are not. We are . . . free to mould or remould our moral system so as better to promote whatever it is that we do value."[4]

This romantic enthusiasm is matched only by the cautious uneasiness of those who see the subjectivist conception of political and moral life, including news reporting, as the road to arbitrariness and caprice and away from freedom. Along these lines, Herbert Brucker wrote, "it is time for all who denounce objective news to stop and think, before American journalism reverts to the primitive practices from which objectivity rescued it," namely, the practices that turned news reporting into mere propaganda.[5] It is not uncommon to find philosophers taking a similar position not only about news reporting but about the entire gamut of moral life. For example, Ronald Milo states that if moral judgments are subjective because they depend on our particular desires and preferences, then "we cannot convince someone that what he proposes to do is morally wrong—even if it is a case

40

of torturing someone solely for the sake of amusement—provided that he has perverse enough preferences."[6]

The disagreements just described raise various questions: Is objectivity possible in news reporting? If so, how? Is it a good thing? To what extent and in what sense, if any, should objectivity serve as a ground for policy- and decision-making about news reporting? And whatever the role of objectivity in news reporting, can and should it have the same role in policy-making? These are the questions I address. In addressing them, I distinguish between the personal, institutional, and social testing senses of objectivity. In the *personal* sense, to be objective is for a person to be free from prejudice and bias. In the *institutional* sense, to be objective is for news reporting to follow a set of rules, for example, by being merely factual or, alternatively, by practicing interpretive reporting. It amounts to a reporting policy or groups of policies and practices. In the *social testing* sense, to be objective is for news reports and reporting practices, policies, decisions, and, in general, ideas and social arrangements affected by them to be open to critical scrutiny by anyone.[7]

I offer reasons in support of four main theses. First, though all these senses of objectivity are relevant to news reporting, they are inadequate as a sufficient ground for policy- and decision-making about it. Second, what is also, and often more significant is the political context in which discussions concerning objectivity take place, and how these discussions affect not just news reporting but the public. Third, there is currently no good reason for accepting the hypothesis advanced by some philosophers that, in such discussions, conflicting, coexistent points of view are irreducible. Fourth, even if this hypothesis is true, it does not entail that objectivity in the social testing sense is impossible or a bad thing in news reporting or policy-making.

THE OBJECTIVITY CONTROVERSY IN NEWS REPORTING

There is abundant evidence that both journalists and nonjournalists are sharply divided on whether reporting can be objective and, if so, whether it ought to be. The situation amounts to a controversy that often centers around whether reporters can or ought to have such psychological traits as detachment or empathy. In other words, it often is about objectivity in the personal sense. Those who berate objectivity argue that since no one can be totally free from prejudice and cultural biases, no one can be detached; therefore, no reporter, and hence no reporting, can be objective. To them, there can be only involvement: Objectivity is impossible, so it ought not be pursued. Subjectivity is king. In this vein, Bill Moyers is reported to have written:

Of all the great myths of American journalism, objectivity is the greatest. Each of us sees what his own experience leads him to see.[8]

This position does not go unchallenged. Some hold that though no one can be totally free from prejudice and cultural biases, nearly everyone can be significantly free from them. Hence, they argue, reporters can be partially detached and objective. Objectivity is possible in the personal sense, and the reporting of those who develop such an objective attitude concerning the news is, as a consequence, objective. This position is typically held by those who believe that reporting ought to be objective. The reason offered in support of this view is that news reporting ought to give us the truth, and objectivity attained through detachment is the way to truth. Involvement is the way to partisanship and hence untruth. "Objectivity is the supreme pursuit," they say. Alan Barth took this stand when he stated: "The tradition of objectivity is one of the principal glories of American journalism."[9]

Others are not skeptical of objectivity but cynical about it. They think that objectivity is possible in the personal sense, as detachment. They further think that such objectivity leads to impartiality and balance in the presentation of the news. However, they consider this a misfortune. Indeed, they believe that news reporting ought not to strive at being objective, for if it succeeded in this attempt, it would give us only part of the truth and also something worse: acquiescence in the status quo. A more restrained view along similar lines was formulated by Roberto C. Goizueta, chairman of the Coca-Cola Co., who told an editors' meeting:

The single most damaging trait in today's journalism . . . is that in the search for, and preoccupation with, objectivity and balance, the important elements of context, perspective and judgment often suffer.[10]

The positions just described do not exhaust those taken in the controversy. Still others believe that although objectivity attained through detachment is indeed a misfortune, there is another new objectivity that "does not come by self-effacement, but by self-transcendence, and . . . it is . . . the objectivity of the ever-questioning, ever-empathetic reporter."[11] How and to what extent this objectivity is possible, and why it is good, however, are left obscure. At any rate, the controversy, as described so far, is about the possibility and value of objectivity as freedom from prejudice and cultural biases in reporters, and as impartial and balanced presentation in news reports.

Still other positions taken in the controversy go beyond the concern with the character and conduct of individual reporters. They call for specific reporting policies, thus involving objectivity in the institutional sense. Before addressing these views, let us clarify the social context in which the controversy develops, because the reasons for adopting some form of institutional objectivity can best be understood and assessed in such a context. In particular, let us focus on the fact that the controversy tends to come to the fore when significant policy-making problems arise in the United States or other societies. For example, it recurrently comes to the fore in the United States, if not elsewhere, whenever the Israeli-Arab confrontation in the Middle East flares up.[12] An examination of the controversy in this type of context should help realistically evaluate the questions formulated at the outset. It should also help realistically evaluate the positions taken on the matter. In carrying out this examination, I focus on the reporting of political events, particularly during electoral campaigns. In such circumstances, both news reporting and politics tend to converge, and objectivity and news reporting are often tried by fire.

THE POLITICS OF OBJECTIVITY

Discussions of objectivity in the reporting of political events are themselves part and parcel of politics, not discussions in a world above it all. They become especially heated, biased, and lacking in empathy during electoral campaigns. The 1952 U.S. presidential campaign was no exception. On September 18, it reached its hottest point. By and large, things were calm on that day. Most papers had little of significance to report. The *New York Times* reported that the Republican candidate, General Dwight Eisenhower, was in the Midwest quoting the scriptures and calling for an "honest deal." The Democratic candidate, Governor Adlai Stevenson, was in Connecticut upholding "ethics in politics ahead of victory." And the Republican vice-presidential candidate, Senator Richard Nixon, was in California denouncing Democratic corruption and calling for higher ethical standards in government. Most other papers' reports were equally dull. But there was an exception: On the third page of the *New York Post*, there was a story revealing that a private fund was operating for Nixon's benefit; that there was a millionaires' club exclusively devoted to the financial comfort of candidate Nixon. The front-page banner read: SECRET NIXON FUND! The inside headline said: "Secret Rich Men's Trust Fund Keeps Nixon in Style Far Beyond His Salary." Later that day, the United Press and Associated Press wired the story throughout the country. The political battle had begun. It was going to last for ten days, and it was going to embattle the press itself.

Republicans called the story a smear of their communist-fighting vice-presidential candidate. Senator Karl Mundt called the *New York Post* "a left wing smear sheet," even though Nixon confirmed the existence of the fund that day.[13] Republican newspapers followed suit. The *Boston Herald*, for example, put the story in the middle of page seventeen under a single-column headline saying, "Politics Took Nixon Fund." The *New York World Telegram and Sun* put it on page twenty-three, in the editorial section. The *Detroit News* squeezed it into a narrow spot above a large advertisement on page nine.

Pro-Stevenson papers did quite the opposite. The *St. Louis Post-Dispatch* and the *Milwaukee Journal*, for example, gave the story front-page treatment. The *Dispatch*'s headline read: "'Angels' Paid Nixon $16,000 to 'Sell Free Enterprise,' Paper is Told."[14]

These events took place ten days after Stevenson had called the U.S. newspapers a "one-party press" in a speech in Portland, in the midst of the heated debate his statement provoked. Soon afterwards, President Truman added to the fire when he said:

> News papers, especially daily news papers, have become big business, and big business traditionally has always been Republican. I suggest that Americans bear this in mind, and add a dash of salt to every Republican helping of the news, especially in those many papers and magazines which do not give a fair balance of news between the two major parties.[15]

His accusation was clear: By and large, newspapers and magazines had made a practice of slanting the news in order to favor Republicans and big business. Truman's statement was also slanted. As our previous examples indicate, major newspapers, whatever their political leanings, slanted the news not just through the reports' main text but through the headlines, relative size and shape, and position of the reports.

The controversy spread like fire—a fact that has more than anecdotal import. This was but one moment in the recurrent controversy about objectivity in news reporting. And, it is realistic to believe that the controversy will stay with us for quite a while. For it has been with us for at least half a century and has become more widespread and sharper during the 1960s, 1970s, and 1980s, proving, so far, to be quite intractable. Why? I suggest that this is so because the controversy reflects—indeed, is fueled by—persistently conflicting concerns of the individuals and societal sectors involved, and because these concerns are affected by the reports.

My hypothesis is supported by various facts. For one, few alternative newspapers, if any, engage in objective news reporting. They believe that such reporting would rule out advocating the concerns—the interests and ideas—they intend to advocate. Further evidence is provided by the fact that quite a few mainstream newspapers support objective reporting. The reasons for this are either, as President Truman argued, that it is good for the mainstream newspaper business or, as others would have it, that mainstream ideals and ideas, in the United States and elsewhere, rule out advocacy and uphold objectivity. Regardless of whether these claims are true, the controversy is not simply about objectivity but also about economic interests, political positions, moral claims, moral rules and principles, ideals, and, in some cases, the wants or demands of various constituencies. Real and persistent conflicting concerns underlie claims about objectivity and contribute to people engaging in the controversy.

The preceding discussion indicates that all participants are put at risk by the conflict, for it disrupts both the media and society—at least in the form of generalized distrust of the media or the policy-making process. Such disruption matters both morally and socially, and it suggests that one should not rely merely or primarily on views about objectivity in trying to determine what to do or what policies to adopt concerning objectivity in news reporting. *The fact of the controversy, and the conflicting concerns that fuel it, should be squarely addressed and given due weight.* Disregarding them can have consequences for the media and society that are at least as intolerable as those of disregarding the social need for accurate and complete information about matters of public interest. In case there is doubt about this point, let us consider some historical evidence that supports it.

MCCARTHYISM AND CHANGES
IN INSTITUTIONAL OBJECTIVITY

The policy of not editorializing the news was thought to uphold objectivity and was thereby adopted and retained in Senator Joseph McCarthy's time, despite the disagreements and eventual controversy about it and the conflicts that underlined the controversy. Senator McCarthy was a master at taking advantage of this policy. He would charge that certain people in the State Department were communists, and the media, in accordance with their policy, would simply report what the senator had said. This policy of objective reporting required that only the bare facts be reported, without comment. Of course, this does not explain why his charges got front-page coverage. The point is that a strict application of the policy, coupled with the leeway newspeople had concerning placement and headlines, contributed to misleading the public and had disastrous consequences for a number of innocent citizens. Conrad C. Fink describes the situation as follows:

> It was an agonizing experience for reporters of the "who-said-what-and-when" school. They could see the senator jumping ahead, from charge to charge, never letting rebuttal catch up. A person attacked today tried to respond tomorrow, but by that time McCarthy was attacking someone else, again seizing headlines. McCarthy, who thoroughly understood the mechanics of news agency and newspaper operations, often timed press conferences just before presses rolled. Day after day, newspapers carried his latest charge before they could obtain balancing comment.[16]

As a result, the critics of the policy multiplied, the controversy spread, and news reporting reached a state of crisis. Had newspeople addressed the fact of the controversy about objectivity and the conflicts of concerns it reflected, these consequences for people and for reporting might have been avoided. By merely using some exaggerated notion of objectivity (for example, complete detachment)—whether in a utopian or a skeptical vein—one fails to address the controversy, let alone the underlying conflicts. This amounts to being lost in abstractions and caught up in the controversy, and is likely to contribute to bringing about intolerable consequences for news reporting institutions and policy-making in general.

Some of the consequences of merely factual news reporting were recognized at the time and, as a result, changes in the institutional conception of objectivity occurred:

> From the McCarthy experience came a true turn in American journalism, a realization that traditional efforts to balance charge with response by quoting the other side a day or so later were inadequate. There evolved a new, much wider definition of objectivity that requires a reporter to provide a dimension of analysis or interpretation in addition to factual reporting. . . . This is done by inserting balancing material within a single story, or writing an interpretive story labeled "news analysis" for a newspage, often next to the spot news story itself.[17]

The controversy, however, did not end here. Interpretive news reporting as just described proved inadequate to cover the Vietnam War and cover-ups during the Nixon administration. Analysis was then included in the news report itself.[18] This raised the question: How is objectivity possible when interpretation is included in news reports? As a result, the so-called new journalism developed in the 1960s and 1970s, where only advocacy was left.[19] But such advocacy also amounts to being caught up in the controversy and, just like detachment, is likely to lead to intolerable consequences for news reporting and policy-making. It breeds public distrust of these activities, which easily leads to alienation from the policy-making process—a sad prospect for democracy, individual rights, and the common good alike.

New journalism advocacy, however, has not overtaken the media. A position that shifts the emphasis from reporters' detachment or empathy, and reports' factual or interpretive balance, to features of the reporting *process* itself is gaining currency. Conrad C. Fink describes it as follows:

> The writer . . . with a paragraph or two on how a story was researched or which sources were contacted, can add for reader or viewer a dimension of understanding that helps establish trust in the story, and thus in the journalist and the newspaper or television station.[20]

Establishing this trust is certainly needed if news reporting is to have the function it must have, if societal policy-making is to make room for reason and an informed, critical public. Citing a story's sources and describing how it was researched open it to the public's critical scrutiny. This publicity, which takes place at the social level, goes beyond any particular individual's limitations of emotion, passion, or information, making room and setting the boundaries for objectivity in the process. But does it suffice to assess news reporting?

Looking back at the past forty years or so, each news reporting change that took place in the United States seems merely to have reflected a given position taken in the controversy, whether about objectivity alone or some selected consequences of some form of objectivity. There seems to have been no attempt to deal with the *social fact* of the controversy itself. Yet, as previously argued, this fact ought to be squarely addressed in making policy and decisions about news reporting. Otherwise, it will be unintelligently, because thoughtlessly, addressed, because newspeople must implicitly adopt some news reporting practice, if not policy, as soon as they report the news. Short of not reporting the news at all, they must report it factually, or interpretatively, or in an advocatory manner, or in some combination of these or other types of reporting. This is bound to have some effect on the conflicting concerns that fuel the controversy. Hence, for the sake of intelligently dealing with the fact of the controversy, its underlying concerns, and the disruption all this brings upon news reporting, policy-making in general, and sometimes the lives of individuals, it is crucial to establish what questions to ask in evaluating news reporting practices, policies, and decisions.

The preceding discussion provides grounds for concluding that the questions should not simply be: Does this news reporting policy promote objectivity in news reporting? Should it do so? Nor should it be: Does this news reporting policy address the concerns I believe ought to be addressed? Rather, it should first be acknowledged that there is controversy about objectivity in news reporting, that this controversy is fueled by various recurrent underlying concerns, and that it disrupts news reporting, policy-making, and people's individual lives. Then, it should be asked: What news reporting policies are newspeople morally permitted—or required—to adopt in dealing with the policy problem posed by the controversy, its underlying concerns (only one of which is objectivity), and the disruption it causes? This question is not simply about the objectivity of policies but also about a variety of circumstances that must be balanced against one another in sound policy-making. Of course, merely asking such a question will not automatically put the controversy to rest, but it is likely to be addressed in a manner free from excessive idealization, political and moral irrelevance, and simple self-righteous or self-interested intolerance.

So far, I have argued for the first two theses of this essay: that, though all senses of objectivity are relevant to news reporting, they are inadequate as a sufficient ground for policy- and decision-making about news reporting;

and that what is often more significant is the political context in which discussions concerning objectivity take place and how these discussions affect not just news reporting but the public. This essay's remainder examines some philosophical implications of this position and argues for the remaining—third and fourth—theses: that there is currently no good reason for accepting the hypothesis that when there is disagreement, some conflicting coexistent points of view are irreducible, and that even if such a hypothesis were true, it does not follow that objectivity in the social testing sense is impossible or a bad thing in news reporting or policy-making.

OBJECTIVITY WITHOUT AGREEMENT

Whenever a long-worshipped idol falls, everything else seems doomed to fall with it. This is the feeling one may get from the preceding sections, whose upshot is that objectivity, however significant, is not a decisive ground for establishing sound news reporting policy. A nagging question arises: Is any news reporting policy justified, so long as it contributes to decrease (or, if a crisis would tend to promote the common good, so long as it contributes to increase) social conflict?

Of course not. First, it is not justified simply from a common-sense point of view. A policy of engaging in libelous news reports, for example, is not justified, even if it would increase social conflict that would, in the long run, promote the common good. To think otherwise would be analogous to thinking that if framing the innocent would lead to the common good, then it is morally permissible. It is not. Second, like framing the innocent, libel would lead to social and personal consequences that ordinary people of sound mind—those not carried away by passion or emotion, and whose reasoning is unimpaired by coercion or manipulation—would find intolerable.

The fact that ordinary people would pass such judgments presupposes a type of objectivity in news reporting that is a feature not of any particular reporter or report but of the news reporting process and policy-making in general. This is objectivity as social testing. To say that news reports and news reporting practices, policies, and decisions are socially testable is to say that they are public. That is, they are open to the previously discussed test of critical scrutiny and of people's interaction with the reports, practices, policies, decisions, and their consequences. In other words, at a very minimum, it is always possible for anyone to give reasons for or against such practices, policies, and decisions and to test them against actual social practice.

However, mere possibilities are among the greatest sources of neuroses and philosophical delusions. Is the possibility of critical scrutiny one of these sources? Since, in the midst of controversy, people are often biased, and their views and concerns are affected differently by different reporting policies, is critical scrutiny of these policies actually possible? Or are people bound to take sides merely because one policy reflects their preferences regardless of reason?

The answer to the latter question is no. People's preferences matter, of course, but people are not always carried away by passion or emotion. Nor is their reasoning always impaired by coercion or manipulation. A modicum of objectivity in the personal sense is not just possible, but often actual. And if people lack information, this is not always insurmountable.

In addition, the objectivity involved in critical scrutiny does not depend on the reporter's objectivity at the time of reporting or ever. In fact, reports are likely to be scrutinized because they may mislead members of the public and affect them in ways they find undesirable. It does not matter whether those who produced the reports or adopted or followed the policies leading to such reports are detached or empathetic. Nor does it matter whether the reports are balanced. It does not even matter whether the members of the public who engage in scrutinizing the reports are detached or empathetic. In any case, their reasons (at least reasons that formulate personal preferences, interests, wants, attitudes, or commitments to such things as moral rules, principles, and ideals) will often be publicly formulated in criticizing the reports. And the process will continue, with these reasons themselves now open to critical scrutiny. This process often leads to a settlement of differences and conflicts. Objectivity as social testing is at the core of this ongoing process.

One might object that, as various philosophers have argued, the reasons given are sometimes bound to remain mere formulations of personal preferences, interests, wants, attitudes, or commitments to moral rules, principles, and ideals. There may be no common ground among those involved in the dispute on the basis of which their particular reasons can be transcended. Hence, objectivity is undermined. We already saw that Mackie takes an extreme view in this regard. A philosopher who has taken a moderate position on the objectivity-subjectivity debate, but would nonetheless agree with the objection, is Thomas Nagel. He writes:

> The distinction between subjective and objective is relative. A general human point of view is more objective than the view from where you happen to be, but less objective than the viewpoint of physical science. The opposition between subjective and objective can arise at any place on the spectrum where one point of view claims dominance over another, more subjective one, and that claim is resisted. In the dispute over consequentialism in ethics, it appears in the clash between internal and external views of human life, both fully admitting the importance of human concerns and ends.[21]

No doubt, the clash between what one individual considers morally overriding given his or her moral beliefs and what others (often policymakers) consider morally overriding given their concern with a good social life poses complex ethical problems. Decisions having moral import must be made in the midst of disagreement about who is right because, even if the matter could be resolved, there is not enough time to wait until well-grounded agreement has been reached. But this does not undermine objectivity. Lack of agreement on what takes precedence—an individual's moral commitment or a good social life—does not in any way entail that judgments cannot be made about the subject. Nor does it entail that reasons for or against the judgments cannot be formulated. That the judgments can be made is evidenced by the fact that they often are made, however heated the disagreement might be. In addition, they are always open to critical scrutiny by appeal to reasons and social practice. This is all that objectivity in the social testing sense requires.

One might object that the preceding discussion misses the point, for given the fragmented nature of today's world, the reasons some persons or groups understand are not understood by others. Indeed, different persons and groups use different languages to formulate their own reasons. Think, for example, of the linguistic, conceptual, methodological, and practical differences concerning moral matters between the technology, business, policy-making, and philosophy communities.[22] Upon realizing the extent and depth of these differences, one might add, as Nagel does, that the "coexistence of conflicting points of view, varying in detachment from the contingent self, is . . . an irreducible fact of life."[23]

In response, it can be said, first, that the irreducibility Nagel describes is just a hypothesis. Pointing to recurrent sharp differences of opinion between philosophers or members of the general public on matters of moral import is no good ground for believing that these differences are irreducible. They may *now*, given our current linguistic, conceptual, methodological, and practical differences, be irreducible. But neither languages nor conceptual frameworks, methods, and practices are static. They can and do change. Indeed, as I argue later, they can change through dialogue and social interaction so that today's incommensurables are superseded by tomorrow's common ground.

Second, even if the described construction of a common ground of reasons through social decision procedures were, at least on occasion, unworkable, the mutual irreducibility of moral points of view does not mean that there is no objectivity. It would if objectivity entailed shared reasons, but objectivity at most entails that good reasons can be formulated in the process of critical scrutiny and trial by practice. In this sense, objectivity is embedded in the process, because it is possible to formulate good reasons for or against the reports or the policies leading to them. In fact, such reasons are often formulated even in oppressive social environments, and there seems to be little doubt that this is a good thing. Otherwise only arbitrariness would remain. Hence, objectivity as social testing is not only possible but actual and, since it helps make better policy and decisions, a good thing.[24]

BUILDING COMMON GROUND

What should we do, if anything, about objectivity? As for objectivity in the social testing sense, there are some things we can do. Though it is a fact of social life that reasons can be given for or against news reports, news reporting actions, practices, policies, and, indeed, any aspect of social life, it is important that such give-and-take of reasons be vigorous. So freedom of speech and political activity should be encouraged to help objectivity in the social testing sense flourish.

Even if no such measures are taken, the test of actual practice can be applied to those reports, actions, practices, and policies. Of course, without reasoning individuals, no such thing will happen. But this simply means that, without reasoning individuals, objectivity in the social testing sense will have no application, just as in a world without any sentences, truth as a feature of declarative sentences is inapplicable. It does not mean that objectivity in the social testing sense makes no sense, nor that it plays no role in actual social life. Indeed, it makes critical scrutiny possible.[25]

In addition, a common ground of reasons can be built, which is evidenced in the process of scrutinizing news reports and reporting policies. The reports' and policies' perceived shortcomings are often described in ways people—not necessarily the reporters or the individuals directly affected by the reports—can understand and reason about. Third parties not caught up in a passionate, emotional, inadequately informed, or manipulated discussion of reports and policies—or those simply engaged in the controversy from a different perspective—can provide critical balance to the scrutiny. This can happen even if the third parties are not detached (after all, if they are involved in the discussions, they will not be entirely unaffected by them).

The point is not simply that mediation and arbitration, together with other social decision procedures, play a role in settling the disputes for policy purposes.[26] The point is that these procedures, which are not sheer dialogue, involve and develop a commonality of practices that mutually adjust the initially clashing points of view. As a result, the languages, concepts, and methods of those involved merge, and a common ground of readjusted reasons is built.[27] As in many a successful marriage, mutual conceptual, linguistic, and practical adjustments develop as a by-product of discussions that need not be, and rarely are, about the adjustments themselves.

As for objectivity in the personal and institutional senses, we can and should strive to make adequate room for it. It permits and promotes critical scrutiny, the use of reasons, and the development of common grounds among individuals and groups with widely different moral views. And these are badly needed if civilized societies are to survive today's complexities and changes. To say this, however, is not to say that everyone or anyone should always be objective. Indeed, there are cases in which a person may be permitted, if not required, to be quite subjective. Along these lines, in reviewing Serge Groussard's *The Blood of Israel*, which discusses the massacre of Israeli athletes at the 1972 Munich Olympic games, Elie Wiesel wrote:

> He does not attempt to be objective; he invokes no political philosophy to justify the Commandos' actions, and for that we are grateful. In certain extreme situations one has no right to be objective, for objectivity leads to neutrality and indifference.[28]

This is the type of situation in which personal objectivity might be morally objectionable.

But it is not my aim here to establish whether Wiesel's position is sound. Rather, it is to illustrate how certain cases may constitute an exception to the rule of generally striving for objectivity, and to explain how the position advanced in this essay makes room for such exceptions. This essay focuses on the often heated controversies involving news reporting and does not rule out any views on the grounds that they are irrational or formulated by entirely biased individuals. Instead, it recognizes that they are formulated in the context of objectivity as social testing, where any view is open to critical scrutiny by anyone and to the test of actual practice. In this context, Wiesel's claim may well survive the challenge of critical scrutiny and trial by practice. And so may the weaker view William James formulated in "The Will to Believe": That in certain extreme situations—whenever one faces a genuine option, evidence and proof are absent or mixed, and one's happiness is contingent on one's belief—one has the right to believe as one pleases.[29] When it comes to policy and decision manifestations of these views, one can, in the ways previously indicated, distinguish what is permissible from what is not. And the views themselves are subject to the test of critical scrutiny and social interaction, not merely of individual opinion. In fact, the very possibility of establishing Wiesel's or James's views on the basis of reasons rather than arbitrarily preferring them is grounded in objectivity as social testing. So are the various positions taken about news reporting and their manifestations in conduct, practice, or policy. This is fortunate, for otherwise, against Will Rogers's hope, this would be the day when things are worse than the most pessimistic of our newspapers make them.

Dialogue

— Your position concerning shared and good reasons makes me uneasy. I agree that objectivity entails good, though not necessarily shared, reasons. Yet I am uneasy with the fact that opposing parties will not always agree on what constitutes a good reason, or on what reasons are good. When this happens, the disagreement may become irreconcilable. This is not a hopeful prospect.

— I entirely agree that such a prospect provides reason for uneasiness. Yet, as I argued, it does not undermine objectivity, however much it may undermine the actualization of a moral community among those whose disagreements turn out to be irreconcilable. Besides, we should not jump to conclusions. As I also argued, it is merely a hypothesis that they are irreconcilable. And even if they are irreconcilable now, this situation may change later, depending on what we do about it now.

— My uneasiness, however, persists. What should I do about it? Do you have any suggestions?

— If your uneasiness results from a desire to attain certainty on the matter, I suggest that you reconsider the soundness of such a desire. After all, as I mention in a note to the essay, my position has a precedent in John Dewey's *The Quest for Certainty*, where he sharply criticized this quest as misguided and a significant pitfall in Western philosophy. Life is risky, our future is uncertain, and a sound theory should both reflect these facts and help us deal with them. This is what the theory I am formulating attempts. I would consider it a failure if it disregarded or misrepresented these obvious risks and uncertainties. If it did, it would be unrealistic and of little help in dealing with them.

— It occurs to me, however, that part of the uneasiness I feel concerns your approach itself. It focuses on the logic of judgments and decisions more than I think it should. Maybe I have been unduly influenced by the work of MacIntyre and others, but I think that a different approach to moral philosophy should be favored. In this alternative approach, the logic of judgments would play a secondary role, and the character and well-being of persons would be paramount.

— No doubt, the ethics of character and the well-being of persons should be given more prominence than they have been given during much of the twentieth century. Many quandaries would be avoided if people's attitudes and traits, and their fit in a moral community, were a significant focus of attention and if, through education, this led to the actualization of a more cohesive moral community. I have no doubt that we should strive to approach this situation. Yet we are a long way from living in such a community right now, and the issues I discuss call for policy-making in the meantime. Indeed, I think the notion of objectivity in the social testing sense offers a workable connection between these short-run and long-run prospects.

— Maybe so, but you have not discussed it sufficiently for readers to be able to tell. Besides, your focus on news reporting detracts a bit from the role of social testing in overall philosophical discussions of subjectivity.

— I am aware of that, and I will address the matter further in the next essay. Let me mention, however, that unless we focus on particular cases or types of cases as I did in the previous essay, we will hardly be in a position to take more general stands concerning objectivity or any other matters of philosophical and political interest. Without careful attention to particulars, such stands will be little more than a lot of hand waving.

— Am I to infer that you are an empiricist?

— You are to infer that I am trying to formulate a realistic theory, partly because unrealistic theories for dealing with policy and decision problems are irrational. Indeed, they are as irrational as the Italian Renaissance cities' reliance on astrologers to decide whether and when to wage war on each other. In contrast, in the attempt to be rational, hence realistic, I pay attention to particular cases and, in general, to the results of empirical research on matters of policy and decisions.

5 Critical Interaction: Judgment, Decision, and the Social Testing of Moral Hypotheses

The role of judgment in moral and political life has been widely questioned during the twentieth century. In philosophy, this has been done by holding that the distinction between evaluations or judgments on the one hand, and decisions on the other, is a mere distinction of words, without any practical substance to it. In short, so-called judgments and evaluations are, or in the end depend on, arbitrary decisions or something very much like them.

Positions such as this are a source of elation to some and uneasiness to others. Some hail the decision aspect of political and, indeed, all moral life as the road to freedom from the authoritarianism they perceive in political and moral doctrines based exclusively on universal rules of right judgment.[1] This romantic enthusiasm is matched only by the cautious uneasiness of those who see the decision aspect of political and moral life as the road to arbitrariness and caprice, and away from reason.[2] Pitting reason as authoritarian rule mongering against freedom as arbitrary and foolish caprice, however, is a mistake. It is the path of good sense not to expose an exaggeration by falling prey to another. In what follows, I seek such a balance.

VIRGINIA HELD'S ACCOUNT OF MORAL EXPERIENCE

A hypothesis that, as I will argue, undermines the place of judgment, hence of critical scrutiny, in moral and political life has been advanced by Virginia Held in "The Political 'Testing' of Moral Theories." She says:

> Moral experience . . . is the experience of consciously and conscientiously choosing to act and to refrain from action, the experience of voluntarily accepting or rejecting moral positions, the experience of willingly approving or disapproving in a moral sense. . . . In moral experience, we decide to take "I ought to do x," or "y is morally wrong," or "you ought not to

do z," etc., as morally valid or invalid. We do so by voluntarily acting or refraining from action, by committing ourselves to moral stands.[3]

Held's position is clear: Choice and the will are basically all there is to moral experience. This is an exaggeration. As I will argue, it does not describe, as the article's title indicates, how moral theories are politically tested. Rather, it makes them untestable, and it makes the critical scrutiny of moral ideas and actions and the policies embodying them impossible.

A PRACTICAL INCONSISTENCY

The exaggerations in Held's account do not just give choice and the will a central place in moral experience (which is indeed their place), but the *exclusive* role. As her statement indicates, we *decide* to take ought statements and statements of right and wrong as valid or invalid. We decide to do this by acting voluntarily or withholding approval.

One might grant that we decide to take certain statements as morally valid or invalid by acting voluntarily or withholding approval. But one might add that our giving or withholding approval is based on moral judgments and not on arbitrary decisions or on blind acts of the will. This might be a defensible position, but this is not what Held maintains. The judgments are also a matter of choice, as she says in trying to distinguish the testing of scientific theories from that of moral theories:

> In the case of perception we ought, in some sense at least, to let the world impose its truth on our observations, we ought to be relatively passive recipients of the impressions that lead us to consider observation statements true or false. In the case of action and of approval, on the other hand, we ought to shape the world actively in accordance with our choices. We ought to be relatively more active than passive . . . we ought, in actively and voluntarily choosing how to act and what to approve of, to impose on the world our choices of the prescriptions and judgments to consider valid, instead of letting the world impose its facts upon us.[4]

This is an exaggeration, hence inaccurate. And since exaggerations are often sources of practical inconsistencies, it is not surprising that there is one here. Notice, first, that Held says that we *ought to shape the world* in accordance with our choices, and we *ought to impose our choices of what* prescriptions and *judgments* to consider valid in the world. That is, based on Held's position, even her judgments of what we ought to do must themselves be based on an arbitrary choice or a blind act of the will.

But if, as Held herself says, "To test something is to see how it stands up under critical scrutiny," her account rules out the possibility of testing any moral theories and, for that matter, any moral ideas at all.[5] By putting sheer caprice at the basis of moral inquiry, her account makes critical scrutiny and the testing of moral theories and moral ideas impossible. It does this because it rules out a central characteristic of critical scrutiny: that whenever this scrutiny is possible, it is possible to give reasons for or against whatever is subject to scrutiny.[6] If the determination of which judgments and prescriptions are to be considered valid is a mere matter of our own individual choice or of individual decision, then no reason can be given for or against such judgments and prescriptions.

One might object that I am selecting too unsympathetic an interpretation of Held's position. After all, she says that, in the case of action and approval, *we* ought to shape the world actively in accordance with *our* choices. *We* ought to impose on the world *our* choices of the prescriptions and judgments to consider valid, instead of letting the world impose its facts upon *us*. A more sympathetic interpretation would acknowledge that the terms "we" and "our" are crucially ambiguous: Do they mean we (or our) one by one, we (or our) together as a given group, or we (or our) together as all human beings? This would make room for a less subjectivist interpretation.

In response, I must say that, in discussions such as this one, ambiguity is not an excusing condition. Held's account can still be faulted for not explicitly excluding the extremely subjectivist interpretation I have attributed to her. And even if the appropriate interpretation were not subjectivistic in this extreme sense, it would still be thoroughly voluntaristic. According to Held, even the determination of which judgments and prescriptions are to be considered valid is a mere matter of our choice or decision, even if this choice or decision is somehow collective. It is nonetheless the case that no reason can be given for or against such judgments and prescriptions. Hence, they cannot be subject to critical scrutiny. Held's account makes critical scrutiny impossible. Therefore, it makes not simply the testing of moral theories but, more importantly, moral inquiry itself—which is a form of critical inquiry—impossible. Only *uncritical* scrutiny remains.

POLITICAL AND MORAL QUESTIONABLENESS

Accounts such as Held's are not merely inaccurate or sources of practical inconsistencies. They are also politically unwise and morally objectionable for various reasons. First, they impoverish the notions of policy assessment and moral scrutiny. Second, they relegate conflicts such as those about the arms race and, after the end of the cold war, about regional hegemony and the proliferation of high-tech weapons to the realm of the arbitrary. Indeed, non-war-related conflicts about such matters as abortion, environmental deterioration, and race relations are also relegated to this realm. Third, as a result of its narrow reliance on the will, such accounts as a rule tend to make things even less governable and more conflictive than they already are. They invariably bring things to a head, unless some arbitrary change of mind does away with the conflicts. In other words, such accounts are not only untrue to the facts of politics. They are also a sure prescription for catastrophe.

Policy and decision problems concerning the proliferation of nuclear, chemical, or biological weapons and regional conflicts, as well as those concerning abortion, environmental deterioration, and race relations, can be soundly addressed by relying on judgment (as well as decisions and determination). They cannot be soundly addressed, as Held posits, through what amounts to romantic—however collective—passion. But the question arises: What leads to such romantic exaggerations? No doubt, an adequate explanation of this fact will refer to personal and social features. But linguistic features appear to play a role too. I next examine some linguistic ambiguities that, at least in Virginia Held's account, appear to contribute to its exaggerated nature.

AMBIGUITIES OF APPROVAL

In presenting her position, Virginia Held uses the term *approval* in a manner that exemplifies a common linguistic pitfall. This pitfall would not be a cause for concern if it simply led to theoretical confusion, or even moral and political irrelevance in moral theory. But developments in moral theory, even if irrelevant in content, have consequences in practice. Given some time, they may well spill over into moral life. And in the case of the above term and its related terms and concepts, it opens the door to mere self-righteousness where reflection and a sensitive critical approach are needed.

Let us take a closer look at the term *approval* as well as related approval and disapproval terms and concepts. I focus on actually operant moral and political reasoning and use the results of the analysis as an indicator of the extent to which accounts such as Held's fail to reflect the realities of moral and political thinking.[7]

The verb *to approve* has at least two senses: a judgment sense and a decision sense. These are: "1. to speak or think favorably of, pronounce or consider agreeable or good, judge favorably; 2. to confirm or sanction formally, ratify."[8] In the first sense, *approve* is often followed by the preposition *of*, as in: He approves of the administration's policies. This is the same as saying that he "judges favorably of" the administration's policies. In the second, decision sense, *approve* is never followed by the preposition *of*, as in: The Senate promptly approved the bill.[9] This is not a judgment but a decision the Senate made and an action it accordingly took. Its opposite is not, The Senate promptly judged unfavorably of the bill, but The Senate promptly rejected the bill. Hence, to approve something in this decision sense is to sanction it.

A parallel point can be made about the verb *to disapprove*. In its judgment sense, it means "1. to think (something) wrong or reprehensible; censure or condemn in opinion."[10] In its decision sense, it means "2. to withhold approval from; decline to sanction: 'The court disapproved the verdict.' "[11]

Accordingly, approvals and disapprovals in the decision senses of these terms are decisions or actions that create legal situations. They do so by, for example, sanctioning or refusing to sanction bills into laws.[12] In contrast, someone's approval or disapproval *of* something is a favorable or unfavorable judgment of it, not a decision. It is the outcome of an activity basically aimed at finding out or establishing rather than merely instituting something. A parallel ambiguity can be found in policy assessment.

AMBIGUITIES OF POLICY ASSESSMENT

The ambiguities of approval have a parallel in policy assessment that is reflected in the senses of the verb *to assess*. In one sense, it means the activity of estimating the value of something, as in: We need to assess the value of this property in order to calculate the tax the owner owes.[13] In this sense of *to assess*, the outcome of the assessment or estimate is an evaluation or judgment of value and, as such, is capable of error. Either the property is worth that much or nearly that much, or it is not. In this case, the value may be either more or less accurately reported. Since a report is involved, and it is capable of greater or lesser error, there is a judgment at work and, accordingly, this sense of *to assess* can be called its judgment sense.

In contrast, *to assess* is sometimes used in its decision sense.[14] An example of this use is: We need to assess tax percentages for residential property. In this sense, *to assess* means the activity of fixing or imposing the value of something. The outcome of this activity may be justified or not—for example, because it is fair or not—but it is in no way capable of error. The tax percentage is what it was decided that it would be through the said activity. In this case, the activity creates the value instead of reporting it.

EXAGGERATING THE ROLE OF JUDGMENT

Someone overly zealous in defending judgments might think that it all comes down to a matter of judgment, because one can pass judgment on values fixed or imposed in the above manner. No doubt, the values thus created can sometimes be subject to critical scrutiny and thought to be justified or unjustified. That is, correct or incorrect judgments can be passed on them, and these judgments may be based on good, or not so good, reasons. This, however, does not eliminate the decision sense of *to assess*. Though the judgments would themselves *be* outcomes of an assessment in the judgment sense, they would still be *about* an outcome of an assessment in the decision sense.

The preceding discussion begins to place judgment and decision in their proper moral and policy-making perspectives. Later essays explore their respective policy-making functions. There is, however, a line of thought that grants the points just made, but argues that the irretrievable subjectivity of ethics is to be found at a higher level. This is the level of the principles or other general criteria that we use to make particular judgments about, among other things, what decisions to make. It is argued that, though particular practical judgments are not simply and arbitrarily chosen, the principles and criteria on which they are based are.

ERROR THEORIES AND REASONING

In his *Inventing Right and Wrong*, J. L. Mackie states, "Morality is not to be discovered but to be made."[15] Accordingly, Mackie holds that, in some important way, all policy-making and, indeed, morality itself is irretrievably subjective and basically arbitrary because of the element of choice or preference it involves. He says:

> [M]any of the most controversial first order moral issues ... are ... questions about changing or preserving economic and social structures, and about conflicts of interest between organized groups within a state or between states or races; and even when one has chosen what seem to be laudable goals, questions about the methods one may use to pursue them, how to defend legitimate but threatened interests, to vindicate rights that have been violated. Similar problems come up in somewhat different forms for private citizens. ... The argument of this book yields ... no answers to such questions. It cannot, since its main thesis is that there is an inescapable subjective ingredient, an element of choice or preference, in the reasoning that supports any policy decision. What it does offer is only a framework of ideas within which such reasoning can go on.[16]

This passage's talk of reasoning should not lead one to believe that Mackie's position makes room for reason at every level of morality. In explaining his statement that morality is not to be discovered but to be made, he says:

> [W]e have to decide what moral views to adopt, what moral stands to take. No doubt the conclusions we reach will reflect our sense of justice, our moral consciousness. ...
>   But that is not the object of the exercise: the object is rather to decide what to do, what to support and what to condemn, what principles of conduct to accept and foster as guiding or controlling our choices and perhaps those of other people as well.[17]

According to this view, to invent morality is to decide not only what to do, support, and condemn, but also—and most crucially—what principles to use. The question then arises: Are these various decisions arbitrary? Mackie's answer is double-edged. On the one hand, he says:

[T]here is no merit in pretending that our choices are rationally constrained in ways that they are not. We are . . . free to mould . . . our moral system so as better to promote whatever it is that we do value.[18]

On the other hand, however, Mackie cautions:

It does not follow . . . that an individual is free to invent a moral system at will. . . . The prescription "Think of a set of rules and principles the general adoption of which would best promote what you value and see as worthwhile, and then follow them yourself, regardless of what you think others will do" may well be a recipe for disaster.

The prescription "Think of a set of rules, and try to secure their general acceptance" may be impractical. What the individual can do is . . . to put pressure on some fragments of the system, so that they come gradually to be more favorable to what he sees as valuable and worthwhile.[19]

According to this view, reasoning may be involved in deciding what principles to use as guiding our choices: what to support and what to condemn; what moral views to adopt and moral stands to take; and what to do. However, this reasoning at best concerns *how* our preferences or choices, "what we see as valuable and worthwhile,"[20] *will best be promoted by the decisions resulting from our reasoning.* In Mackie's account, the preferences and choices themselves are beyond reason, hence, beyond critical scrutiny.

Mackie does not hold that our preferences and value choices will not change as a result of our reasoning. His position certainly makes room for preference changes as a result of a reasoning process. But if our preferences change as a result of such a process, this is only an interesting psychological development in Mackie's view. It is not a practical *conclusion* reached by weighing the pros and cons of the preferences or value choices themselves, either through our own reflection or through discussions with others. In Mackie's view, in the last analysis, the preferences we have and the value choices we make are both irretrievably subjective and arbitrary.

MORAL EXPEDIENCY: MACKIE'S CONCEPTION
OF POLICY AND DECISION PROBLEMS

Mackie's account involves a questionable conception of policy and decision problems. On this conception, an individual who has a problem of conduct—a behavioral or decision problem—merely has a problem of expediency in attaining or furthering a certain aim assumed not to be at issue itself. A society with a policy problem merely has a problem of expediency concerning what policies will best lead to attaining certain aims assumed not to be at issue themselves. That is, it is characteristic in problems of expediency that the aims are taken for granted and assumed settled. Mackie's account is a perfect example of this *expediency conception* of policy and decision problems: What we see as worthwhile or valuable is not at issue, and the problem is simply that of how best to promote it. It is a mere problem of expediency, even if the expediency involved is moral expediency. This conception, however, leaves Mackie's account open to various objections.

POLITICAL INACCURACY

First, as a matter of fact, problems of expediency in social life are not the most frequent or significant ones. Indeed, they have no place among the range of problems Mackie refers to, concerning such subjects as abortion, world hunger, environmental decay, and the arms race. In these cases, the aims themselves are characteristically at issue, and those involved often sharply disagree about what the aims should be. No doubt, certain individuals or groups may approach the issues as if facing a mere matter of expediency in promoting their own aims: what they see as worthwhile or valuable. However, this is merely an element of higher-level policy and decision problems posed by the fact that there is controversy and even confrontation about these aims. It is in no way an accurate conception of these higher-level policy and decision problems.

POLITICAL AND MORAL QUESTIONABLENESS

Second, there is the problem of what to do about the conflicts of aims and the sharp disagreements and even confrontations that accompany them. This calls for an approach that is not, as a rule, bound to side with one aim or another. But Mackie's position makes no room for such a thing. According to him, one can change aims, but at any one time, one must side with one aim or another. Each and every individual policy-making action must be aimed at promoting what the individual sees as worthwhile or valuable and as having enough support from others so as to have a chance of advancement. Hence, this approach fails to address the political fact of societally disruptive conflicts that policymakers should squarely address. As a consequence, it cannot address the policy and decision problems posed partly by these conflicts. This inadequacy for dealing with the actual problems of the political world is not simply a matter of irrelevance or inaccuracy. Given the enormous risks many of the problems involve, it is also a politically unwise and morally objectionable position.

PREFERENCE CHANGE AND ERROR THEORIES

ERROR THEORIES AND THE COMMON OPINION OBJECTION

In response to these criticisms, one might try to fight charges of irrelevancy and misrepresentation with charges of irrelevancy. One might accordingly say that the preceding discussion is based on ordinary conceptions of policy and decision problems tied to ordinary notions of value. One might add that Mackie's main thesis states that these conceptions are erroneous. And one might proceed to argue that it is therefore irrelevant to point to the fact that those conceptions do not agree with his thesis. Of course they do not. After all, his theory is

> an "error theory," a theory that although most people in making moral judgments implicitly claim, among other things, to be pointing to something objectively prescriptive, these claims are all false.[21]

And it is irrelevant to argue that what an error theory says is false is widely claimed to be true.

REASONS FOR CHANGING PREFERENCES

This response would be well taken if the notions of policy and decision problems, and of moral problems in general, used above as alternatives to Mackie's notions had been shown to be as arbitrary as Mackie indicates. But they have not. Actually, the reasons he mentions as possible bases for deciding what principles to use in guiding our choices, what to support and what to condemn, what moral views to adopt, what moral stands to take, and what to do are relevant reasons for changing our preferences and value choices. As Mackie correctly states:

> Privately imagined rules or principles of action are worthless. . . . What counts is rules that are actually recognized by the members of some social circle, large or small, and that thus set up expectations and claims. Innovations and reforms are not excluded, but they must be possibly actual, not purely utopian.[22]

This already points to reasons for establishing which preferences or value choices, as embodied in given rules or principles, are worthless and which are not. In addition, and quite curiously, Mackie says:

> Notoriously, the same people and the same activities look very different from opposing points of view. A first step is made when both sides see that there are points of view from which each of the rival descriptions makes some sense. A second, harder, but necessary step is made if they can each see some force in the opposing point of view, that is, give some weight to the values and ideals that underlie the aims of their opponents.[23]

To give weight to values and ideals that one did not give weight to in the past is not simply to decide not to promote one's preferences; it is to *change* one's preferences. To say, as Mackie does, that this step is *necessary for fruitfully dealing with societal conflicts* is to point to a reason for changing one's preferences by changing their relative weight. No doubt, in a trivial sense, this involves an irretrievably subjective element, since subjects must be involved for it to happen. But this type of subjectivity is harmless, because it does not make things arbitrary at all. On the contrary, it is compatible with pointing to reasons for taking a less uncompromising and inflexible position in one's moral thinking.

A PARADOXICAL ACCOUNT

To Mackie's credit, it ought to be mentioned that he did not remain silent concerning the feeling of paradox his discussion prompts. He attempts to address it by saying that, when involved in a conflict of values and ideals like those described above:

> Trying to frame maxims which can be endorsed from all points of view, or which represent a compromise between radically different points of view . . . you decide that after all you ought to stop and help. Your moral conclusion, thus arrived at, now owes much less to any of your subjective preferences. But as they have dropped out of the picture they have been replaced by another subjective element, your endorsement of the substantive practical principle of third stage universalization.[24]

According to Mackie, then, one's subjective preferences do not change. They are replaced by one's endorsement of a principle of universalization that enjoins a compromise between radically different points of view in dealing with the conflict.

The paradox remains, however. According to Mackie, the universalization principle must be preferred and replace old preferences. Such a replacement amounts to attributing less weight to the preferences one used to endorse uncompromisingly. Further, this change in their weight is not a merely arbitrary matter because, as indicated, reasons can be given for it. Indeed, Mackie himself has given them. One is that individual preferences are not overriding because their change is necessary for fruitfully dealing with the conflict. Hence, the suggested defense of Mackie's and other error theories refutes the theories.

TOWARD A CRITICAL AND INTERACTIVE APPROACH: THE SOCIAL TESTING OF MORAL HYPOTHESES

The preceding discussion points to an approach that takes discovery and invention, judgment and decision, reason and choice to be closely interconnected with each other and with action in the policy-making process. In this context, moral hypotheses—from proposed rules to principles and entire theories—and policy-making hypotheses—from proposed policies and decisions to theories—can be significantly confirmed or disconfirmed through a social testing process. I next outline some of the constraints on social testing and the features that social testing must have.

HARD-TO-FIND DATA

First, a crucial fact of social testing is that, at assessment time, it is often unfeasible to spell out all significant implications of the policy (or theory). Lack of knowledge or descriptive or predictive ability (if not lack of time) prevents it, even if the details happen to be available for inspection or discovery at the outset. Just think of predicting the specific implications of a policy—or projecting the implications of a moral rule for assessing policies—about the nearly 60,000 chemicals in the U.S. market (among which about 1,000 are new) every year. In effect, only a few can be monitored. And it is extremely difficult to infer which chemicals cause which harms, or even what statistical risks are associated with the chemicals. This difficulty is compounded when one considers the myriad other matters relevant for concluding what would be the side effects of given policies regulating the chemicals or the implications of morals rules for assessing the policies.

UNSETTLED DATA

Second, the above information is not merely hard to find. It is not always available. This is characteristically the case when new technologies are involved—for example, as discussed in Essay 3, the automobile at the beginning of the twentieth century, and personal computers at the end. At the time of their introduction, some relevant considerations—for example, public adaptability to the new technologies—are still unsettled. In any such situation, many significant details still have to be worked out, quite often in unpredictable fashion. This can be done only through a pragmatic process that may include bargaining, negotiation, interaction among those involved, and their limited and only partially controlled experience of the technologies or business or political arrangements under discussion. This is a process of critical scrutiny and social interaction through which reasons for assessing practices, policies, and decisions are settled.

A PRAGMATIC PROCESS OF CRITICAL INTERACTION

The social testing process helps work out policy-making details in a manner that involves critical scrutiny and interaction. That is, it relies on judgment, on individual or collective decisions to interact, and on the resulting interaction with the new technologies and with people through them. In doing so, it leads to the settlement of reasons for further testing moral and policy-making hypotheses. If the details worked out do not fit the general reasons the hypotheses specify, these hypotheses become questionable. None of this, however, is tested, let alone settled, without critical scrutiny. The details become settled when they survive the test—often a recurrent test—of critical scrutiny by those going through the bargaining, negotiation, and interaction process.

SOCIAL TESTING AND GOOD SENSE

No doubt, one group of individuals may settle on something that another group would not settle on at all. This does not depend simply on the particular concerns at issue but also on how much care, imagination, moral sensitivity, and political savvy the members of each group have. Some groups may be so prone to confrontation that nothing will ever be settled among their members. These will simply work themselves into societal extinction (perhaps through argumentative exhaustion). But this is no reason to fault the social testing process. Expecting the process to work regardless of the specific people involved in it is a mistake. Indeed, it is as hopeless as expecting sound criteria for preventing, diagnosing, and treating disease to have their intended effect when used by careless or ignorant doctors on equally careless or ignorant patients. Though guidelines are helpful and, quite frequently, necessary, they are no substitute for a basic modicum of good sense.

Since social testing is to be carried out in the actual political arena, it is likely to involve people with various degrees of care, imagination, moral sensitivity, and political savvy. Indeed, some are likely to be very careless, unimaginative, morally insensitive, or lacking in political wisdom. But this is no obstacle to carrying out the test or reason for questioning its validity. So long as, on the aggregate, a basic modicum of good sense is predominant or shared by a few influential individuals in the group, the test should yield reliable results. The more critical scrutiny and trials a hypothesis survives under such circumstances, the more confirmed it is; the less it survives them, the less confirmed it is. If a hypothesis fails more than it survives, then there is reason to modify, supplement, or substitute it. At no point during or after the testing, however, should one expect total convergence of opinion or coincidence of concerns. Nirvana and perpetual peace are not part of the real world of politics, but reason and basic good sense can find room in this world and work through its conflicts.

Dialogue

— I suppose you have made your position concerning objectivity clear enough, but at the cost of losing sight of the overall picture. Your focus on news reporting in Essay 4 was somewhat too narrowly drawn. And your distinction between the role of judgment and that of decision in policy-making left me wondering what use it has. How are these things relevant to the larger framework? And what is this framework?

— As for the narrowness of my discussion of objectivity in news reporting and war-related matters, I already explained why it applies to objectivity in policy-making generally. The applicability of objectivity in the cases I discussed, which are among the most confrontational ones, gives us reason to infer that it is also applicable in other policy-making cases that are less confrontational and subject to bias. Now, concerning the use of distinguishing between the role of judgment and that of decision in policy-making, I have said a bit in discussing the social testing process. But, granted, more needs to be said. The upcoming essays will expand on the topic.

— OK, but that was not the main point of my question. It was how does the discussion so far relate to your overall purposes, as stated in the preface? For example, how does it relate to the notions of issues and issue-overload? And how does it relate to the notion of philosophy as diplomacy? You mentioned it in the preface, but so far have hardly developed it.

— Let us consider issues and issue-overload first. The previous essays provide reasons for believing that policy-making about them need not be hopelessly subjective and arbitrary, though sometimes—such as when time is of the essence—decisions (including decisions made in substantial ignorance of the circumstances) may be crucial. It is at this point that the philosophy as diplomacy approach most definitely comes into play.

— I still need some clarification of what you just said. I am quite puzzled about the notion of philosophy as diplomacy. Are you trying to help or harm philosophy by drawing an analogy between philosophy and diplomacy?

— My purpose is to formulate a conception of philosophy, especially as regards ethics and sociopolitical philosophy, that is applicable, sensitive to the concerns involved, and effective when dealing with policy-making problems. Diplomacy can serve as an analogue to formulate this conception.

— But, as you know, people often hold diplomacy in low esteem.

— Some people hold many worthwhile activities in low esteem, but this is no reason to stop engaging in them, supporting them, or using them as models when doing so promises to be fruitful.

— But is diplomacy itself effective? Why use as a model something that is ineffective or in a state of crisis?

— Diplomacy has been in existence in policy-making for quite some time and is reasonably effective.

— Some will question its current effectiveness. With the advent of such things as nearly instantaneous communication, summit meetings, and individual efforts at parallel mediation, diplomacy is not what it used to be.

— The question is whether diplomacy is in a crisis of growth or an insurmountable crisis. At any rate, philosophy is characteristically in a state of crisis (its very role and rules are continuously at issue). So why should the fact that diplomacy is (if it indeed is) in a state of crisis make it an inadequate analogue to clarify the functions and applications of philosophy in policy-making?

— There is, however, another reason to question your analogy. It is not unusual for people to loathe diplomacy because of its immorality. To the extent this attitude is well-founded, how can diplomacy serve as an analogue for philosophy, especially for moral philosophy?

— The view you mention is based on just one, not necessarily accurate, conception of diplomacy. As I will explain, when accurately and not cynically described, diplomacy is not a morally questionable activity. Indeed, it is often sensitive to the various concerns involved in policy-making problems. After all, it needs to be sensitive in order to be effective.

— I suppose this leads to discussions of the term *diplomacy*, the various senses in which it is used, and the sense in which I am using it.

— That's right. And, to some extent, you will find such a discussion in the next essay.

6 Philosophy as Diplomacy

The conception of philosophy as diplomacy has rarely been discussed by writers in ethics and moral and political philosophy. It is not my aim to formulate an exact, let alone definitive, definition of this conception. First, I formulate a rough and tentative characterization of philosophy as diplomacy. Then, I contrast it with more traditional approaches to problems in ethics and sociopolitical philosophy, the areas of philosophy where the conception of philosophy as diplomacy seems to be more readily—though perhaps not exclusively—applicable.

In particular, I characterize the uncompromising approach to policy-making, together with the expediency conception of policy and decision problems and the categorical conception of moral injunctions the approach involves. I contrast them with the diplomatic approach and the conceptions of policy and decision problems and moral injunctions associated with it, and argue for three theses. First, the diplomatic approach is politically and morally better suited for dealing with policy and decision problems posed by abortion, fetal research, and other pressing and controversial matters of social concern. Second, the conception of policy and decision problems associated with the diplomatic approach accurately construes these problems, and the expediency conception presupposed by the uncompromising approach misconstrues them. Third, the categorical conception of moral injunctions involved in the uncompromising approach is questionable and, at any rate, irrelevant to actual policy-making.

All along, I refer to cases that should help clarify what moral philosophy as diplomacy is. This, rather than exact definitions, should suffice for the time being. After all, exact definitions stand or fall with the theories in which they are eventually formulated, and no full-fledged theories embodying the notion of philosophy as diplomacy exist today. This book simply outlines the basic elements of one such theory and gives reasons for preferring it to current alternatives.

A WORD ABOUT DIPLOMACY

As stated in the preface, by *diplomacy* I do not mean, as cynics would have it, the activity of doing and saying the nastiest things in the nicest way.[1] I mean, quite broadly, the activity of dealing with relations between states, nations, other social groups, or even individuals so that ill does not prevail. In this activity, open-ended social decision procedures such as bargaining, negotiation, mediation, arbitration, and others are crucial.

The question might arise: Why use this definition instead of the former or some other one? One reason concerns historical accuracy. The broader characterization seems more in accord with the wide variety of efforts taken to be diplomatic efforts in human history, especially today. No doubt, there is more than one current sense of the term *diplomacy*, as Sir Harold Nicolson made plain in his *Diplomacy*:

> In current language this word "diplomacy" is carelessly taken to denote several quite different things. At one moment it is employed as a synonym for "foreign policy," as when we say "British diplomacy in the Near East has been lacking in vigour." At another moment it signifies "negotiation," as when we say "the problem is one which might well be solved by diplomacy." More specifically, the word denotes the process and machinery by which such negotiation is carried out. A fourth meaning is that of a branch of the Foreign Service, as when one says "my nephew is working for diplomacy." And a fifth interpretation which this unfortunate word is made to carry is that of an abstract quality or gift, which, in its best sense, implies skill in the conduct of international negotiation; and in its worst sense, implies the more guileful aspects of tact.[2]

Actually, Nicolson was not consistent in his use of the term *diplomacy* himself. As José Calvet De Magalhães put it, after vehemently denouncing the confusion between diplomacy and foreign policy, Nicolson ends up confusing the two in several passages, both in the aforementioned essay and in another book (published in 1954) called *The Evolution of Diplomatic Method*.[3]

De Magalhães goes on to argue for a notion of diplomacy defined by four main features. He writes:

> The concept of diplomacy . . . can be defined as follows:
> a. an instrument of foreign policy
> b. for the establishment and development of peaceful contacts between the governments of different states
> c. through the use of intermediaries
> d. mutually recognized by the respective parties.[4]

This definition may be adequate for studying diplomacy in the relations between modern states up to the 1930s or 1940s, but not before the modern period, and certainly not after the first half of the twentieth century. In other words, it is quite ahistorical. Let us see why.

First, the above definition rules out contacts by intermediaries that have not yet been recognized as intermediaries. The reason De Magalhães gives is that, "if this envoy is not recognized by the receiving state as a legitimate representative of the sending state, he will not be able to carry out his mission for want of that initial official contact indispensable to start a dialogue between states."[5] However, this reason is overly legalistic and politically unconvincing. Diplomacy can take place when a state attempts to mediate between nations or ethnic groups that are not—but may become—states and therefore cannot officially recognize the mediator as an envoy. This is the case of the United States' 1992 diplomatic efforts to intercede between Serbians and Croatians. Another example is the United States' efforts to start a dialogue between Israel and the PLO.

Second, as current summit diplomacy makes plain, though intermediaries are typically part of the diplomatic picture, they need not always be present. Of course, this is not to say that they are not desirable. As De Magalhães reminds us, exchanges through intermediaries would have been less risky to the world community than the famous May 1960 meeting between President Dwight D. Eisenhower and Nikita Khrushchev in Paris, where Khrushchev made violent accusations about the U2 plane that had just been shot down by Soviet air defenses.[6]

Third, mediation efforts can be effectively carried out by self-appointed intermediaries through contacts with representatives of foreign states, even without official recognition by any state as being legitimate representatives of any other state. Just think of the many such missions Pope John Paul has carried out just about everywhere, without being an official representative of any of the parties involved. Think also of Armand Hammer in Moscow and Jesse Jackson in Damascus. One might be inclined to classify these efforts, as James Der Derain does in *On Diplomacy*, as para-diplomatic rather than diplomatic.[7] Yet even then, the fact that they are seen as para-diplomatic makes plain that they are significantly analogous to diplomatic efforts. Hence, they are useful in this essay's attempt to draw an analogy between philosophy and diplomacy that proves fruitful to the application of ethics and sociopolitical philosophy to policy-making.

In this attempt, what matters is not to formulate a definition of diplomacy that gives us its essence—if it has one—or distinguishes it clearly and precisely from all other activities. Rather, what matters is to characterize those salient features of diplomacy that make the analogy between diplomacy and philosophy fruitful to the application of ethics and sociopolitical philosophy to policy-making. Such a description will suffice.

This brings us back to the characterization I favor. The salient feature displayed by diplomatic as well as para-diplomatic activities is an emphasis on such social decision procedures as negotiation, arbitration, and mediation, pursued so that ill does not prevail in the relations between states, nations, ethnic groups, other groups, and individuals. In this activity, open-ended social decision procedures such as bargaining, negotiation, mediation, arbitration, and others are crucial.

Analogously, as I will further explain, philosophy as diplomacy is a type of philosophical approach—a family of philosophical theories rather than any one theory—whose aim is to help deal with the relations between individuals, between groups, and between individuals and groups so that ill does not prevail. This initial characterization makes it plain that the primary locus of philosophy as diplomacy is in moral philosophy. Indeed, in what follows, I focus on moral philosophy and discuss the notion of moral philosophy as diplomacy. Yet, as previously stated, I leave open the question of whether the scope of philosophy as diplomacy extends beyond moral philosophy into, for example, aesthetics, the philosophy of culture, the philosophy of language, and, through it, metaphysics and epistemology. Now let us narrow our focus and begin to place philosophy as diplomacy in the context of traditional ethical and sociopolitical theories.

FEATURES OF PHILOSOPHY AS DIPLOMACY

NOT SIMPLY CONSEQUENTIALIST:
A CIVIL RIGHTS CASE

To say that moral philosophy as diplomacy aims at avoiding ill is not to say that it is primarily consequentialist. Ill may consist in the violation of a right or failure to act in accordance with principles of justice, which are deontological considerations.

In the conception of moral philosophy as diplomacy, the avoidance of socially undesirable consequences does not invariably or even frequently override the violation of rights. For example, in September 1962, Governor Ross Barnett refused to allow a black student, James Meredith, to enroll at the University of Mississippi. President Kennedy sent in federal marshals and federalized the Mississippi National Guard. As a result, on September 30 and October 1, a bloody confrontation took place between frenzied segregationist whites and the federal marshals, the federalized Mississippi National Guard, and the regular army troops protecting the campus. It would be preposterous to argue that it was worth sacrificing James Meredith's civil rights for the sake of avoiding the bloodshed that ensued.[8] After all, peace is not justified at just any cost. This is reflected in actual diplomacy and, by analogy, in moral philosophy as diplomacy.

NOT SIMPLY DEONTOLOGICAL:
A NUCLEAR WAR CASE

The conception of moral philosophy as diplomacy is also not merely deontological. It does not rule out the possibility that in certain cases—for example, conflicts threatening nuclear holocaust—the social consequences of the conflicts would be so catastrophic as to take precedence. In such a case, otherwise relevant deontological considerations—for example, a country's self-determination or sovereignty rights—would be overridden. And this need not be so because other deontological considerations take precedence. Suppose that the international crisis threatening nuclear holocaust is already a conventional war. It is, therefore, a state-of-nature situation. And in any such situation, it is at least questionable whether rights or the obligations correlated with them carry much, if any, weight. Collective consequences appear to have decisive weight. Indeed, they are grounds of both overriding moral injuctions and prudential courses of action.

REALISTIC AND PRAGMATIC

The conception of moral philosophy as diplomacy does not exclude moral rules, laws, and principles from the process of morally dealing with policy and decision problems. However, as stated, it crucially includes social decision procedures that go beyond such primarily argumentative procedures as discussion of merits and negotiation. These additional procedures include mediation, arbitration, outflanking, manipulation, boycotts, and strikes. In fact, in highly confrontational situations such as that exemplified by the previously mentioned Mississippi case, they may even include combat.

This is crucial for distinguishing moral philosophy as diplomacy from traditional approaches such as those I discuss later. First, as indicated, moral philosophy as diplomacy is sensitive to the varieties of policy and decision problems and the concurrent varieties of social decision procedures. This makes it realistic.

Second, moral philosophy as diplomacy aims at specifying the types of conditions under which given procedures are likely to address the problems feasibly, effectively, and in a manner sensitive to the various concerns involved. That is, it is an alternative to approaches that hopelessly seek consensus, or invariably opt for confrontation, in dealing with issues and issue-overload. This makes it realistic and, also, pragmatic.

Third, in contrast with alternative approaches, moral philosophy as diplomacy is realistic because it does not merely or primarily dwell on abstract ideas. For example, in the case of abortion, it does not focus on whether the human fetus is a person. And regarding preferential treatment, it does not focus on whether such treatment is compatible with abstract principles of justice. Instead, it focuses on the social *fact* that there is a recurrent issue that something should be done about. (I return to this later.)

Fourth, moral philosophy as diplomacy does not presuppose that policy and decision problems such as those previously mentioned are primarily— let alone exclusively—settled by appeal to principles. Nor does it presuppose that they are fairly settled depending only or primarily on whether principles are invoked and whether they are valid. In fact, such an appeal to principles is but one aspect of the previously mentioned discussion of merits, or rational discussion. This procedure includes appeal to reasons that may or may not be principles. Only the force of the better argument is supposed to count. Inducements and threats are to be left out. As indicated, however, there are other decision procedures. And it is a task of moral philosophy to establish which procedures are suited for dealing with which issues. This leads to additional, crucial ways in which moral philosophy as diplomacy is pragmatic.

Fifth, moral philosophy as diplomacy recognizes the central fact of policy-making that, as discussed in Essay 5, at assessment time it is often unfeasible to spell out all significant implications of a policy (or theory). This points to the sixth and most crucial feature for distinguishing moral philosophy as diplomacy from traditional approaches: Moral philosophy as diplomacy takes seriously the fact that, as discussed in Essays 3 and 5, certain unsettled data are worked out in the process and are not available at the time initial policy discussions take place. Indeed, they often result in part from such discussions. The process of critical scrutiny and social interaction leads to the settlement of reasons for assessing policies and decisions. These are new, previously nonexistent, and hardly predictable data.[9]

A TENTATIVE CHARACTERIZATION

The preceding remarks provide grounds for a tentative characterization of moral philosophy as diplomacy in contrast with traditional approaches— strictly consequentialist, strictly deontological, or merely pragmatic—in moral philosophy. It should be added that moral philosophy as diplomacy is, first of all, moral philosophy—moral theory, ethical theory, ethics as a branch of inquiry, reflection on morality. That is, it is a critical and self-critical study aimed at soundly dealing with problems of right and wrong, good and bad, justified and unjustified, that arise in people's lives.[10] Further, it is not identical to any one theory in ethics or sociopolitical philosophy. Rather, it is an approach within which a great variety of theories can fit, such as the one I am formulating. Having said all this, the following appears to be a sound characterization: Moral philosophy as diplomacy is a branch of inquiry aimed at dealing with problems of right and wrong, good and bad, justified and unjustified, in ways that are feasible, effective, and crucially sensitive both to the often unsettled and conflictive nature of the concerns that contribute to pose the problems and to the variety of open-ended social decision procedures that may help settle these concerns and deal with the problems through policies and decisions, and on the basis of reasons worked out in the policy-making process.

The specific ways that are permissible or even required when dealing with given problems depend on the specific economic, political, and other pragmatic constraints involved. Such constraints are especially pressing when dealing with problems posed by issues or, as in issue-overload, by their combination. A more detailed examination of some contrasts between philosophy as diplomacy and traditional approaches concerning issues and issue-overload will help clarify the notion of philosophy as diplomacy and its applicability in ethics and sociopolitical philosophy.

UNCOMPROMISING VS. DIPLOMATIC: TWO APPROACHES TO POLICY AND DECISION PROBLEMS

Policy discussions are far from detached exchanges between phlegmatic observers. Discussions on such topics as abortion, fetal research, animal welfare, the environment, international development, the international debt, and the arms race involve sharp disagreements accompanied by heated controversy and, sometimes, outright confrontation between those involved. The question is: What approach is morally and politically best suited for dealing with the policy and decision problems such situations pose? As previously argued, the philosophy as diplomacy approach and the specific theory this book outlines do not exclude deontological considerations— quite the contrary. Yet the question still remains: How are deontological considerations regarded in the present context? In particular, are they categorical or not? This leads to an additional question: What kinds of moral reasons enjoining or proscribing a policy or a decision are relevant for dealing with the problems: categorical or noncategorical ones? These are the main questions I address next.

In doing so, I focus on two policy-making approaches and the conceptions of policy and decision problems associated with them. One approach is *uncompromising*. It treats policy and decision problems as mere matters of moral expediency—when not of simple expediency—involved in carrying out injunctions based on reasons that are considered categorical, inescapable, final. The other approach is *diplomatic*. It treats policy and decision problems as including unsettled questions not just about the policies and decisions at issue but about the reasons used to favor or oppose them. With the diplomatic approach, reasons for or against policies and decisions are always open to critical scrutiny and are not considered to be (let alone known to be) categorical, inescapable, final.

Concerning these approaches, I argue for three interconnected theses. First, the diplomatic approach is politically and morally better suited for dealing with policy and decision problems posed by abortion, fetal research, and other pressing and controversial matters of social concern. Second, the conception of policy and decision problems associated with the diplomatic approach accurately construes these problems, and the expediency conception presupposed by the uncompromising approach misconstrues them. Third, the categorical conception of moral injunctions involved in the uncompromising approach is questionable and, at any rate, irrelevant to actual policy-making.

Concerning the first thesis, I argue that the diplomatic approach is politically better suited because it is more effective in reducing unnecessary conflict. It is morally better suited because it realistically upholds—rather than inflexibly undermines—morality. In contrast, the uncompromising approach is ineffective in reducing conflict and undermines morality.

Regarding the second thesis, I first argue that the diplomatic conception of policy and decision problems is accurate, because it treats the reduction of social conflict as a consideration that can carry more weight than others. That is, it treats social conflict itself on a par with policy and decision considerations that concern merely specific subjects of social conflict, such as abortion or fetal research. In contrast, the expediency conception of policy and decision problems is inaccurate because it makes no provision for weighing such considerations against each other. Instead, it inaccurately treats policy and decision injunctions about such things as abortion and fetal research in a political vacuum devoid of conflict.

As for the third thesis, I first argue that the categorical conception of moral injunctions involved in the uncompromising approach is questionable because it presupposes—rather than establishes—the preeminence of the moral point of view. I then argue that it is irrelevant to actual policy-making. Even if such moral injunctions turn out to be categorical, in some abstract sense, at policy-making time, there are no good reasons for identifying them as being so.

A CLOSER LOOK AT THE UNCOMPROMISING APPROACH AND THE EXPEDIENCY CONCEPTION

To say that the uncompromising approach treats policy and decision injunctions as categorical is not to say that these injunctions are based on selfish grounds. They can be, but need not be. The expediency conception of policy and decision problems these injunctions lead to is often moral expediency. Indeed, the grounds and the injunctions are often altruistic or fall somewhere between the extremes of altruism and egoism. For example, people argue about abortion by appeal to rights: those of the fetus if anti-abortion, those of the mother if pro-choice. In any case, they are certainly not selfish arguments. Nor, judging by the individuals who offer them, is their use motivated by selfish or self-interested considerations.

In addition, to say that the uncompromising approach treats policy and decision problems as problems of expediency is not to say that individuals who adopt such an approach are lacking grounds to think their injunctions categorical. Actually, they often have carefully thought out reasons for the finality of their position. In any case, in this conception of the problem, the injunctions are not at issue; their justification is presumed settled. The reasons, if recited, are simply aimed at persuading others to adopt the same aims and, thus, supposedly contribute to a resolution of the problem. Let us consider some examples.

With this approach, an individual may have the decision problem of whether to demonstrate against the use of baboons for research purposes, without having any doubt that the elimination of such use is overriding. The only question is whether demonstrating will help attain it. Analogously, a group or society may have the policy problem of how to preserve national security at any cost, without there being any doubt that this aim is overriding. In this approach, then, policy and decision problems are merely problems posed by practical obstacles or uncertainties in the attainment of aims that are assumed to be settled, because moral or other injunctions to seek these aims are taken to be final, inescapable, or categorical.[11] This prompts the questions: Can reasons, at least moral reasons, about policy and decision be final, categorical, or inescapable? Can they be known to be so? If they can, is an uncompromising approach to policy-making thereby justified?

THE PHILOSOPHICAL CONTROVERSY ABOUT CATEGORICAL MORAL REASONS

Discussions of the finality of reasons have tended to focus on moral injunctions, that is, moral reasons to act one way or another. Kant, most notably, thought that the categorical imperative presented some moral injunctions as ends in themselves, "objectively necessary, without regard to any other end."[12] In contrast, the apparent finality that reasons of etiquette, prudence, or politics may possess is conditional on the ends or purposes of etiquette, prudence, or politics. According to this view, one ought to do what etiquette, prudence, or politics requires in given circumstances, if the ends of etiquette, prudence, or politics are ends that one wants. One ought to do what morality requires regardless of one's wants, desires, or interests.[13]

It has been objected that, at best, moral reasons are final *all moral things considered*, but not from the nonmoral standpoint of, for example, etiquette, prudence, or politics. Along these lines, Philippa Foot has argued that "moral judgments have no better claim to be categorical imperatives than do statements about matters of etiquette."[14] In response, Lawrence C. Becker has argued that the moral point of view, moral reasons, moral justifications, and the like are not separate in kind from nonmoral ones. They simply broaden the scope of considerations that are relevant in principle. In certain cases, however, reasons such as those of etiquette may have too little weight to make a difference. From this, Becker concludes, "a valid moral judgment is by definition overriding. Its action-guidance is 'inescapable' or 'binding' in the sense that there is nothing more to consider—nothing which might be introduced to enlarge the inquiry further and make the prescription subject to withdrawal."[15]

Whatever its virtues, Becker's view on the no-holds-barred nature of moral considerations hardly makes valid moral judgments categorical. For it does not establish that the inquiry should indeed be broadened and that practical reasons should not be merely of etiquette, selfish, or political. Simply saying that all such considerations are relevant from the moral point of view does not establish the priority of such an all-encompassing point of view over other, narrower ones. Hence, it has not been disproved that, at best, moral reasons are final *all moral things considered*, but not from nonmoral—narrower—points of view.

HOW CATEGORICAL CAN REASONS IN POLICY-MAKING BE?

My present concern is something other than determining the status of moral judgments. It is to argue that even if valid moral judgments formulating moral injunctions are categorical, this is irrelevant to whether people are moral or not and to policy-making in the actual world.

First, suppose that valid moral judgments are categorical. This would be a logical, not a motivational, feature of moral judgments. It would be incapable of preventing moral people from ceasing to be moral and of convincing the immoral to be moral. Thinking otherwise amounts to what Philippa Foot described as "trying to give the moral 'ought' a magic force."[16]

Second, suppose that valid moral judgments are not categorical. This logical, not motivational, feature of moral judgments would not incline people to cease to be moral. Nor would a motive to be moral be lacking that would have been present had valid moral judgments been categorical. Morally inclined people would still do what they ought to do, regardless of whether they ought to do it categorically or simply because the circumstances, relevant moral rules and principles, and their commitment to living a good life with others require it.

Third, concerning the claim that the status of moral injunctions is irrelevant to policy-making, suppose that at least some moral injunctions are categorical. This would have no effect on policy-making unless there were conclusive grounds for believing which ones were categorical. In policy-making, however, one does not come easily or definitively by such grounds.

Fourth, identifying categorical injunctions is especially difficult, if not impossible, when new technologies are involved. As previously argued, at the time of their introduction, some relevant considerations are still unsettled. Without clairvoyance, one could not possibly conclude beyond all reasonable doubt what ought to be done, categorically, about a new technology.

To offer the last two arguments is not, of course, to argue that one cannot have very good reasons for reaching certain conclusions. Rather, it is to argue that, in policy-making, these reasons are not simply open to critical scrutiny but are characteristically conditional. Even if there were a set of reasons that served to establish some categorical moral injunction, those reasons would be difficult to know without any doubt. And some reasons are not worked out or predictable at the outset.

The arguments just given provide reason to believe that categorical injunctions are irrelevant to whether people are moral and whether policies are sound. But the previously discussed uncompromising approach to policy-making, and its associated expediency conception of policy and decision problems, crucially depend on the assumption that moral injunctions are not only categorical and relevant but also decisive for policy-making. Since this assumption is false, the approach and its associated expediency conception of policy and decision problems are unwarranted. An adequate approach and conception should begin by being realistic.

I next develop the more realistic—diplomatic—approach sketched at the outset and its associated—conflict government—conception of policy and decision problems. In carrying out this task, I focus on the case of abortion. Given its intractability, abortion serves as a test for the uncompromising as well as the diplomatic approach. Indeed, it is one of those cases in which such approaches are tried by fire.

THE CASE OF ABORTION: TOWARD A DIPLOMATIC APPROACH TO POLICY AND DECISION PROBLEMS

An urgent matter of social concern can be the focus of a variety of moral problems. Consider abortion. When a woman is faced with the problem of whether (and not simply how or where) to have an abortion, she has a moral decision problem—that is, a behavioral moral problem, or a moral problem of conduct. So does a physician faced with the problem of whether (and not simply how most effectively or profitably or without legal liability) to perform an abortion. These are not mere problems of expediency. Those who have the problems are being torn up by the fact that some of their moral notions (e.g., their moral values) have come into conflict; they must make up their minds about what to sacrifice to what, and they find it distressingly difficult to do so. Their lives are disrupted by an internal conflict, whatever the source of the conflict is.

This does not mean that such problems are not political. In fact, they often are. They are often partly the result of political arrangements. However, the conflicts of moral notions—of values, interests, ideals, rules, principles, and the like—that contribute to pose the problems are internal to the persons. Indeed, their lives are being disrupted by these conflicts, which are central constituents of the moral decision problems being faced.

In cases such as that of abortion, the conflicts significantly disrupt a person's life and may even threaten a moral crisis. In less pressing cases, such as when life or basic liberties are not at stake, they may cause only momentary disruption. Yet they are never practically indifferent matters. They are never mere matters of preference, such as whether or not to grow petunias in the garden. Nor are they mere matters of arbitrary decision, such as whether to go into a building through the right or the left of two adjacent doors.

Although such moral decision problems are often political, they are not identical with policy problems. The latter, of course, are also political but, unlike moral decision problems, they are not about the conduct of particular individuals. In fact, they arise beyond the realm of any one individual's personal experience.

Consider, for example, the matter of whether the federal government should provide funding for abortions. When this point is raised, the problem does not arise simply within the confines of any one individual's personal experience. It arises in society at large, at the most encompassing levels of the public policy realm. It is a societal problem, and an individual's experience in and of itself is of no help in conceptualizing the problem. We may indeed wonder whether we could bring ourselves to pay for an abortion, but this is to wonder about an importantly different matter: about what our values, ideals, obligations, duties, moral rules, or principles are. Or we may try to imagine the suffering of a woman forced to have an unwanted baby because of her inability to pay for an abortion. But this, though it may raise (and has raised) policy problems about abortion, is not itself a policy problem. To conceptualize policy problems about abortion realistically, one needs to consider policymakers facing abortion policy decisions. For example, one needs to consider a legislator facing the decision of what abortion funding policy to have, or a Supreme Court justice facing the decision of what abortions, if any, to interpret as permitted by law.

In these cases, the problems are not simply about what policy to have in a political vacuum. They are partly about social conflicts concerning these policy problems—conflicts that are significantly disruptive of society. To what extent they are disruptive is a policy concern and contributes to pose the actual policy problem: what abortion policies to have, *given that there is a societally disruptive conflict about abortion*.[17] This is the actual policy problem, because, like any policy and decision problem about controversial matters, it arises and must be dealt with *in the midst* of conflicts in which the aims themselves are at issue. The conception of policy and decision problems associated with the diplomatic approach is accurate because it captures this crucial feature of the problems.

In contrast, the expediency conception fails to capture precisely this feature. First, it treats the conflicts as mere political externalities—simply as obstacles, or help, in the carrying out of categorical injunctions and the striving to attain aims not themselves at issue. But in the actual world of politics, conflicts about the aims—whether based on wants, claims, interests, needs, advantages, values, ideals, attitudes, traits, rules, obligations, rights and duties, or principles—are unresolved. Hence, from the standpoint of political reality, the expediency conception of policy and decision problems is false. This is a good reason to reject the nonmoral expediency conception of policy and decision problems.

Second, it follows that, from the standpoint of morality, the expediency conception of policy and decision problems is unsound. Since moral injunctions about policy- and decision-making are presumably meant to guide us, they must be sensitive to the actual political circumstances in which the policy and decision problems we face arise. But since, as previously argued, the expediency conception is politically false, it prevents moral injunctions from being sensitive.

Third, the expediency conception misconstrues moral problems, which are typically prompted by conflicts of concerns that involve such things as mutually conflicting rules, obligations, claims, rights and duties, needs, interests, wants, advantages, desires, attitudes, and traits. And in failing to reflect the conflicts, the expediency conception conspicuously fails to make room for moral problems about the conflicts. Hence, the expediency conception is false from a moral standpoint.

Fourth, the expediency conception undermines morality. Its failure to make room for moral problems about conflicts—this lack of moral circumspection—partially, if not entirely, undermines critical scrutiny and the openness of moral discourse. This undermines morality and moral reasoning by turning them into mere dogmatic—however well-articulated—mores. It follows that, in policy-making, the expediency conception should be rejected, together with the uncompromising approach to policy-making that presupposes it.

Is there room for this conception and approach at the individual decision level? Hardly so. As the previous discussion of policy problems concerning abortion indicates, in many policy problems individuals are not isolated. A crucial characteristic of policy problems is that people are collectively— even if not individually—faced with them. Their society is disrupted. In the case of abortion, society is disrupted because people are sharply divided about which abortion policies should be introduced, and they confront each other in trying to bring about adoption of the policy they want. Society is disrupted by a societal conflict of values or demands and by what people do to uphold their values or satisfy their demands. Many individuals, however, manage to live through it without having their personal lives disrupted by this societal conflict at all. They live through it without any internal conflict of values. Some go ahead and have or help others have abortions without questioning whether it is right for them to do so. Others go ahead and have or help others have babies without questioning whether it is right for them to do so. However, some of those who have or help others have babies say that abortion is murder and want it outlawed. And some of these who have or help others have abortions say that having babies is irresponsible and outlawing abortions sheer intolerance. These people have answers about the moral notions at issue.

It is characteristic of such policy problems that many of the people who are collectively faced with them have answers about the moral notions at issue. Although they may have questions about the most expedient way to uphold those notions, they have no moral problems of conduct. The soundness and finality of their moral injunctions to pursue whatever individual aims they pursue are presumed settled. Indeed, some people seem to have simply demands and no questions whatsoever about what they are entitled to demand; they presuppose the expediency conception of individual decision problems. Yet when people have moral problems of conduct, they characteristically have distressing questions about which of their moral notions they ought to sacrifice, not answers or mere demands. Hence, the expediency conception does not adequately capture the nature of moral problems of conduct.

Nor does the expediency conception capture the nature of the political decision problem these people face. This is the problem of what policy to support, given that there is social conflict about what policies to have; that the conflict disrupts society to some extent; and that policy-making should try to curb this disruption, and that inflexible or thoughtless support of an uncompromising position does precisely the contrary.

The path of both political and moral realism, circumspection, and wisdom points to the previously described diplomatic approach and conception of policy and decision problems. From their standpoint, policy and decision problems are treated as including unsettled questions not just about the policies and decisions at issue but about the reasons used to favor or oppose them. Here, reasons for or against policies and decisions are always open to critical scrutiny and are characteristically conditional. It is not presumed (let alone known) that they are categorical, inescapable, final.

CONCLUDING REMARKS

The philosophy as diplomacy approach to policy-making and its associated conflict government conception of policy and decision problems are in no way a cure-all. They do not preclude the possibility that an official policymaker—or anyone, for that matter—may have a problem of conscience in dealing with a policy problem crucially posed by a societal conflict. This can certainly happen. For instance, a Catholic Supreme Court justice who believes that laws that stop Medicaid funding for poor women's abortions are unconstitutional may have one such personal problem when having to vote on a case covered by these laws. The policy problem partly addressed by the decision, however, is different from the justice's problem of conscience. The policy problem is partly posed by the societal disruption resulting from the clash of demands or opinions about public funding for abortions, together with what people do to uphold their opinions and satisfy their demands. It is not at all posed by the fact that the judge has certain religious beliefs, although the problem of conscience is posed by these beliefs in combination with the duties attached to the judge's office and the civil law.

In addition to matters of conscience, the philosophy as diplomacy approach and the conception of policy and decision problems bring into focus a variety of related problems. As this essay's discussion indicated, these include the problems of whether ethics is autonomous and whether ethics is always overriding. This is a virtue rather than a shortcoming, for it helps address the problems in a manner directly relevant to the actual world of politics and morality and avoids the risk of reducing them to some meta-meta-ethical equivalent of detached exchanges between phlegmatic observers.

Dialogue

— Your notion of philosophy as diplomacy is clearer now than before, but I am still not sure that it works. You have tried to show how it works in a few cases. Are there any principles according to which one should put it to work?

— I believe so. In Essay 8, I will formulate and give reasons in support of the principle of practical equity and various laws that fall under this principle and apply to special types of policy-making cases. Of course, even after I have given all such reasons, the principle and the laws will still be largely hypotheses, which is what I call them. To establish that they are actually principles or laws, it will be necessary to confirm them sufficiently through the critical scrutiny and social interaction process I have been describing.

— Why is it that, instead of feeling that I now have some answers, I feel that the questions have multiplied to the point of making me dizzy? Let me explain what I mean. You just said that the principles depend on the type of case. How many types are there? Are there as many principles as types? On what basis do you distinguish between types? I wanted one question answered, and your response has led me to ask three more.

— That is the nature of inquiry. The more answers we get, the more questions arise. However, as we get more answers, we presumably attain greater knowledge. As for the additional questions you just asked, I cannot answer them at once, but I could tell you a bit about the types of cases I have in mind.

— It seems to me that, if the application of your theory's principles depends on the type of cases involved, your theory should include not merely some impressionistic discussion but a taxonomy of these cases. Otherwise, how could we apply the principles in a reliable manner? This would raise questions about its application, hence about whether philosophy as diplomacy, your overall approach, actually works.

— I agree, but I am curious to know the reasons for what you just said.

— My reasons are simple. You can establish that the approach works only by formulating a theory that falls under this approach and testing it through its applications. Such testing, if at all possible, is inadequate without a taxonomy of the types of cases to which the theory is supposed to apply.

— You are absolutely right. Fortunately, I think I can satisfy your curiosity. I next try to present the needed taxonomy.

7 A Delicate Balance: Reason, Social Interaction, Disruption, and Scope in Ethics and Policy-Making

Social conflict is a source of abhorrence to some and hope to others. Some abhor it on the grounds that it undermines social progress. Auguste Comte, for example, thought that social conflict involved a tendency toward insurrection that "would be fatal to humanity, and distract all progress," if left unchecked.[1] Others find hope in social conflict on the opposite grounds: that it is the way to social progress. Karl Marx and Friedrich Engels, for example, saw the proletariat "struggling for mastery" with other classes toward "the abolition of the old form of society in its entirety and of mastery itself," that is, toward liberation.[2] Here, I seek to investigate the moral and policy-making significance and limits of social conflict, consensus, and their varieties. In addressing this topic, I also inquire whether other variables are equally or more crucial for describing policy-making problems in a manner helpful for morally sensitive, yet effective, policy-making. The essay further expands on the descriptions and examples of policy-making problems and their levels provided by the previous essays and outlines a taxonomy of the problems.

I ask: How should policy and decision problems be described to help make not just politically effective but morally sensitive policy and decisions about them? Should they all be described as conflictual or, alternatively, as consensual? Or should social conflict be highlighted in some cases and consensus in others? For what purposes? At any rate, how crucial are these forms of social interaction in posing policy and decision problems? Are other variables (e.g., the scope of a given conflict and the social consequences it has for individuals and groups) equally or more crucial? For what purposes? What questions do all these variables prompt, and what policy-making guidelines do they suggest?

I argue for eight theses, all of which reflect the fact that from both a policy-making and a moral standpoint, what is needed in describing policy and decision problems is balance. First, policy and decision problems arise in the midst of various types of *social interaction* that are not adequately described by referring simply to conflict or, alternatively, to consensus. Second, it also matters whether the interaction is rational or nonrational, that is, whether or not it predominantly involves meaningful dialogue and critical scrutiny. Third, given this additional variable, social interaction can range from predominantly conflictive and nonrational, through predominantly conflictive but rational, to predominantly consensual, which can also be rational or nonrational. Fourth, the specific type of interaction a policy and decision problem involves is crucial for establishing which social decision procedures to employ in dealing with the problem. Fifth, the specific scope of a policy and decision problem is also crucial for establishing which social decision procedures to employ. Yet, sixth, none of these is individually or jointly sufficient for establishing how urgent it is to do something about the problem. Seventh, crucial for assessing this urgency is the combination of the *social scope* of interaction—that is, whether it is local, regional, national, international, or global—and the *social consequences* of this interaction—that is, whether this interaction harms individuals or disrupts groups and, if so, how much. Eighth, the more urgent a policy-making problem that predominantly involves nonrational interaction (e.g., one posed by military oppression), the more applicable and, arguably, more morally justified are social decision procedures that bypass meaningful dialogue such as civil disobedience, external sanctions, and, in certain cases, force. This latter thesis also brings out the policy-making significance of all the above features, which has already been evidenced by the various cases discussed in previous essays and will be reflected by the taxonomy I will sketch.

As a by-product of my main discussion, I explain in some detail various exaggerations in traditional conflict and consensus models. I also mention limitations of such theories as ethnomethodology, phenomenology, and exchange theory, which tend to focus on the microlevel of social life.

SOME CAUTIONARY REMARKS

ABOUT THE TAXONOMY'S PURPOSES
AND SIGNIFICANCE

The essay's theses and the taxonomy they involve should be useful to policymakers concerned with engaging in policy-making in a morally sensitive and effective fashion. In the ensuing discussion, this is what I mean when I say that the taxonomy is useful to policymakers. As the book's preface and previous essays make plain, I do not mean that it is useful for promoting the factional or sectarian aims of this or that policymaker, or of this or that group of a given policymaker's liking.

As I argued at length in the previous essays, an exclusive concern with such aims is both a recipe for policy-making disaster and morally objectionable. Hence, the position I am taking is in conflict with the cynical approach suggested by conflict theories, according to which every policy-making motive is egoistic or sectarian, and moral considerations are a mere matter of ideology. My position is also in conflict with consensus theories, which take consensus to be a touchstone of social desirability. As I will argue later, from a moral standpoint, consensus is sometimes unjustified.

The book's preface and previous essays make plain that this book is concerned with policy-making—a characteristically forward-looking activity. It is not designed to help explain or pass judgment on social change, its history, or any of its stages. Though these are intellectually valid enterprises, and their results are relevant to the present study, such studies are primarily backward looking.

To say, as I do in this essay, that, in order to establish the urgency of policy-making problems, it is crucial to focus on their social scope and social consequences, is not to say that these suffice to solve the problems. Indeed, in order to deal with the problems soundly, one must establish which type of social interaction is predominantly involved in the situation posing the problems. Without doing this, one cannot establish which social decision procedures are likely to be effective in dealing with the problems. More specifically, in order to select effective social decision procedures, one needs to establish whether the social interaction involved in a given problem is primarily conflictive or consensual and whether it primarily involves meaningful dialogue and appeal to reasons.

Of course, after having established all this, a crucial moral question still remains: What policies, decisions, and social decision procedures are permissible in dealing with specifiable policy problems? Since this essay does not address this question, it does not attempt to provide complete criteria for finding morally sensitive solutions to policy-making problems. Essay 8 will do this, subject to the various qualifications formulated in previous essays and partly systematized in the current one. The present essay is a systematic prolegomenon to such a task; this is its point and that of the taxonomy it formulates. Its justification is obvious: A sound moral assessment of policies and decisions depends on the establishment of a morally sensitive classification of the problems that the policies and decisions address.

The previous essays have provided a variety of descriptions and examples of policy-making problems and discussed their levels. The present essay aims at outlining a taxonomy of the problems in a manner that reflects those descriptions, examples, and discussions.

In this connection, a further point of the taxonomy and this essay is to help clarify how the crucial components of policy and decision problems—not the least of which is their scope—are frequently ignored both in ethical and in policy-making discussions and theories.

ABOUT THE ESSAY'S METHOD

The method this essay uses was previously discussed concerning the book as a whole. It has been employed in both philosophy and social process studies and consists in merging description and argument. That is, it involves describing a number of cases or observations to exemplify categories and classifications, and then using the same or similar cases or observations as evidence for the utility or accuracy of the categories and classifications.[3]

This method may cause impatience among both philosophers and social scientists. Philosophers, eager to reach the thick of philosophical arguments, may find it too sketchy and argue that it fails to address in a useful manner the moral issues it purportedly classifies. Social scientists, eager to deal empirically and in great detail with particular cases, may find it too theoretical. In response, I can only say that a sound moral assessment of policies and decisions depends on the establishment of a morally sensitive classification of the problems that the policies and decisions address. The present essay aims at outlining this classification.

One might object, however, that the search for such classifications is the type of study social scientists—not philosophers—would pursue. But this objection is mistaken. Hypotheses and theories in moral philosophy, especially those concerned with policy-making, are significally confirmed or disconfirmed through their applications. Hence, a concern with cases and observations, and the taxonomy issuing from them, is philosophically crucial.

As for the impatience from a social science standpoint, the taxonomy this essay formulates should prove useful in structuring the enormous body of available case studies in a manner readily applicable to policy- and decision-making. This meets a policy-making as well as a scientific need. Without such a taxonomy, the results of these studies remain largely unstructured data rather than a body of knowledge applicable to new policy and decision cases. And with inadequate categories and classifications, the applications to policy-making are questionable.

To be sure, taxonomies exist in both social science and philosophy. But their purpose has been primarily geared to the study of social change, its history, and stages, not to the moral assessment of policies and decisions. In addition, when concerned with policy-making, various existing categories and classifications are incomplete and, at times, slanted toward a conflict or, alternatively, a consensus model of society. Hence, there is a need for this essay's task.

CONSEQUENTIALIST OR DEONTOLOGICAL?
AN OPEN QUESTION

To say that the social consequences of a conflictive (or consensual) type of social interaction contribute to pose policy and decision problems is not to take a consequentialist position. It is not to say that policies and decisions aimed at addressing problems should be evaluated on the basis of the desirability or undesirability of their consequences alone, if at all. They could, without inconsistency, be assessed on the basis of principles of justice or other deontological notions.

No doubt, policymakers doing their job have to address the fact that a certain type of social interaction (e.g., the abortion controversy) has consequences for society and individuals. But this is not to say that policymakers should address this fact because, otherwise, undesirable consequences would follow. They could be required to address it because of deontological considerations. One such consideration is the fact that, in some cases, policymakers took an oath of office and the duties of that office include that obligation. Another consideration is the fact that the said interaction may involve the violation of individual rights or, at the level of groups, undermine the conditions for the applicability of individual rights.

Alternatively, policy-making need not be based on these or any other deontological reasons but, instead, on the previously mentioned consequentialist reasons. Accordingly, this essay leaves open the possibility of relying only on deontological reasons, only on consequentialist ones, or on a combination of both. My concern here is simply to sketch categories and classification criteria—a taxonomy for characterizing policy and decision problems in a manner that makes room for morally sensitive, yet effective, policy-making.

THE CONSENSUS-CONFLICT DEBATE

Opposite views and attitudes about social conflict have been displayed in recurrent debates in both philosophy and social science. In 1958, for example, Ralf Dahrendorf spearheaded an attack on the consensus model associated with functionalism:

> As with change, we have grown accustomed to look for special causes or circumstances whenever we encounter conflict; but . . . a complete turn is necessary in our thinking. Not the presence, but the absence of conflict is surprising and abnormal.[4]

Not long afterwards, in a book coedited by Talcott Parsons, the leading functionalist at the time, Edward Shils, wrote in one of the essays:

> Modern society, especially in its latest phase, is characteristically a consensual society.[5]

The debate raged for some years. In 1968, Robin Williams pointed out the simplistic exaggerations in Dahrendorf's and Shils's views:

> Actual societies are held together by consensus, by interdependence, by sociability, and by coercion. The actual job is to show how actual social structures and processes operating in these ways can be predicted and explained.[6]

An analogous position was taken by the functionalist Robert Merton:

> It is not enough to refer to the "institutions" as though they were all uniformly supported by all groups or strata in the society. Unless systematic consideration is given to the *degree* of support of particular institutions by *specific* groups we shall overlook the important place of power in society.[7]

Shortly after these remarks were made, the consensus-conflict debate in sociology began to decline.[8] At the same time, studies of conflict in social organizations developed, but some areas were left largely untouched.[9]

As I argue next, there were good reasons to put aside the consensus-conflict debate in the manner in which it had been formulated. Yet theoretical discussions in the social sciences shifted their focus in a manner that amounted to throwing out the baby with the bathwater. Some significant questions were not even asked, for example: What are the varieties, significance, and limits of social conflict and consensus for the assessment of policies and decisions? To address questions such as this, one needs to go beyond the currently predominant concerns of ethnomethodology, phenomenology, exchange theory, and any other studies that tend to focus on the microlevel of social life. I turn to some of these largely forgotten questions in the ensuing discussion.

CONSENSUS SITUATIONS: A BLIND SPOT
IN THE CONFLICT MODEL

Some policy-making problems cannot be interpreted in conflictual terms without overstepping the bounds of common sense and the constraints of observation. Consider the problem of whether foreigners visiting the United States should be allowed free entrance to national parks. Or consider the problem of determining the number of commemorative stamps to be issued in a given year. Ordinarily, although cases of this type may not involve unanimity, they rarely involve conflict. Consensus is predominant, and the problems can be addressed simply by discussion of merits.

One might object that these cases involve hidden conflict. To say this, however, is to fly in the face of perfectly good evidence and common sense and, at the very least, calls for argument. But no such argument is given, and until a sound one is given, the hidden-conflict view will remain mere speculation.

In response, one might attempt to shift the burden of proof by arguing, along the lines of Dahrendorf's previously mentioned statement, that "the absence of conflict is surprising and abnormal."[10] But this response would beg the question. Even if we grant that the absence of conflict is surprising and abnormal because conflict is frequent, it does not follow that there are no significant cases involving little or no conflict. One might as well argue that since air is common where we normally live, the absence of air—say, at high altitudes—is surprising and abnormal and, therefore, there is no such thing as situations in which air is absent. Such cases as those mentioned in the first paragraph of this section provide good reason to conclude that the wholesale conflict model is an exaggeration. Accordingly, any policy-making positions that presuppose it (e.g., some Marxist positions as well as, arguably, Schumpeter's market version of social choice theory) are flawed.[11]

In defense of the conflict model, one might grant that consensus situations are theoretically significant because they make plain the simplistic nature of conflict models, but ask: Are they practically and morally significant? The answer is that they are practically significant because they help establish that, however infrequent, consensus is not entirely unattainable in the real world. And this, in turn, makes them morally significant. Let us see why.

Since consensus is not entirely unattainable, it is not entirely relegated to the realm of unrealistic moral ideals. Indeed, it often exists and is sought among small groups such as families, Quaker groups, and even a few philosophy departments. In addition, it can arguably be said that consensus exists across entire societies concerning such things as humanitarian aid to victims of natural calamities (e.g., floods and earthquakes) and Red Cross aid to victims of some human activities, such as wars.

Hence, it is sometimes realistic, and therefore morally sensitive, to recognize the existence of consensus in assessing policy-making. In addition, it is realistic, hence morally sensitive, to recognize those situations in which, though not existent, consensus is attainable. These points are crucial for avoiding moral cynicism. Indeed, the alternative—unrealistic, wholesale denial of consensus—leaves the door wide open to the worst excesses of realpolitik.

It is also obvious, however, that some policy-making problems concern highly conflictive situations. Think, for example, of those concerning abortion, preferential treatment, and environmental deterioration. Hence, a wholesale consensus model is equally exaggerated, and my first thesis follows: Policy and decision problems arise in the midst of various types of social interaction not adequately described by simply referring to conflict or, alternatively, to consensus.

UNCRITICAL ACQUIESCENCE OR CRITICAL ACCEPTANCE

The complexities of actual policy-making situations go deeper than sometimes primarily involving conflict and other times primarily involving consensus. Let us first focus on consensus.

There is a further reason why consensus is morally significant in policy-making: Consensus is not always a good thing. Consensus is sometimes good, or at least morally defensible, when it has been reached through an open, critical process of reasoning and exchange of opinions. No doubt, the views reached through consensus may still be false, and the consensus reached may be weak. It may be merely an excessively tentative, unconvinced, and hesitant willingness to go along with certain views. Whatever its shortcomings, however, this form of consensus is morally defensible, because appeals to reason and meaningful dialogue have been instrumental in reaching it, and there is room for correcting current views through further appeals to reason and meaningful dialogue.

In other cases, consensus may be morally questionable if not outright objectionable. It may be based not on reason and critical scrutiny but merely on fear, blind faith, unreflectiveness, sheer tenacity, or many other varieties of unreason. No doubt, the views thus reached may happen to be true, and the circumstances (e.g., confusing evidence, together with the urgent need to reach consensus) may justify the manner in which consensus was reached. However, there is a social cost involved: inflexibility, imperviousness to reasoned-out social change, generalized unreflective acquiescence. This prompts the morally valid question: Is such a consensus justified? The fact that this question is morally valid is evidence that the said consensus is morally questionable, that it is open to challenge and in need of justification from a moral standpoint.

Further, if the answer turns out to be that the circumstances did not justify reaching consensus in such a nonrational manner, then the consensus thus reached, even if the opinions on which there is consensus are true, would be morally objectionable. Regardless of whether a given form of consensus is morally defensible, the mere fact that it may or may not be so indicates that it is significant for morally sensitive policy-making. Analogously, it is morally crucial to face up to the varieties, in both nature and moral significance, of those policy-making situations that involve conflict.

CONTROVERSIES AND CONFRONTATIONS

A controversy (e.g., the preferential treatment controversy) is a social conflict that involves sharp differences of opinions or conflicts of demands. Yet, however heated these may be, there is significant room for the use of reason and meaningful dialogue between those whose opinions or demands are opposed. That is, such things as manipulation, threats, and the use of sanctions or force may be present, but they are not predominant. Were they predominant, one would be faced with a confrontation (e.g., a conspiracy, a violent strike, or a war), and negotiation or discussion of merits would have little, if any, effect on the situation. That is, negotiation and discussion of merits, which involve appeals to reason and meaningful dialogue, are predominant in controversies and secondary, if at all present, in confrontations. Hence, confrontations, like controversies, are social conflicts, but they differ from controversies in the *degree* to which appeals to reason and meaningful dialogue play a role in them.

Accordingly, social decision procedures that center on appeals to reason and meaningful dialogue have little, if any, application in confrontational situations. When dealing with confrontations, procedures that bypass appeals to reason and meaningful dialogue are more likely to be effective, which does not mean that just any of them is therefore justified. The features of the situation are crucial for establishing which procedure to use; but the justified ones will be among those that are effective. Otherwise, policy-making would not be in accordance with its practical aim of doing something about a situation.

The facts that there are two crucial types of conflict, that there are two crucial types of consensus, and that different social decision procedures are applicable in each type of case serve to establish this essay's second, third, and fourth theses. The second thesis is that, in morally and politically characterizing a situation that prompts a policy-making problem, whether it involves predominantly conflict or consensus is not the only consideration; whether the interaction is rational or nonrational, also matters. The third thesis is that, given this additional variable, social interaction can range from predominantly conflictive and nonrational, through predominantly conflictive but rational, to predominantly consensual, which can be rational or nonrational. The fourth thesis says that the specific type of interaction involved is crucial for establishing which social decision procedures to employ in dealing with the problem.

MACROSOCIETAL MATTERS: A FORSAKEN
CONCERN IN SOCIOLOGICAL STUDIES

The features of policy problems these theses describe, however, are not sufficient to establish how urgent it is to do something about a problem. Also crucial are the social scope of interaction, and its social consequences. Yet these, as well as the various types of consensus and conflict, are largely ignored in many current social studies.

As Thomas J. Bernard states in *The Consensus-Conflict Debate*, the "criticisms that conflict theory raised against functionalism have generally been sustained, and now have entered into the mainstream of sociological thinking."[12] Yet, as he also says,

> conflict theory has not assumed a major role in academic sociology; rather, attention has shifted to new topics that are largely unrelated to either consensus or conflict theories—ethnomethodology, phenomenology, exchange theory, and other theories . . . that tend to focus on the "microsociological" world of everyday life, rather than on "macrosociological" phenomena such as social structure and process.[13]

From a policy-making standpoint, this situation is unfortunate. Many significant policy and decision problems—from those about abortion, through those concerning the ozone layer or the greenhouse effect, to those posed by the many ongoing regional wars—arise at the macrosocietal level. And microsociological studies are of little help concerning them. In addition, as previously stated, the results of such microsociological case studies remain largely unstructured data, not a body of knowledge applicable to new policy and decision cases.

This is not to say that microsociological studies are without merit. On the contrary. But they are of little use in the moral evaluation of policies and decisions meant to address problems at the macrosocietal level. Hence, wisdom suggests that balance and structure be restored. The ensuing discussion is meant to contribute to attaining these things.

MACROSOCIETAL VS. MICROSOCIETAL:
A SIGNIFICANT MATTER OF SCOPE

To say that a situation is *macrosocietal* is to say that it affects one or more societies or large societal sectors, such as business and the scientific community. That is, it is not limited to the microlevel of everyday individual lives, localities, or minor regions. This distinction is analogous to that between microeconomics and macroeconomics in economic theory.[14] As for other social sciences, they draw the distinction but do not all currently focus on the macrosocietal level. For example, much of current sociology does not.

An analogous development can be found in moral philosophy. A distinction between the macrolevel and the microlevel of social life has been drawn, and the significance of macrosocietal facts (e.g., individual freedom and responsibility) has been discussed.[15] Yet, during the twentieth century, much emphasis has been placed on individual action, which takes place at the microsocietal level. To be sure, there is now a greater readiness, if not a trend, to emphasize policy matters in engineering ethics, technology ethics, and science and society studies.[16] And health care ethics, with an emphasis on the entire health care system and all those involved in it, is replacing medical ethics, with its exclusive emphasis on the physician-patient relationship and the no doubt valid problems of conduct it prompts. However, this growing emphasis on policy is unlikely to bear fruit unless policy problems that arise at the macrosocietal level (e.g., those posed by volatile international markets) are distinguished from those that arise at the microsocietal level (e.g., the problem of how much money to allocate for education in a town's budget). These different types of problems cannot be addressed realistically, let alone in a morally sensitive manner, with the same type of policy treatment.

Hence, there is good reason for inferring this essay's fifth thesis: The specific scope of a policy and decision problem is crucial for establishing which social decision procedures to employ in dealing with the problem. For example, it is feasible to have a referendum to resolve a town's budgetary problem, but a referendum would hardly be a realistic way of addressing international economic policy problems such as those posed by international market volatility. Indeed, given the highly technical nature of this problem, a referendum would be a morally questionable way of addressing it.

NONDESTABILIZING VS. DESTABILIZING CONSEQUENCES

Conflicts can be disruptive and, in cases of significant disruption, they can destabilize a locality, region, social sector, or one or more societies. When a social conflict is destabilizing it not only inconveniences a lot of people (who have to deal with the demonstrations and protests involved) but also it tends to threaten the well-being or very existence of a social group either economically or politically. In what follows, I focus primarily on destabilization that takes place at the macrosocietal level. The destabilizing effects range from such things as poverty leading to widespread discontent, to armed insurrection or mass migrations. These effects make societies politically or economically unstable by undermining predictability and cooperation.

DESTABILIZATION AND PREDICTABILITY

Conflicts undermine the predictability of others' behavior because, at least in some conflict situations, one has little knowledge of what others will do.

This is especially so in or near extreme state-of-nature situations. In such situations, as Hobbes said, there are no common ways of doing things, and all one can expect is that others will do what they think is in their own self-interest.[17] But lack of knowledge is not the only source of unpredictability. Jon Elster has usefully described cases in which unpredictability results from having too much knowledge about others, failing to use the knowledge we have, or being in a situation with no, more than one, or highly unstable equilibria—that is, states in which no agent has an incentive to behave differently.[18]

DESTABILIZATION AND NONCOOPERATION

Conflicts and noncooperation also undermine societies. Widespread discontent and mass migrations—think, for example, of the East Germans' 1989 exodus to West Germany—constitute a situation in which individuals and groups emphasize their own concerns to the detriment of those of others. For example, in the 1989 migration, the actions of individuals or groups created externalities that were not better for all—at least not better for West German workers who faced increased competition for jobs. Such a situation is not extreme but, nonetheless, is a bit closer than before to the state of nature Hobbes described as "solitary, poor, nasty, brutish, and short."[19]

ASSESSING URGENCY

The preceding discussion makes plain that there is a range of situations that vary by type of interaction, scope, and degree of social disruption and that these variations are morally and politically significant. The disruption they cause may take the form of violations of individual rights or political or economic disruption, which may amount to destabilization of entire groups, social sectors, or societies. Simply focusing on the type of interaction, however, tells us nothing about how urgent it is to find a solution. Urgency depends on the degree of social disruption and the extent and nature of individual rights violations the situation involves. That is, the assessment of urgency depends partly on the scope of the problem, but crucially on the consequences for the individuals and groups affected. Does the conflict, for example, tend to destabilize one or more societies, as war would? Does it tend to undermine programs in whose absence societies or large social sectors would be disrupted and their members undergo intolerable hardships?

The points just made are good reasons for inferring theses six and seven: Neither the type of social interaction nor the scope of the policy-making problem is individually or jointly sufficient for establishing how urgent it is to do something about the problem. Crucial for assessing this urgency is the combination of the *social scope* of interaction—whether it is local, regional, national, international, or global—and the *social consequences* of this interaction—that is, whether this interaction harms individuals or disrupts groups and, if so, how much. Let us examine some salient cases that clarify and provide evidence for the latter points and set the stage for establishing this essay's last thesis.

SOME SALIENT CASES

CASE 1. ABORTION AS POPULATION CONTROL: A NONDESTABILIZING CONTROVERSY

In August 1984 at the Mexico City United Nations International Conference on Population, the U.S. delegation prompted controversy at home and abroad by announcing that it would withhold aid from organizations that promoted abortions, thus endangering the funds the United States provided to the International Planned Parenthood Federation through the United States Agency for International Development.[20] The demand for assurances that abortion programs would not be promoted was met to the U.S. delegation's satisfaction, and a conference report was adopted, but not without further controversy and a two-and-a-half-hour debate about the propriety of including an Arab-supported resolution that implicitly condemned Israeli settlements on the West Bank of the Jordan River.[21]

The type of social interaction involved in this case was a controversy. However heated and loaded with political manipulation, the conflict made predominant room for appeals to reason and meaningful dialogue. It may have been the case that no amount of reasonable dialogue would have changed the Reagan administration's position on the matter, but this is sheer speculation. And even if it were true, it does not mean that reason and meaningful dialogue had only a secondary role in the dialogue. Indeed, whatever changes took place in the other participants' positions were not primarily the result of threats or the use of force, but of bargaining, which significantly involved the use of reason and meaningful dialogue.

The fact that the conflict was a controversy, however, provides no grounds for assessing how urgent it was to do something about it. The controversy might have had no significant effects. To establish whether it would have had them, one has to examine the conflict's scope and likely consequences. As for its scope, it was macrosocietal, since it affected various societies. But how serious were its likely social consequences?

The conflict would appear not to have destabilized any society or large social sectors, though it no doubt affected the societies targeted by the policy decision. To come to terms with it, these societies had to adapt to the new situation. The controversy also had consequences for individuals, because it resulted in an agreement that led to changes in the countries involved, and these changes affected their inhabitants.

These, however, were consequences of agreeing to the U.S. demands, not consequences that made it urgent to do something about the controversy the United States had started. What created this urgency was, primarily, the likely consequence that, if the demands were not met and the controversy continued unsettled, the funds the United States provided to the International Planned Parenthood Federation through the United States Agency for International Development would have been endangered.

The consequences that were likely to result from the controversy itself for both individuals and society were morally significant. In general, consequences such as these, and their weight relative to each other, crucially matter in establishing the urgency of doing something about the situation. In addition, in order to establish how to deal with the situation, it is morally and politically crucial to establish what type of conflict is leading to such consequences. Policy-making cannot be effective or morally sensitive— indeed, it can backfire politically and undermine morality—if a controversy is mistaken for a confrontation, or vice versa. Hence, since they help clearly focus on these crucial matters, the distinctions drawn and categories described here should be of use in the ethics of policy-making.

CASE 2. NUCLEAR WASTES:
A PARTLY DESTABILIZING CONTROVERSY

In October 1984, controversy broke out in Canyonlands, Utah, over the then likely prospect that at least one of two nearby sites would be selected, in accordance with the 1982 Nuclear Waste Policy Act, to store radioactive wastes expected to remain toxic for at least a hundred centuries.[22] In December 1984, the Energy Department picked sites in Texas, Nevada, and Washington as the leading candidates to be the United States' first permanent burial ground for nuclear waste, but it immediately ran into legal and political opposition and was submerged in controversy—a conflict still raging years later.[23]

The type of social interaction in this case is, like in the previous one, a controversy. Though its scope is macrosocietal, it does not go beyond the national level. The controversy's consequences, in themselves, are not destabilizing. Yet the nuclear waste controversy is but a moment in the United States' nuclear energy controversy. And, as I discuss in Essay 10, the consequences of this recurrent controversy arguably have included a relative destabilization of the U.S. nuclear energy industry. In this regard, the policy situation seems to be different from that in Case 1, since a sizable business sector is destabilized. And this result is morally significant because individual lives—those of nuclear employees who, as a result of this destabilization, will probably lose their jobs—are likely to be undermined. These consequences are crucial for establishing the degree of urgency for dealing with the problem. So are the health risks the waste would pose for those living near the sites and the possible correlative violation of their right not to be made to take avoidable health risks without their participation in the relevant policy-making process.

In addition, policymakers need to establish how to deal with the problems posed by the above situation. That is, they need to establish whether to resolve it through negotiation, mediation, arbitration, a referendum, or other social decision procedures. In order to establish all these things, it is crucial to determine what type of social interaction the situation involves. As discussed, it is a controversy. Hence, though some or other of the social decision procedures just mentioned may be both effective and morally sensitive, others would be politically unsound and morally questionable if not outright impermissible.

For example, given the history of the nuclear energy controversy in the United States, it would be imprudent to try to settle the matter by decree. This would lead to a public outcry, if not lawsuits against the agencies involved. Further, it would be morally questionable and, arguably, imper-missible for a variety of reasons. One is the fact that such an autocratic decision would disrupt individual lives, and possibly regions, and further disrupt the nuclear industry by increasing the controversy. Another is the fact that individual rights to participation in the nuclear policy-making process would be violated. Just as, at the time of the American Revolution, there was no justification for taxation without representation, there is now no justification for taking public health risks without participation. In any case, all these considerations are clearly brought into focus by the distinc-tions and categories this essay develops, which, therefore, are of use in the ethics of policy-making.

CASE 3. ANIMAL RIGHTS CONFRONTATIONAL ACTIVISM: NONDESTABILIZING CONFRONTATIONS

In July 1985, scores of animal rights activists occupied the offices of the National Institutes of Health in Bethesda, Maryland, to publicize the plight of baboons used for research purposes at the University of Pennsylvania's Head Injury Clinical Research Center in Philadelphia. They charged that the research pursued at the Center was inhumane and without scientific merit. Their evidence was based on sixty hours of videotapes stolen from the lab in 1984 by the underground Animal Liberation Front.[24] In November 1988, a bomb was planted near the parking spot used by the chairman of U.S. Surgical in Norwalk, Connecticut, because the firm demonstrates its surgical staplers on about 1,000 anesthetized dogs each year, killing them afterwards.[25]

In contrast with the previous cases, the conflict involved here is a con-frontation, not a controversy. That is, the use of reason and meaningful dialogue is not predominant in the social interactions between the activists and the representatives of the powers that be. This is a significant difference for the moral assessment of policy and decision, because as long as current attitudes persist, discussions of merits or simple negotiations are unlikely to work. Hence, other approaches may be justified. This is a morally significant aspect of the situation that an excessive emphasis on consensus is likely to miss, but the distinctions and categories in this essay easily bring it out.

In addition, though the acts described are somewhat isolated, the conflict's scope reaches the macrosocietal level, since it affects the U.S. science and technology sector. Concerning its consequences, there is reason to believe that the conflict has harmed (though hardly destabilized) science and technology in the United States. This is a consideration relevant for establishing how urgent it is to address the problem. An overall judgment of urgency should also establish such things as how far such harm has gone, how serious it is, and how it harms either nonhumans or the interests of those who stand up for nonhumans. Finally, in establishing how to deal with the policy-making problem posed by the situation, the type of social interaction involved—confrontation—is also crucial.

The preceding discussion gives reasons to part company with the previously mentioned microsociological studies in ethnomethodology, phenomenology, and exchange theory. It also gives reasons to part company with moral theories that focus exclusively on individuals, the actions they perform, the obligations or rights they have, and the consequences they undergo. In contrast with all these, the approach taken here is politically and morally more helpful. Without disregarding the effects on individuals, it also pays attention to the macrosocietal aspects and consequences of the situation.

CASE 4. THE IRANIAN CRISIS:
A DESTABILIZING CONFRONTATION

When conflicts bring about or threaten imminently to lead to consequences that amount to states of nature, they are often called *crises*. For example, when Iran took U.S. citizens hostage, there was a crisis called "the Iranian crisis." This was a macrosocietal confrontation that seriously destabilized not just the United States with sudden oil shortages, or Iran with enormous military pressures, but the world community at large. The crisis constituted a serious threat to world peace and to the character of the world community itself.[26]

In light of the preceding discussion and the fact that the conflict was a crisis, it would have been a mistake to treat it as a mere controversy or as involving nondestabilizing consequences at the macrosocietal level. Avoiding these mistakes, of course, does not guarantee success in addressing it. But it at least points in the right direction by focusing on the conflict as a macrosocietal confrontation whose very occurrence is destabilizing at that level. In cases of this type, dialogue characteristically is not meaningful, and the consequences to individuals and large social sectors or entire societies are serious. Hence, these situations pose urgent policy-making problems that are unlikely to be effectively addressed through discussion of merits or negotiation. Other, more confrontational policy-making approaches—from economic and political sanctions to combat—are both politically more realistic and morally more sensitive than less confrontational ones.

No doubt, negotiated solutions are preferable if they are possible. But in cases of this type, other, more drastic policy approaches are often necessary before meaningful negotiations are possible. These crucial political and moral matters are discussed in some detail in Essay 12. At any rate, the taxonomy here developed helps focus on them.

CASE 5. THE BHOPAL CONTROVERSY:
A MICROSOCIETAL, YET INTERNATIONAL, CONFLICT

In February 1989, Union Carbide and the Indian government reached a settlement whereby Union Carbide agreed to pay $470 million for the 1984 Bhopal methyl isocyanate leak that killed more than 3,300 people and injured tens of thousands. This settlement sparked a controversy on the grounds that the victims had been betrayed.[27]

Although this controversy is international and involves legal actions taken under two legal systems, it does not affect entire societies or societal sectors. It would appear to be microsocietal, that is, primarily having to do with the everyday lives of individuals or small social units such as towns and firms.

As for its consequences, the conflict over Bhopal's legal settlement has harmed the victims. They received little or no economic compensation or access to adequate health care. Whatever they did receive came too late for many of them. This is a good reason to redirect strategies away from seeking redress through courts of law in similar cases. Although it was urgent to do something about the victims and the conflict, the court action was inadequate for helping the victims and helped increase the conflict unnecessarily. Here, as in the other cases discussed in this essay, the taxonomy proposed helps redirect attention to these politically significant and morally sensitive matters.

CASE 6. ARGENTINA'S DIRTY WAR: POWER ELITES
AND MACROSOCIETALLY DESTABILIZING CONFLICTS

The preceding cases are not meant to imply that conflicts posing policy problems at the macrosocietal level must necessarily be widespread—only that the scope of their effect must be. In fact, there are macrosocietal policy and decision problems posed by conflicts between only a few, but highly influential, people or groups. These are *power elite* conflicts, such as the one that took place in Argentina mostly between 1974 and 1983. It was a conflict between a number of military officers actively supported by a few small extreme right groups and the constitutionally elected though widely discredited government of President Isabel Perón. A military takeover was staged, President Perón was arrested, and, beginning on March 24, 1976, military officers and their extremist supporters carried out their extermination policies against a great number of people.

Extermination policies were, no doubt, morally impermissible when dealing with active opponents to the military regime. But the policies went far beyond that, on the assumption that the goal of exterminating the opposition justified the cost of eliminating people who might turn out to be innocent. As a result, a great number of Argentines, among them many bystanders caught off guard, were, as the phrase went, "taken out of society." The infamous "dirty war" had begun.

A large societal sector in Argentina—indeed, the society as a whole—experienced the consequences of the conflict. The military government's policies left somewhere between 9,000 and 30,000 people tortured and killed (the official word was "disappeared"), plus many others tortured or exiled or both. They also led to fraudulent acquisition of property through repression, a generalized loss of public trust, and, after the South Atlantic armed conflict with Great Britain and the economic and political chaos it hastened, the collapse of the regime.[28]

These facts leave no doubt that the conflict, though restricted to a small elite of active participants, posed a macrosocietal policy and decision problem. It made Argentinian society both politically and economically unstable and caused widespread harm among individuals. Indeed, it eventually became an extreme form of a macrosocietal policy problem: a macrosocietal crisis. Hence, it was no doubt urgent to deal with it.

However, as the events that transpired made plain, the thorough governmental oppression and terror involved, the nature of Argentinian territory, and the size and nature of Argentinian armed forces and police made internal violent resistance unlikely to succeed. Only other confrontational social decision procedures such as foreign sanctions and citizens' nonviolent resistance had a good chance of being politically effective. Arguably, they also were morally sound and, to some extent, had the desired effect of slowly forcing the regime to weaken its stand. Finally, the worsening economy and the South Atlantic war and its aftermath overtook the regime.

The implications discussed concerning this and the previous cases provide grounds in support of our remaining—the eighth—thesis. It says: The more urgent a policy-making problem that predominantly involves nonrational interaction (e.g., that posed by military oppression) is, the more applicable and, arguably, more morally permissible are social decision procedures that bypass meaningful dialogue such as civil disobedience, external sanctions, and, in certain cases, force. This thesis, whose implications will be developed in the ensuing essays, further brings out the policy-making significance of all the features of policy problems crucial to our taxonomy.

ASKING POLICY-MAKING QUESTIONS
BASED ON THIS ESSAY'S TAXONOMY

The main thrust of the preceding discussion is to bring out the moral and policy-making significance of a number of features found in policy-making situations. Given their significance, those features prompt a series of policy-making questions that, for the sake of making politically sound and morally permissible policy and decisions, policymakers—both official ones and ordinary individuals in a position to influence policy-making—would do well to ask:

1. Is the situation predominantly conflictual or consensual?
2. Does the situation predominantly make room for appeals to reason and meaningful dialogue—that is, is it predominantly rational—or not?
3. Does the situation arise at the macrolevel or microlevel of social life?
4. Is the situation destabilizing of one or more groups—possibly entire societies—or not?
5. Does the situation involve violations of individual rights and, if so, what is the nature and extent of these violations?

There are, no doubt, additional questions worth asking. Yet the ones just formulated are invariably crucial to achieving a politically and morally sound perspective on the policy-making problems posed by the situations faced. All of them ought to be asked, though not necessarily in the order in which I have formulated them. However, the order I chose reflects a manner in which policy-making problems can more easily be understood in all their complexity.

People, however well-meaning, often get caught in a policy-making situation and argue merely about who has the right to what or, alternatively, what will or will not work. In this manner, they lose perspective. Whenever this happens, shifting people's attention to such things as whether the situation is conflictive or not, and whether it makes room for appeals to reason and meaningful dialogue or not, helps their understanding of the problem. This, in turn, puts them in a better position to appreciate the various features of the problem and assess their relative weight from both a policy-making and a moral standpoint.

No doubt, such an approach does not guarantee certainty. Nor will it work in a society (fortunately only an imaginary society) where most people are idiots, lunatics, crooks, or utterly callous. However, it has a good chance of helping ordinary people in the various types of policy-making situations that arise in societies as we know them.

The questions just formulated presuppose a taxonomy of policy and decision problems whose main features are indicated in the flowchart located on page 107. Each special type of policy-making situation can then be subdivided into various subtypes. Consider, for example, those that are nondestabilizing. They include, first, those that primarily involve violations of individual rights, hence, disrupt individuals. Second, there are those that primarily disrupt groups, that is, they have undesirable though not catastrophic consequences for groups but do not violate individual rights, such as conflicts about the deficit. Third, there are those that both disrupt groups and involve violations of individual rights. In a parallel manner, further specifications are needed in dealing with destabilizing policy-making situations. For example, some situations destabilize groups that already violated individual rights; others destabilize groups in which individual rights were not previously violated and, in destabilizing the groups, they thus undermine the conditions for respecting individual rights in these groups. In any case, a taxonomy such as that here developed suggests various policy-making guidelines.

SOCIAL DECISION PROCEDURES AND THE TAXONOMY OF POLICY-MAKING PROBLEMS

Those situations that are destabilizing at the macrosocietal level pose problems that require policy-making that is quite different from that required by administrative policy or decision problems, such as how to print commemorative stamps most economically. In general, which procedures are suited for dealing with which problems depends on the type of problem. For example, the 1988 chlorofluorocarbons treaty, however inadequate its requirements (given the extent of ozone-layer depletion disclosed by new evidence), indicates that, when the threats are planetary, well-established, and likely to be manageable, confrontations may be avoided. Indeed, discussions of merits coupled with negotiations that focus on everyone's interests can lead to a sound policy beginning. This is further supported by recent commitments by Europe and Japan to provide financial assistance so that other countries can abide by the 1992 agreements signed by members of the European Community, and by the weaker Rio de Janeiro Treaty.[29] Similarly, negotiation seems to be the central procedure used in dealing with the internationally disruptive controversy about acid rain between the United States and Canada.[30]

In other types of cases, different procedures may be suitable. An attempt at insulation is exemplified in the National Institutes of Health's initial

Policy-Making Situation

Primarily Conflictive

Predominantly Rational

Macro Level

Dest. Non-Dest.

Micro Level

Dest. Non-Dest.

Predominantly Nonrational

Macro Level

Dest. Non-Dest.

Micro Level

Dest. Non-Dest.

Primarily Consensual

Predominantly Rational

Macro Level

Dest. Non-Dest.

Micro Level

Dest. Non-Dest.

Predominantly Nonrational

Macro Level

Dest. Non-Dest.

Micro Level

Dest. Non-Dest.

directive to proceed with fetal research that does not offer incentives for women to have abortions. This treats the controversy as disruptive of a societal sector—a significant part of the scientific community—and tries to circumscribe it. It also tries to contain its consequences for this sector, to uphold the freedom of inquiry of individual scientists in the group, and to take the lives of fetuses seriously. Hence, it is morally sensitive in that it pays attention to the significant moral concerns involved. From a political standpoint, it is still an open question whether it will succeed despite constraints introduced by Bush administration officials.[31]

In contrast, the Bhopal settlement points out the shortcomings of court proceedings, negotiation and compromise, and the need for accompanying emergency arrangements and funds to aid victims of industrial accidents.[32] At any rate, judging by the ongoing increases in litigiousness in the United States and abroad (despite the recent increase in peaceful superpower relations), the above or related procedures are not used as often as desirable. The taxonomy this essay sketched should facilitate their use. It should help keep a balance—a delicate balance—between the exaggeration of abhorring all social conflict and that of finding hope for social progress only in conflict, however irrationally motivated, societally destabilizing, and undermining of individual rights it might be.

Dialogue

— I have no doubt that policy and decision problems can be classified in the manner you describe. However, I am still unconvinced of the utility of such classification.

— Your hesitation puzzles me. I have given a number of reasons why the taxonomy I formulated would be of use to policymakers from both a moral and a political standpoint. I have made clear the policy-making and moral mistakes that can result from treating all policy and decision problems as confrontational; from treating them all as posed by controversies or, even worse, as merely administrative; from treating them all as microlevel problems; and so on. What else do you think I should have done?

— I believe that, for example, you should have shown when and, if ever, why macrosocietal consequences override individual rights and, if so, which rights.

— I will do so in Essay 8. Please be patient. But even if what I say in the eighth essay turns out to be mistaken, it should not undermine the entire taxonomy. The points I have made so far will still hold. At most, moral evaluation criteria other than those I will formulate will be needed.

— As I said before, however, your taxonomy tends to multiply questions to the point of making one dizzy.

— No doubt, it prompts many questions. But what else should be expected? Social life is not simple. It's a virtue of my taxonomy that it brings out the complexities of social life in a manner that helps us deal with them with a sense of proportion. It's neither simplistic nor chaotic.

— You'll grant me, though, that it's not nearly conceptually economical and precise enough to be of use in applying highly abstract theories.

— True, but as I said, what else should be expected? Neither political life nor moral life is a simple and precise affair. In being applicable to them, the taxonomy reflects this fact, which explains its complexities and imprecisions. If these make it useless for applying highly abstract theories, too bad for the theories. As I argued concerning rational choice, decision, game, and social choice theories, their abstract simplicity and precision make them unrealistic and undermining of morality.

— You realize, however, that many sophisticated philosophers and social thinkers prefer those simple, precise theories.

— Yes. But what do they have to offer instead: the tyranny of order at any cost, or the tyranny of disregarding this or that individual or group in the rush to attain results? There are no morally redeeming qualities in these approaches. Besides, in the not so long run, all such approaches tend to lead to so much opposition that they undo themselves. In contrast, an approach like the one I am proposing, in which critical scrutiny and interaction are central, has a good chance of working both morally and politically.

— Not so fast. You grant me, I suppose, that even such an approach would yield objectionable results if those involved were idiots, lunatics, crooks, or utterly callous.

— True. Yet, to stay with my line of argument, that case is not realistic. Indeed, the very notion of a society with primarily such members may be incoherent. My approach is meant to work in actual societies, which characteristically involve a mixture of intelligent individuals and idiots, reasonable people and lunatics, morally good people and crooks, as well as caring and callous people. How else could you explain the very existence of societies if this mixture were absent and all or most of their members were unreasonable, unintelligent, crooks, or callous?

— I see your point. The problem is that even with the mixture of good and bad qualities you claim to be present in actual societies, your approach may sometimes yield questionable results.

— Granted. But in actual policy-making circumstances, these results are invariably open to (and, given the population's makeup, subjected to) further criticism and testing through social interaction. This makes room for correcting them and, eventually, is likely to lead to both politically sound and morally permissible policies and decisions.

— Such corrections, however, cannot wait forever. As Lord Keynes said, in the long run, we are all dead.

— True. As I indicated, my approach is meant to be sensitive to this fact. However, it is not meant to eliminate all chances of human error or wrongdoing. Such an aim would be foolish because it is unrealistic.

— Still, I have no idea of how your approach would make room for critical scrutiny and social interaction.

— I'm glad you asked. These questions bring us to the topic of my next essay.

8 Practical Equity: Dealing with the Varieties of Policy and Decision Problems

The excesses of social order always limit individual freedoms, if not well-being. Those of social disorder always limit well-being, if not individual freedoms. As a matter of both moral and political wisdom, policy-making is invariably faced with finding a politically sound and morally permissible way between these and any other excesses. Hence, the question I will address in this essay arises: What criteria can help us establish which policies and decisions are both politically sound and morally permissible in the actual world of politics? My aim is to specify conditions under which policies and policy-making decisions are permissible *given existing time constraints; political pressures; economic, technological, and other relevant conditions; the people involved; the information they can be expected to have at decision-making time; and the moral and political implications of the policies or decisions.* I am *not* concerned with specifying features that make policies or policy-making decisions politically sound and morally permissible with hindsight. Nor do I specify what these features would be in ideal conditions, independent of the said circumstances.

Although I am not concerned with specifying these features, this does not mean that they cannot be specified. Nor does it mean that my account is incompatible with any such specification, or that it makes it redundant. I am simply addressing the entirely different problem of how to go about engaging in making politically sound and morally permissible policy and decisions in the actual political world.

In this world, ideal or nearly ideal conditions that are largely devoid of scarcity, conflict, and irrationality sometimes develop. Frequently, however, one or more conditions typically used to characterize ideal societies are absent. First, scarcity is often worse than moderate. Second, conditions are often so harsh that all policy-making alternatives are relatively undesirable

112

and, in some cases, tragically catastrophic. Third, people often do not respect rights or comply with principles of justice or even with utilitarian principles. Fourth, current social arrangements, whose change would cause significant loss, harm, or serious general deprivation to some people, are often the result of previous injustices to which the said people are not always accomplices.[1] As the discussions in previous essays indicate, the hypotheses I formulate in answer to the above question are intended to help address situations such as those just described in all their variety.

In doing so, the hypotheses will rely on the taxonomy formulated in Essay 7, which made plain that sensitivity to the varieties of policy and decision problems is crucial. For example, it matters whether a given problem is prompted by a societally destabilizing confrontation, as in Iraq's invasion and annexation of Kuwait in 1990, or by a merely administrative, nonconflictual matter, as in trying to establish how many commemorative stamps to issue in a given year. Although the above question can be asked regarding problems of each type, this essay focuses mainly, though not exclusively, on policy and decision problems that arise at the macrosocietal level. That is, I concentrate on problems that affect large social sectors (e.g., agribusiness or the scientific community) or entire societies.[2]

All but one of the hypotheses I formulate and propose as policy-making guidelines apply to policies and decisions meant to address problems of specific types. In addition, as an upshot of my discussion, I formulate and provide reasons in support of an overall hypothesis, the *principle of practical equity*. Together, these hypotheses are a main component of a satisficing theory in the sense introduced by Herbert Simon and discussed in previous essays. That is, they are not meant to characterize absolute rights. Nor do they formulate, or serve as a basis for formulating, fixed, sub specie aeternitatis moral rights, obligations, laws, or principles such as those of justice or of utility. Nor, indeed, are the essay's hypotheses presumed to be definitive themselves. Rather, they are the main components of a theory according to which the freedoms and well-being to be sought are not fixed, though they normally involve meeting a minimum standard of provisions. The main purpose of the said hypotheses is to help us, at least temporarily, deal with those matters that are not fixed in a politically sound and morally permissible way.[3] A crucial way in which they help is by suggesting the appropriate moral questions to ask in specific policy-making situations. I formulate some of these questions (which build on those formulated in Essay 7) in the remainder of the essay. More detailed questions are suggested by the hypotheses themselves.

Though I am primarily concerned with the moral and political assessment of policies and decisions for dealing with macrosocietal problems, I do not entirely disregard problems affecting only individuals or small groups such as towns or localities. After all, the policies and decisions addressing these microsocietal problems are neither politically nor morally irrelevant or insignificant. Hence, the hypotheses I formulate are meant to be sensitive to how policies and decisions affect individuals; the relations between them; those between individuals and the small groups, societal sectors, or societies affected; and those between the social groups, societal sectors, and societies themselves.

These relations characteristically involve matters of fairness, desert, and well-being, which are covered by the various senses, both moral and legal, of the term *equity*.[4] This is why *equity* is used in the overall hypothesis I formulate. As for the use of *practical*, it reflects the recognition that economic, technological, political, and moral reality sets constraints on which policies and decisions are likely to be both feasible and effective. As indicated, I am concerned with assessing policies and decisions that fall within the scope of these constraints, for if they do not, they have little chance of being applicable or doing any good in the real world.

LIMITING CONDITIONS VS. SINGLE-SOLUTION CRITERIA

In accordance with the purposes just discussed, the hypotheses I formulate are intended to describe *limiting conditions* for assessing policies and decisions. In other words, they are meant to work as filters through which any politically sound and morally permissible policy and decisions to which they apply must pass. Of course, more than one alternative policy or decision may satisfy such limiting conditions. In this case, according to the hypotheses, each is permissible.

One might, however, insist on establishing which alternative is the only permissible one. The hypotheses I formulate may, but need not, meet this demand. Whether they do depends on the facts of the case. It may turn out that for a given policy problem, only one policy solution satisfies the criteria the relevant hypothesis formulates. But there is no logical, political, or moral reason why this should be so. Indeed, single-solution requirements amount to policy-making simplicity and, ethically, to a lack of realism and intolerance if not to self-defeating perfectionism.

I should add that single-solution requirements often go hand in hand with the requirement that freedoms, well-being, or some combination of these be maximized. Such a requirement, however, has the effect of turning the best that can be done into a duty. But if it is a duty, then nothing can be done that is beyond the call of duty. This flies in the face of ordinary moral thinking as well as political and moral wisdom. First, people ordinarily think that some decisions, including policy-making decisions, are admirable because they go beyond what is required. For example, a person without dependents to look after might leave a very successful and well-remunerated career at a financial institution in order to become director of a nonprofit housing-related organization where the pay is much less and the hours worse, simply because he or she wants to help improve housing options for those in need.

Second, the single-solution requirement goes against political and moral wisdom, for it entails that any policy and decision that falls short of optimization is both politically unsound and morally wrong. But most, if not all, actual policies and decisions will fail to be optimizing. As a result, the said requirement can only increase cynicism about the prospects for politics and morals, thereby undermining both. And since, presumably, it is meant to improve both politics and morality, it is but another instance of self-defeating perfectionism. Hence, in order to remain sensitive to the turns and twists of policy-making reality, and the scope and flexibility of the morally permissible, the hypotheses I formulate in this essay are of the limiting conditions (not the single-solution, let alone optimization) type.

THE ROLE OF CRITICAL SCRUTINY AND OTHER DECISION PROCEDURES IN POLICY-MAKING

PRIMARILY ADMINISTRATIVE SITUATIONS

Consider the policy and decision problems formulated by the following questions: What yearly deadlines should exist for deciding what commemorative stamps to issue? What commemorative stamps should there be? Should foreigners visiting our country be allowed free entrance to its national parks? These problems arise at the macrosocietal level, in situations involving little or no societal disruption, and are typically addressed through meaningful dialogue and appeal to reasons.

Ordinarily, dealing with such policy problems as these in a sound manner need not limit the freedoms or well-being of those likely to be affected. In fact, the situation is *primarily administrative*. If any controversy arises concerning policies for dealing with the problems, it typically concerns the most effective way of using available means for purposes that are hardly questioned. It infrequently, if ever, centers on a person's or group's forgone, perhaps desirable, but clearly unneeded extravagant advantages such as the luxury of being able to buy one of those $40,000 bracelets or one of those $30,000 watches advertised in the *New York Times*.

At this primarily administrative end of the spectrum of policy and decision problems, critical scrutiny and therefore judgment by those likely to be affected are, as always, relevant. However, critical scrutiny about the purposes of the policies or decisions envisioned is generally unnecessary, because it is generally known what judgments it will yield. These judgments will acknowledge that there is a desire for the ends involved, but they will not ordinarily describe the attainment of such ends as crucial. Indeed, the ends are extravagant, and if anyone expressed a different view on the matter, it would be an eccentricity and require further argument in its support.

CONTROVERSIES AND ECCENTRIC WANTS AND NEEDS

To take the position just taken is not to deny, however, that within limits, people are entitled to their extravagances and eccentricities. And, no doubt, they sometimes have eccentric or even embarrassing wants or even needs.[5] In such a situation, even if there is general agreement, consensus, or conformity about a certain matter, critical scrutiny may nonetheless be necessary. It may still have to be established in what regard, and to what extent, policies and decisions should make room for satisfying the wants or needs of the eccentric, the nonconformist, the weird, and even those who, from the standpoint of personal morality, are morally objectionable. The possibility of satisfying these wants or needs deserves consideration, at a minimum.

Considering the possibility of satisfying such wants or needs, however, does not mean that they ought to be satisfied. Nor does it mean that policy-making measures ought to be taken so that they can be satisfied. My point is simply that, in the type of situation described, critical scrutiny involving those likely to be affected or their representatives is both morally and politically crucial. It is morally crucial because, otherwise, those out of power (e.g., those who, though living in a democracy, are in the minority) could simply be disregarded and railroaded into acceptance. It is politically crucial because of two combined factors. First, though railroading unusual people into acceptance may seem effective in the short run, it is likely to breed instability and conflict. After all, the unusual of today have a way of becoming the commonplace of tomorrow. Second, in the type of situation described, there is time to seek alternative arrangements that are sufficiently tolerable to all who are likely to be affected.

Let us consider an example. Among U.S. suburbanites, wearing a medieval helmet while mowing one's front lawn in full view of neighbors and passersby would normally be considered eccentric. Suppose someone does this simply for kicks, or to shock or puzzle the neighbors. It harms no one. But suppose that the neighbors, bothered by the odd sight, press for a local ordinance outlawing the eccentric behavior. The eccentric neighbor might not consider wearing the helmet crucial, but he or she might consider the freedom to wear the helmet crucial and find it intolerable not to be able to enjoy such a freedom, however frivolous it might be. So it deserves consideration.

From the standpoint of arguing the merits of the case, the neighbors or their representatives must try to show that the eccentric's reason for desiring such a freedom is not as strong as their reason for finding his wearing of the helmet intolerable. In other words, they need to show that their finding it intolerable is justified and that their reason is stronger than the eccentric's reason for wanting the freedom to wear the helmet. To establish this, they might try such things as showing that the neighbor's behavior decreased the value of their homes or scared their young children. Yet these considerations would be unconvincing.

Of course, the matter would not thereby be definitely settled. Critical scrutiny would still be relevant in dealing with the conformist neighbors' intolerance, if not with the eccentric neighbor's silly preferences. In addition, such social decision procedures as negotiation, bargaining, and compromise would be of use in working out a modus vivendi that all those affected would find tolerable enough, however ideally dissatisfying.

The example just discussed is not isolated or unreal. Instead of wearing a medieval helmet while mowing the front lawn, someone might want to cover the front lawn with red and black signs or other paraphernalia praising the Church of Universal Anarchy (as I saw someone had done in Madison, Wisconsin, in the late 1970s and early 1980s). Here again, negotiation, bargaining, and compromise, when not sheer coping, are good candidates for dealing with neighborhood conflicts.

Not all cases of eccentric ends, however, are alike. For example, on a more dangerous note, someone might want to keep a pet lion chained to a large tree in his or her yard (as I saw someone had done in Plano, Texas, in the mid-1970s). Suppose the neighbors complain, or an official of the state considers it a public risk. Regardless of whether there is an ordinance outlawing the presence of the lion in the yard, a basic policy question is: Should there be such an ordinance? In this case, critical scrutiny concerning the merits of the case is likely to suffice. What could the lion's owner possibly say to establish that having the lion in the yard is more crucial than the safety of the neighbors, their dependents, their visitors, or people who simply happen to pass by? The case for keeping the lion in the yard would be extremely weak.

THE FALSE SECURITY OF STRONG VIEWS

The approach just outlined may elicit distrust on the grounds that, given the appropriate conditions, people will make the wrong choice. For example, suppose the lion's owner is wealthy and extravagant enough to promise an Olympic swimming pool for the town in exchange for permission to keep the lion in the backyard. Many might find it appealing, even if public or personal safety would be jeopardized. As a result, stronger views that, in general, appeal to inflexible or absolute moral rights, obligations, laws, or principles (whether of a strictly deontological or of a strictly teleological nature) may seem more promising. But do they constitute an alternative? Not by themselves. Let us see why not.

For the purposes of our argument, let us consider a stronger view that, though widely different from many others, shares with them a strong character. That is, it involves an appeal to moral rights, obligations, laws, or principles that, in some regard, are inflexible if not absolute. Since we are not concerned merely with this aspect of the view, nor with any specifics that make it different from other such views, nothing in our argument depends on its peculiarities. That is, our conclusions apply to all strong views.

In accordance with the methodological remarks just made, let us consider the following view: *There is at least prima facie reason for satisfying any wants and needs that are attainable when those who have the wants or needs would find the policies or decisions that keep them unattainable intolerable, and their satisfaction would not seriously deprive others.*[6] Even assuming that this view is valid, it may not always be obvious that it applies to a particular situation. Or it may be obvious to some, but quite controversial to others. Or it may be controversial that, given pressures to address other matters, there is enough time to address this one.

In cases of this type, controversy frequently develops about the applicability of the said view, even when there is agreement on the view itself. Accordingly, the view is of little, if any, help in assessing policies and decisions. At best, it is an abstract guideline whose applicability and, occasionally, validity is to be established in the process. This is also the case for all other views like it.

In contrast, various social decision procedures can help settle the abovementioned applicability matters. For example, regarding the view just discussed, social decision procedures besides discussion of merits and the narrow type of critical scrutiny it involves are crucial. Hence, they are politically sound and morally permissible in dealing with the said matter.

However, the fact that decision procedures other than discussion of merits are crucial does not open the door to the use of just any procedure. For example, discussion of merits, negotiation, compromise, or coping are less appropriate now than before because, by manipulating the town with the promise of a swimming pool, the eccentric neighbor has given the conflict more of a nonrational character. Hence, those seeking to get the lion out of the yard are faced with having to use more drastic procedures, including organized action involving a publicity campaign, demonstrations, boycotts (the lion's owner presumably has business interests), and appeals to higher authorities. These procedures are likely to be both politically feasible and effective and morally permissible in the circumstances.

How does this alternative help? Though it does not provide definitive closure, it helps by creating presumptions. So long as those likely to be affected are represented in the process and, directly or through their representatives, consent to it, there is good reason to presume that the resulting policies and decisions are permissible.

CONTROVERSIES AND NONEGCENTRIC WANTS AND NEEDS

Cases like those just discussed can no doubt prompt controversy. More often than not, however, controversies center on individuals' or group's noneccentric disadvantages. For example, they may center on current disadvantages that prompt the proposal of a new tax, versus the disadvantages that would be created if the proposed tax were introduced. Controversies such as this often become heated and involve public demonstrations and, sometimes, acts of violence. More often than not, however, conflicts about taxes are predominantly addressed through meaningful dialogue, reliance on reason, and such options offered by the political process as negotiation, bargaining, compromise, and voting.

As we previously saw, this situation is still a controversy, not a confrontation. Nor is it a matter of consensus, let alone one leading to societal disruption or destabilization. An example of a societally disruptive consensus would be a country's consensus on pursuing agricultural deep tillage and related practices that lead to widespread soil erosion and thus slowly undermine the country's agricultural system in a manner likely to acquire crisis proportions in a few decades.

As for the appropriate way of dealing with such a situation, there is ordinarily no good moral or political reason to bring about serious societal disruption now for the sake of later improvements. If the society needing policy-making about the controversy is not so objectionable as to deserve being dismantled, it would be unjustified to disrupt it, let alone destabilize it. Here again, the role of judgment on the part of those likely to be affected is crucial, but reaching it may take a great deal of critical scrutiny. Often it is not obvious who may be deprived, or in what respects and to what extent the deprivation may take place. Indeed, as before, decisions may have to be reached through social decision procedures that go beyond critical scrutiny. In many cases, negotiation, bargaining, compromise, and voting are both politically feasible and effective, and morally permissible. However, as argued in previous essays and further exemplified by the latter example, the more nonrational a situation becomes—that is, the more appeals to reason and meaningful dialogue lose predominance in it—the more appropriate drastic procedures become.

CONFLICTS IN OBJECTIONABLE SOCIETIES

Suppose that the society in which the soil erosion policy and decision problem arises is objectionable because its citizens are oppressed, maybe to the point of being victims of state terrorism. That is, suppose that the situation is confrontational in nature, or nearly so. Even here, attempts at destabilizing it through policy-making about its agricultural practices would normally have little, if any, chance of success. Indeed, they might have the unintended but often predictable consequence of making things even more oppressive. Bungled attempts at disrupting oppressive regimes are often followed by greater oppression and even terror.

But the situation may be unusual. That is, if the situation is desperate enough and the indirect destabilization attempt is sufficiently likely to work (as may have been the—presumably unintended—case in the Soviet Union during the late 1980s), such disruptive attempts may be worth considering. Are they, however, politically sound and morally permissible? To answer such a question, the judgment of those likely to be affected is more crucial than ever. And the greater the likelihood that those who will be affected will be harmed or seriously deprived by such attempts, the more crucial it is.

Unfortunately, in this type of situation, the evidence for establishing what this judgment would be is scarce or hard to obtain, partly as a result of public fears about reprisals. When this occurs, decisions about such things as who should be deprived, in what regard, and how much may have to be made before settling the disagreements about the subject matter at issue.

MAKING POLICY AND DECISIONS IN RELATIVE IGNORANCE

The fact that decisions may have to be made and policies introduced with relative lack of information does not mean that the decisions are arbitrary or the policies based on no judgment whatsoever. Judgments, however rushed, are often present. But they sometimes concern only the need to make a decision or introduce a policy, given the pressing political, economic, or technological circumstances. In such circumstances, those making policy or decisions can usually rely on little more than a rough-and-ready evaluation of the likely needs, wants, and life plans of those likely to be affected.

One might want to make additional information a requirement for sound and morally permissible policy-making in these circumstances, but this would be a mistake. If more information were necessary for politically sound and morally permissible policy-making in such circumstances, then no policy-making would be sound or permissible, because no such information would be realistically attainable. This is a preposterous and unrealistic argument for paralysis. Hence, some policy-making (this essay will specify what kind) is sound and permissible in these circumstances, and the currently attainable information is as much as can be required for policy and decision assessment purposes.

Despite the fact that judgment by those likely to be affected or their representatives is significantly needed in these cases, political, economic, technological, and other pressures make it even more crucial to engage in social decision procedures that sidestep some uses of these judgments. That is, policymakers must do such things as negotiate, bargain, compromise, vote, or engage in more drastic methods such as political insulation or manipulation. The question, of course, is: What sort of arrangements and social decision procedures are permissible in the circumstances? One of the problems raised by this question concerns the preemptive consequences of policies and decisions.

THE PROBLEM OF PREEMPTION

As indicated, the likely crucial wants, needs, interests, life plans, and accompanying rights claims of those affected are the reasons people may find given policies and decisions intolerable. However, in the cases just described, this information is significantly missing. All one can do is make certain general assumptions about what those affected are likely to need or to have as crucial wants or interests. They will generally want to stay alive and have adequate food and shelter, but beyond this, predictions become a bit shaky. For example, there is no telling what life style will be crucial to their life plans. This problem becomes more pronounced the more future generations are likely to be affected by current policies and decisions.

The net effect of all this is that, at policy-making time, it is not known which specific wants, presumed derivative needs, interests, and rights claims will be crucial to whom, let alone take precedence. Yet policy-making must go on and, as a result, may lead to situations that are partly or totally intolerable to those they eventually affect. Hence, there is good reason not to go overboard and to make room for future corrections. The problem is that, once certain policies and decisions are in place and remain in place for a sufficiently long period of time, not just any correction is possible, and many are quite difficult. Think, for example, of the enormous complications involved in shifting from a war-time to a peace-time economy in the United States and the ex-Soviet Union. What conditions could be used to assess policies and decisions regarding their preemptive effects? One might be the following: *Those policies and decisions are permissible that address the current policy-making situation feasibly and effectively, while being unlikely to preempt future corrections, whose difficulty or impossibility people are likely to deem intolerable.*

This condition should be of help in assessing a variety of policies and decisions. For example, it would rule out policies and decisions that emphasize nuclear energy use beyond what is needed to meet a certain level of expected energy demand (e.g., because conservation measures could be used to meet the rest). The reason for ruling them out is that such an emphasis is likely to undermine a shift to other energy sources (e.g., solar energy) were they to become viable in the future. Of course, as stated, beyond the basic general concerns about such things as life, food, and shelter, predictions about what people will find intolerable in the future are hard to make. Let us go back to one of our previous examples. Who would have thought at the beginning of the twentieth century that people would find the highway carnage caused by automobile use in the United States tolerable? I return to matters of preemption in Essay 11. Here, however, let us consider some objections to the role of ordinary people's judgment and critical scrutiny in policy-making.

THE LACK-OF-GOOD-JUDGMENT OBJECTION

Various problems arise concerning the reliance on people's judgments to assess policies and decisions. One is that even when the evidence is available and there is time to gather it, how does one go about establishing what this judgment is? No doubt, statistical studies would be helpful, and the existence of generally supported precedents for the measures contemplated would help infer what the judgment of those affected might be.[7] Inded, such information would serve as a test when the judgments are available and as an alternative when they are absent or hard to interpret. But should the judgments of everyone affected count as data for such studies?

No doubt, not just anyone's judgment should count. Some of those affected are incompetent, either because they are children or because they are insane. Others, though sane, are carried away by passion or emotion, like fanatics, to the point that their judgment is unreliable. Still others, though cool-minded, are so uninformed or misinformed that their judgment is likely to be ill-grounded if at all relevant. And there are cool-minded, sane, and informed adults whose judgment is unreliable because they are subjected to coercion or manipulation (as when third parties that depend on them—their employees, for example—are kidnaped for ransom).

However, there are also ordinary people who are of sound and cool mind, free from the influence of coercion and manipulation, and well informed. These are the best sources of evidence. In addition, since they are ordinary people, the suggested constraints are realistic. Indeed, they are very much like those used in selecting people for certain social positions, such as that of a jury.

THE INCOMPETENCE OBJECTION

One might argue that these people's judgments do not take the interest of the incompetent into account. This difficulty can be met by relying on trustees or representatives of the incompetent, so long as they are of sound and cool mind, free from the influence of coercion and manipulation, well informed, and *act in accordance with the requirements of their job of trustee or representative.*

This raises the question: What are the requirements attached to the job of trustee or representative? In general, they amount to acting in a manner that accords with the interest or well-being of those entrusted to or represented by them. So, when it comes to conveying their judgment of policy assessment and policy-making purposes, the trustees and representatives should, first, have sought to acquire adequate information. Second, in light of this information and the interest or well-being of those entrusted to or represented by them, they should carefully and reflectively formulate the judgments they convey. As for what is in the interest of those entrusted to or represented by them, the previous discussion covered that topic to some extent, and it is discussed in more detail later.

THE FACTS VS. VALUES OBJECTION

Another objection to the suggested reliance on people's judgments might be that people's judgments, even when constrained as just described, establish nothing. People's value judgments on given policies or decisions or matters relevant to them are not evidence of their actual value.[8]

To say that the judgment of those affected is crucial in soundly assessing policy and decision is not to say that politically sound and morally permissible policies and decisions deductively follow from the policies and decisions people prefer. Nor is it to say that, on the basis of a representative sample of people's preferences on a given type of policy or decision, we can inductively infer a generalization of the type of policies or decisions that are politically sound and morally permissible. None of these things follows. What we can do, however, is use what is often called "hypothetical reasoning" or "argument to the best explanation," and what Peirce called "abduction," in contrast with deduction and induction. In other words, we start with the observed fact that, under conditions that make their judgments reliable, people judge certain policies and decisions politically sound and morally permissible. If no better explanation is available, we conclude on this basis that people's judgments are explained by the fact that the policies and decisions are indeed politically sound and morally permissible.[9] The same type of argument can be soundly used in support of moral rights, obligations, laws, and principles, one function of which is to explain people's judgments. Of course, such reliance on people's judgments raises the question we already addressed: Whose judgment is supposed to count? Let us see how the constraints of our approach apply in discussing various procedural principles or criteria that constitute alternatives to this book's approach.

THE LIMITS OF PURE DEMOCRACY
AND PURELY PROCEDURAL PRINCIPLES

Schumpeter's argument about democracy is well known. Envision a democratic community that reaches the decision to persecute religious dissent. Or imagine a country that, in a democratic way, introduces policies that institute the persecution of Christians, the burning of witches, and the slaughtering of Jews. These are plausible situations. After all, the democratic republic of Geneva burned heretics during Calvin's time, and democratic Massachusetts persecuted them in a morally repulsive manner during colonial times. We should certainly not approve of these policies on the grounds that they have been introduced according to the rules of democratic procedure. Schumpeter concludes that though democracy has instrumental value, it cannot be an end in itself independent of the results it will produce under given historical conditions.[10]

In his *Tyranny and Legitimacy*, James S. Fishkin generalizes this argument to all purely procedural principles, that is, principles that specify decision rules but do not specify anything about the content of the decisions, other than that the rule never be changed. The generalization is meant to apply only in ideal society situations, that is, whenever scarcity is moderate and the current situation is not primarily the result of past violations of the principle.

Fishkin distinguishes procedural principles requiring unanimity from those that do not require it. In an ideal society, he argues, the latter could lead to impermissible policies or decisions. Such a thing would happen whenever they imposed severe deprivations on those whose agreement, consent, or conformity is not required by the procedure, when other policies and decisions would impose no severe deprivations on anyone. As for procedural principles requiring unanimity, they could lead to impermissible policies and decisions by omission, that is, by the continuation of existing policies. He says:

> Imagine only that some group requires food to avoid starvation (perhaps there has been famine) or some group requires emergency assistance or medical care (perhaps there has been a flood or some other natural disaster) and that such events pose a new policy problem. If there is not an already existing policy, the veto of any new policy could have consequences as dreadful (for all those apart from the blocking coalition) as any acts of commission. Or suppose the issue is not a new one but merely an old one about which agreement has never been reached. Perhaps there is mass poverty and a small wealthy elite who are just sufficiently numerous to block any redistribution. The continuing absence of any redistribution measures (unemployment compensation, medical care, food assistance) could deny the satisfaction of basic human needs of the bulk of the population.[11]

As stated, Fishkin's position is meant to apply to ideal society conditions. In contrast, the present book's approach is meant to help make permissible policies and decisions in the actual, often far from ideal world. Does that entail that purely procedural procedures can do a better job in the actual world? Not at all. First, as argued in previous essays, unanimity may not be workable in the actual world, and the tyranny of the majority is a common occurrence. Consider, for example, a situation of serious scarcity in a democratic country in which famine affects groups excluded from the coalition in power but does not affect the coalition in power. In such a situation, the coalition in power could make policy or decisions that channel available resources to further improve its own well-being. This would involve a serious and avoidable deprivation to those excluded from the coalition in power. Accordingly, they and other ordinary people who are of sound and cool mind, free from the influence of coercion or manipulation, and not carried away by passion or emotion would think it intolerable. Hence, it is morally questionable if not impermissible. But nothing in the process itself could prevent it.

Second, suppose that unanimity were attainable and the process required it. Suppose, further, that famine or the consequences of a natural disaster affect the population of an out-of-the-way region whose representatives are a minority in government. Or suppose that inveterate poverty is widespread in the land, but a small elite is free from it. The veto of any policies or decisions aimed at providing assistance in these cases is a possible omission in such a process.

One might argue that providing such assistance would not be justified until it is established who, among the needy, should get it. But under time pressures and other constraints, this position in effect amounts to saying that it is better to let all die from famine or lack of medical attention than to help anyone who might turn out not to have needed help as much as others. Such passive siding with the status quo would hardly be morally justified. And those likely to be affected, as well as other ordinary people who are of sound and cool mind, free from the influence of coercion or manipulation, and not carried away by passion or emotion, would think it intolerable.

Situations such as those discussed provide reasons for specifying constraints on purely procedural policy-making approaches. However, as already argued, for the approach to be applicable to actual policy-making, these constraints should be such that they make room for the participation of ordinary people in relatively common ways. For example, the excesses of political and legal procedure are a good reason to set constraints. However, they are not a good reason to sever the political and legal process from the moral assessment of policies and decisions. As argued in previous essays, doing such a thing would be both politically and morally irrelevant and a sure recipe for disaster. The constraints this book's approach introduces are simply those ordinarily used to select people for certain social positions, such as that of a jury. They are supposed to work so long as there are enough ordinary people with a modicum of intelligence and moral sensitivity.

APPLYING MORAL PRINCIPLES, LAWS, AND OTHER
CONCEPTS IN THE POLICY-MAKING PROCESS

A SHORT REVIEW OF SOME DIFFICULTIES

To say that critical scrutiny and judgment by ordinary people should be part and parcel of policy-making is not to say that abstract principles of morality (e.g., Kant's categorical imperative) have no role in the process.[12] Nor is it to say that such other moral concepts as rights and individual and collective consequences are irrelevant. They are not. But, as we saw, various problems arise: How should the principles be applied? Should given problems be addressed at the level of moral rules, moral laws, or overall moral principles? We also saw some of the difficulties involved in applying general criteria that specify rights or obligations to particular situations, and how such applications required the employment of various procedures.[13] As already argued, the approach I have been outlining, which includes a wide variety of social decision procedures, is meant to be helpful in dealing realistically with these and related application problems. However, there are other procedural approaches being proposed that should be evaluated.

CONTRACTUAL, EMPATHETIC,
AND ARGUMENTATIVE TESTING CRITERIA

The application problems just mentioned are sometimes addressed by means of mixed procedural accounts that rely on procedures but specify conditions under which people's judgment and critical scrutiny provide answers to the questions just asked. Three types of procedural accounts are predominant. Perhaps the most commonly used is *contractual*. In one of its versions, moral reasoning aims at working out principles that others who are looking for principles would not reject.[14] A second account is *empathetic*. In one of its versions, people identify moral norms by putting themselves in the position of all those who would be affected if the norms were followed.[15] A third is the *argumentative testing* account, in which only the force of the better argument prevails.

Each of these accounts has shortcomings. As Jürgen Habermas has argued, the contractual account assimilates judgments to rational choice decisions. In addition, contractual and empathetic accounts have other, more serious, problems involving the use of the notion of rational choice for policy-making purposes. However, these can be corrected, and the approach in this book suggests how.

As for the empathetic account, Habermas has soundly argued that it assimilates judgments to empathetic acts of understanding. As in the case of contractual accounts, such assimilation is exaggerated. If the approach I am proposing turns out to be better, such exaggeration is avoidable. In addition, the empathetic understanding account has other shortcomings.

To characterize these shortcomings, let us begin by pointing out four facts. First, many ordinary people can understand claims, regardless of how eccentric or questionable the ends sought in claiming them. For example, one can understand that someone claims a right to wear a medieval helmet while mowing the lawn, however eccentric this might be. Similarly, one can understand that someone claims the right to engage in sadomasochistic practices with consenting adults, however far out on the social fringe such an activity might be. Second, ordinary persons can understand what such eccentric or fringe claims mean. Third, ordinary persons can engage in critical scrutiny of policies affecting these claims and even make the judgment that the policies to be introduced should grant the rights they claim. Fourth, if such a person has a cool and sound mind, is free from the effects of coercion and manipulation, and is not carried away by passion and emotion, then his or her judgment (or that of his or her representatives), should not be discounted in the policy-making process.

Yet there is no sense in which a number of such ordinary persons can *empathize* with eccentric ends such as wearing a medieval helmet while mowing the lawn, or socially fringe ends such as sadomasochistic activities. They cannot in any way put themselves in the helmet user's or sadomasochist's shoes. Both experiences are completely and irretrievably alien to them.

One might argue that, in such a case, their judgment should not be used in policy-making. But this undermines critical scrutiny, appeals to reason, and meaningful dialogue by making room only for dialogue among given interest-group members. The only policy-making approach available under such conditions would be the expediency approach criticized in previous essays, which would be politically unwise and would undermine morality.

As for the argumentative testing approach, it is closer to that in this book, but too simplistic. Consider Habermas's account: A policy or decision would pass the test of argumentative testing if it were so judged by people, assuming that "all those possibly affected could participate, freely and equally, in a cooperative search for truth in which only the force of the better argument appears."[16] Although this approach does not have the problems the others face, it has another: It is quite unlikely that *actual* people's judgments will be somehow connected with the highly detached judgments the approach involves.

Given the shortcomings of the accounts just discussed, in what follows I formulate hypotheses that involve a combined approach. That is, they significantly appeal to argumentative testing but also make room for contractual decisions based on mere preferences or, sometimes, on sympathetic understanding, in a manner that attempts to correct the exaggerations in the more simplistic accounts discussed. In particular, first, it involves procedures that include discussion of merits but go well beyond its limits, into procedures involving a greater predominance of decisions. Second, it relies on the judgment of people who are relatively well-informed (but not perfectly informed) about the matters at issue. Third, their judgments count—much as they are supposed to in ordinary societies—if these people are competent, not carried away by passion or emotion, and free from the influences of coercion and manipulation.

The position I am taking, of course, does not in any way entail that politically sound and morally permissible policies and decisions must result from a process in which only people meeting the said conditions take part. The process can include anyone, even the crazy and the evil. However, as discussed in this and previous essays, the condition under which the resulting policies and decisions will be politically sound and morally permissible is that, at policy-making time, those likely to be affected by the policies or decisions (or their representatives) who meet the said constraints on judgment are likely to find the policies and decisions tolerable. Let us proceed to formulate the corresponding hypotheses and place them in context.

PRIMARILY ADMINISTRATIVE SITUATIONS

As previously indicated, some policy and decision problems are administrative. They arise in nondisruptive, predominantly rational situations. Let us initially concentrate on societies in which no radical change is needed, because they make significant room for individual freedoms and well-being and for reforms when improvements are needed. The preceding discussion suggests the following hypothesis for policy and decision assessment in this type of situation:

HYPOTHESIS I: THE ADMINISTRATIVE SITUATION HYPOTHESIS

If, first, a policy-making problem or set of problems arises in a largely nonconflictive, nondisruptive, nonoppressive situation (that is, the situation involves no controversy or confrontation, no likely social disruption, and no serious limitations on individual's freedoms and well-being);

second, the differences of opinion or opposing demands, if any, involved in the situation are predominantly addressed through reliance on reason and meaningful dialogue, not through consensus or consensus building based on such things as indifference and blind faith;

third, a policy, decision, or combination of these is likely to be both feasible and effective in dealing with these problem(s) (that is, there are clear precedents or reliable studies that evidence it—for example, they evidence that, in the available time and with the available resources, a combination of raising taxes and cutting spending will effectively deal with the problem of reducing the national deficit); but

fourth, the policy, decision, or their combination is also likely to lead to societal disruption or to limit the freedoms or well-being of those likely to be affected (in the society or abroad), **roughly as much as, or more than,** *alternative policies, decisions, or combinations of these (including that of not making any policy or decision about the problem(s) at least for the time being);*

and fifth, at least some of the people affected, or their trustees or representatives, when of sound and cool mind, free from the influence of coercion and manipulation, and as informed as circumstances permit, are likely to find the disruption or limitations intolerable (because, for example, there are clear precedents or other evidence strongly indicating that they will do so—for example, in the past, some of these people may have strongly objected when they experienced the hardships that both raising taxes and cutting spending brought about for them),

then *it is not permissible simply to make the decision or contribute to introducing or retaining the policy or combination of policies. But in order to settle on alternatives within the available time, some combination of only nonconfrontational social decision procedures such as discussion of merits, negotiation, rational consensus building, bargaining, mediation, and arbitration, accompanied by coping and waiting, may be used.*

On the other hand, *if the first three conditions are satisfied, but the fourth and fifth conditions are not (that is, the policy, decision, or combination of these is likely to lead to less social disruption or to less limitations of freedom or well-being than the alternatives—(for example, because waiting would precipitate a societal crisis, and the said people are likely to find the resulting situation tolerable, once they experience it),*

then *it is permissible to make the decision and contribute to introducing or retaining the policy or combination of these, despite the misgivings, reservations, or protests that may occur at policy-making time.*

THE NEOCLASSICAL OBJECTION

One objection that might be raised against this hypothesis is that ordinary people of sound mind, free from the influence of coercion and manipulation, and well-informed would object to *any* limitations on their freedoms and well-being. But would they? Let us recall that the situation envisioned here is largely nonconflictive. Any limitations are perceived as comparatively minor. Otherwise, there would be conflict, if not disruption. Hence, the said objections could come only from people concerned with comparatively minute advantages or disadvantages to themselves and lacking sympathy for others. Given this, let us examine the force of the objection.

First, some of the objection's psychological and political assumptions are mistaken. People such as those it describes are few. Indeed, despite claims to the contrary made under the umbrella of the neoclassical model in economics and other social sciences, there is overwhelming evidence that ordinary people are not cold calculators each out to maximize his or her own well-being.[17]

Second, morally speaking, the people envisioned by the objection are not just self-interested—that is, interested in themselves, as presumably everyone is—but selfish. This view of people undermines morality because (1) it is unrealistic, and (2) it undermines a crucial element of morality: the reliance on meaningful dialogue and appeals to reason in addressing problems. Hence, there is good reason for excluding such a position through the above hypothesis.

THE UNJUSTIFIED CONTENTMENT OBJECTION

Another objection grants that some individuals might be content with a policy or decision and not object to the limitations it puts on their freedom or well-being. But it maintains that they *ought* to find them intolerable. However, suppose that some individuals meet the hypothesis's conditions. Since they are ordinary people, they will, in the aggregate, possess a modicum of care, imagination, moral sensitivity, and political savvy. And all this would be exercised in the critical scrutiny process, leading them to find a certain policy arrangement tolerable or not. If they find it tolerable in the type of situation considered, *no better evidence could realistically be expected to establish that it is permissible for them to do so.* Their finding it tolerable establishes that, in the situation described and based on the best available information, it *is* tolerable. And that it is tolerable is the best available explanation for their finding it tolerable in the circumstances.

Those who argue otherwise may point to rights or to abstract principles of obligation in support of their claims. But, as I also argued, there exists no better way of establishing what rights, obligations, and even moral rules, laws, and principles are relevant in given circumstances and how much weight they have (for example, whether, in the circumstances, given collective consequences take precedence over given individual rights or vice versa) than connecting them to people's judgments. The hypothesis formulated above articulates precisely such a connection.

THE IDEAL WORLDS OBJECTION

One might object by appealing to situations in which the policy-making circumstances would be different, the individuals more reflective, better informed, or endowed with greater sensitivity. However, this is to step into the never-never land of excessive idealization and utopia and to abandon the constrained and not always ideal, but reliable and improvable, actual world of policy-making. I have already argued that, from both a political and a moral standpoint, one should remain in the latter world because, among other reasons, corrections are always possible in it. That is, further critical scrutiny and experience may uncover or work out reasons why what was found tolerable at one time ought not to be found tolerable anymore. As for what happens in the meantime, the above hypothesis sets clear constraints, for example, by ruling out certain policies and decisions and, if no better ones are available, permitting the use of a range of social decision procedures to settle the existing differences instead.[18]

THE PERFECTIONIST OBJECTION

The objection might also be raised that one can never be certain whether individuals who do not object are indeed completely informed and free from the influence of coercion and manipulation. No doubt, there is an element of judgment that comes into play here. But this judgment is open to critical scrutiny by those involved. And a variety of political actions conducive to such scrutiny—from congressional inquiries to public debates—are possible so long as there is time left before policies are to be formally introduced. Hence, if there is time, policy-making decisions should not be rushed to the point of precluding viable objections. (In fact, in predominantly rational, nondisruptive situations such as the hypothesis envisions, there is often enough time for the purpose at hand.) However, delays should not reach the point of no return, where neglect takes over and the only policy is no policy, or no effective policy.

In asking for certainty, the objection leads precisely to policy-making failures of neglect. It is but another example of the policy-making paradox of perfectionism: In trying to optimize outcomes by attempting to perfect policies, the outcomes thus brought about are worse than they would have been, had one not attempted to perfect the policies.

THE IDEALISM OBJECTION

It might be objected that the hypothesis proposed is itself overly idealistic, since people are never sufficiently cool or sound of mind, free from the influence of coercion or manipulation, and well-informed. This objection, however, exaggerates people's weaknesses. In fact, many individuals have a sound mind—that is, they are not insane or mentally incompetent—and also have a cool mind quite frequently. That is, they are not normally carried away by passion or emotion; they are not carried away by fear, greed, the will to power, the libido, or fanaticism about a cause, nation, social class, abstract principle, or, as in the case of egoists, themselves.

In addition, these very same people are often free, if not from coercion and manipulation (these are recurrent facts of social life), at least from their influence. For example, some judges ruling on cases involving organized crime in the United States, Italy, or Colombia, have enough courage, presence of mind, and ability to remain above the coercive threats or manipulation exercised by organized crime members or their associates.

As for being well-informed, some individuals (e.g., technology, health care, economic, or legal experts) are well-informed and, with the help of their services, others can become well-informed on matters relevant to policy and decision. This is what members of the U.S. Congress do through such sources as the Office of Technology Assessment and the testimony gathered at committee hearings.

To say that people can be well-informed about a matter of concern to policy and decision is not to say that they can know all there is to know about it. Rather, it is to say that they can learn what can be learned about it at the time and, most importantly, that they can learn about the limits of current knowledge. Hard cases arise when, because of time constraints, not even this much can be learned before policy-making time. But even in this situation, people can be well-informed about the fact that they support or oppose certain policies or decisions, given the existing limited information or uncertainty. In such circumstances, as previously argued and as the previously formulated hypothesis implies, it is wise to opt for cautious policy-making. That is, one should make room for future corrections whenever it is feasible and those who are likely to be affected would find the impossibility or extraordinary difficulty of making such corrections intolerable.

MACROSOCIETAL POLICY AND DECISION PROBLEMS IN SOCIALLY DISRUPTIVE SITUATIONS

Consider policy and decision problems about such technology developments as genetic engineering, nuclear energy, fetal research, the development of RU-486 (the "abortion pill"), the green revolution, and industrial processes leading to the release of chlorofluorocarbons into the atmosphere. They are significantly posed by conflicts of opinion (when not merely of demands) about a variety of these developments and the perceived risks and practices associated with them.

These conflicts are often socially disruptive. In an innocuous sense, it is obvious that the protests involved inconvenience a lot of people. In a non-innocuous sense, it is not always obvious that the conflicts can have a tendency to destabilize one or more large societal sectors, or even entire societies, economically or politically. Examples of these sectors are the biotechnology industry in conflicts about genetic engineering; the utilities

and related industries in conflicts about nuclear energy; scientific research—with an impact on health care, its related industrial and educational
activities, and the thousands who will contract Alzheimer's and other
diseases—in conflicts about fetal research; about half the Earth's adult
population—women—in conflicts about the development and marketing of
RU-486 and cognate drugs; and much if not all of the Earth's population in
conflicts about the green revolution and the release of chlorofluorocarbons
as a by-product of various industrial processes.

One thing is clear: These conflicts pose societal problems in and of
themselves, calling for policy-making that is quite different from that called
for by administrative problems like those previously discussed. At any rate,
as already argued mainly in Essays 1 and 6, the second-order question arises:
What ought to be done about the conflicts?

CONTROVERSY OR CONFRONTATION?

The specific type of policy-making called for by problems involving
societal conflict differs depending on the type of conflicts involved. Accordingly, hypotheses meant to help assess policy and decisions about such
problems should reflect this fact. Consider discussions about matters of
health care costs. In the United States, they affect at least patients, doctors,
corporations, the government, and the insurance industry, and are quite
heated. They frequently involve sharp oppositions of opinions or demands
on the part of members of the various groups affected, coupled with
disputes, debates, or contentions aimed at establishing the validity of the
opinions or demands. However, they do not primarily involve attempts at
mere persuasion through such things as sheer manipulation, sabotage, or the
threat or use of force. Thus they amount to controversies that involve a
strong element of dialogue, however heated.

Certainly, controversy can and often does turn into outright confrontation. Things can go awry, with conflicting demands, the use of force,
sabotage, threats, or manipulation being the main or only elements involved.
Meaningful dialogue loses its predominance, overpowered by a conflict of
wills. Controversies about research on nonhuman animals and research on
human fetuses, for example, have moved in the direction of confrontations,
with bombings and threats becoming quite frequent.

When social conflicts such as those just discussed are significantly disruptive, policy-making is in order, and the policy question arises: Is the conflict
a controversy or a confrontation? And since the degree of societal disruption
matters, questions such as the following also arise: Does the conflict pose a
clear and immediate threat to the existence or well-being of the societal
sectors or societies affected, or does it endanger them to a lesser degree? If
the latter, to what degree does it endanger them?

Danger to society or societal sectors is not necessarily overriding. Some societies, and some societal sectors, are so sick to the root that little can be said in their defense. In other cases, they may be in need of change, but their demise would be unwarranted if not disastrous. In still other cases, they may be worthier of being preserved than any other aspect of the subject matter of the conflict. Hence, a higher-order policy question, one that deals with priorities, arises: How significant is the societal disruption associated with the conflict when weighed against the matters at issue in the conflict? The poignancy of this question, however, will vary depending on what social decision procedures are feasible at a given time.

CONFRONTATIONS, CONTROVERSIES, CONSENSUS, AND TYPES OF SOCIAL DECISION PROCEDURES

The questions just formulated are not the only, or first, policy questions to ask. One must also ask: What policies and policy-making procedures are both viable and morally permissible, given the existing time and budgetary constraints, degree of uncertainty about the procedures' consequences, and probability of public support for the policies and procedures or acquiescence to them? How much time, money, and energy are there? How much should be devoted to answering these questions? If the conflict is a confrontation, through what social decision procedure or combination of procedures is it permissible to address it? Which ones are appropriate if it is a controversy?

In dealing with confrontations and their characteristic breakdown of dialogue, a variety of procedures suggest themselves: outflanking, strikes and demonstrations, threats, war. None of these procedures relies on meaningful dialogue and appeals to reason, though they may be applied by using reasons. Yet they may be politically sound. And they may be morally permissible if the conflict is a confrontation and they are accompanied by requests or demands to reestablish the dialogue. Indeed, the less reliant on meaningful dialogue the situation posing the problem, the more these procedures are permissible—at least so long as they are accompanied by efforts to bring reliance on meaningful dialogue back into the picture. For example, Iraq's invasion and annexation of Kuwait in August 1990 was met with nearly unanimously supported U.N. sanctions while negotiations were still being sought.[19] Whatever the weaknesses of the particular sanctions, as I discuss in Essay 12, there was little or no disagreement throughout the world community that they were politically and morally unobjectionable, so long as they were applied in the search for peace, not for strategic advantages or political or economic gain.[20]

If the conflict is a controversy, however, none of these procedures appears permissible, if at all relevant. Instead, such things as political insulation, arbitration, voting, negotiation, mediation, consensus building, and discussion of merits—which make room for meaningful dialogue—take center stage. And these procedures are also different from those called for by societally disruptive situations in which nonrational or mistaken consensus is predominant. In that case, such things as demonstrations, sit-ins, boycotts, and other consciousness-raising procedures appear most suitable.

At any rate, though the specific policies and decisions that are acceptable vary according to type of case, the same features serve to assess them. Among them, it is most crucial to determine the type of problem being addressed, what the social circumstances are, and what those involved would think if they were of sound and cool mind, free from the influence of coercion and manipulation, and well-informed. This leads to a series of additional hypotheses for assessing the policies and decisions in different types of social situations.

HYPOTHESIS II: THE RATIONAL DISRUPTION, NO RADICAL CHANGE HYPOTHESIS

If, first, a policy-making problem or set of problems arises in a situation that is socially disruptive or involves significantly contested limitations on individual freedoms or well-being;

second, the differences of opinion or conflicts of demands involved in the situation are predominantly addressed through reliance on reason and meaningful dialogue, however heated, not through confrontation or, alternatively, through consensus or consensus building based on such things as unreflective indifference or blind faith;

third, a policy, decision, or combination of these is likely to be both feasible and effective in dealing with the problem(s) (that is, there are clear precedents or studies that evidence it—for example, they evidence that, within the time available, a combination of raising taxes and cutting spending will effectively deal with the problem of reducing the national deficit); but

*fourth, it is also likely to lead to societal disruption, or to limit the freedoms or well-being of those likely to be affected (in the society or abroad) roughly **as much as, or more than**, alternative policies, decisions, or combinations of these (including that of not making any policy or decision about the problem(s), at least for the time being);*

and fifth, at least some of the people affected, or their trustees or representatives, when of sound and cool mind, free from the influence of coercion and manipulation, and as informed as circumstances permit, are likely to find it intolerable (because, for example, there are clear precedents or other evidence strongly indicating that they will do so—for instance, in the past, some of these people may have strongly objected when they experienced the hardships that both raising taxes

and cutting spending for social programs brought about for them),
then *it is not permissible simply to make the decision or contribute to introducing or retaining the policy or combination of policies. But in order to settle on alternatives within the available time, some combination of social decision procedures may be used in the following order of priority:*

First, such **nonconfrontational** *social decision procedures as discussion of merits, negotiation, rational consensus building, bargaining, mediation, arbitration, and simply coping while waiting may be used if they are feasible and likely to be effective.*

Second, if the latter are not feasible or likely to be effective, then nonconfrontational procedures involving **pressure tactics** *such as publicity campaigns, letter writing, demonstrations, and appeals to higher authorities may be used.*

If none of the previous procedures is feasible or likely to be effective, then the situation is probably of a different type, perhaps a confrontation, or one that primarily involves irrational consensus, and it will fall under one of the remaining hypotheses.

On the other hand, *if the first three conditions are satisfied, but the fourth and fifth conditions are not (that is, the policy, decision, or combination of these is likely to lead to less social disruption or to less limitations of freedom or well-being than the alternatives—for example, because waiting would precipitate a societal crisis, and the said people are likely to find the new situation tolerable once they experience it),* **then** *it is permissible to make the decision and contribute to introducing or retaining the policy or combination of these, despite the heated arguments and opposition that may occur at policy-making time.*

HYPOTHESIS III: THE NONRATIONAL DISRUPTION,
NO RADICAL CHANGE HYPOTHESIS

If, first, a policy-making problem or set of problems arises in a situation that is socially disruptive or involves significantly contested limitations on individual freedoms or well-being;

second, the differences of opinion or conflicts of demands involved in the situation are not predominantly addressed through reliance on reason and meaningful dialogue, but instead are predominantly addressed through confrontation or, alternatively, through consensus or consensus building based on such things as unreflective indifference or blind faith;

third, a policy, decision, or combination of these is likely to be both feasible and effective in dealing with the problem(s) (that is, there are clear precedents or reliable studies that evidence it—for example, they evidence that, within the time available, a combination of raising taxes and cutting spending will effectively deal with the problem of reducing the national deficit); but

fourth, the policy, decision, or their combination is also likely to lead to societal disruption, or to limit the freedoms or well-being of those likely to be affected (in the society or abroad) roughly **as much as,** *or* **more than,** *alternative policies, decisions, or combinations of these (including that of not making any policy or decision about the problem(s), at least for the time being);*

and fifth, at least some of the people affected, or their trustees or representatives, when of sound and cool mind, free from the influence of coercion and manipulation, and as informed as circumstances permit, are likely to find it intolerable (because there are clear precedents or other evidence strongly indicating that they will do so—for example, in the past, some of these people strongly objected when they experienced the hardships that both raising taxes and cutting spending for social programs brought about for them),

then *it is not permissible simply to make the decision or contribute to introducing or retaining the policy or combination of policies. But in order to settle on alternatives within the available time, some combination of social decision procedures may be used in the following order of priority:*

First, such **nonconfrontational** *social decision procedures as discussion of merits, negotiation, rational consensus building, bargaining, mediation, arbitration, and simply coping while waiting may be used if they are at all feasible and likely to be effective (as they may be in situations where irrational consensus predominates).*

Second, if the latter are not feasible or likely to be effective, then such nonconfrontational procedures involving **pressure tactics** *such as publicity campaigns, letter writing, demonstrations, and appeals to higher authorities may be used.*

Third, if none of the previous procedures is feasible or likely to be effective, then **confrontational but** *still* **nonviolent** *methods such as civil disobedience, outflanking or bypassing, political insulation, and various forms of manipulation may be used.*

If none of the previous procedures is feasible or likely to be effective, then the situation is probably of a different type, perhaps one requiring radical change, and falls under Hypothesis IV.

On the other hand, *if the first three conditions are satisfied, but the fourth and fifth conditions are not satisfied (that is, the policy, decision, or combination of these is likely to lead to less social disruption or less limitations of freedom or well-being than the alternatives—for example, because waiting would precipitate a societal crisis—and the said people are not likely to find the new situation intolerable once they experience it),*

then *it is permissible to make the decision and contribute to introducing or retaining the policy or combination of these, despite the heated arguments, opposition, and confrontational activities that may occur at policy-making time (for, given the previous conditions, these could not amount to social disruption or limitations of freedom and well-being that are equal to or greater than those of the alternatives).*

THE DISSATISFACTION OBJECTION

The previously discussed objections could be raised here too. However, they would be mistaken for the reasons already given. A new objection, however, might also be raised. It says that the hypotheses just formulated would permit policies, procedures, and policy decisions that some, perhaps all, ordinary persons would find unsatisfactory. But one should realize that, in politics as in life generally, one cannot always, if ever, entirely satisfy everybody. Indeed, sometimes, one cannot entirely satisfy anybody. This is only a matter of common sense and realism. Accordingly, the hypotheses formulated above aim at ruling out those policies, procedures, and decisions that would be *intolerable* to anyone, but not those that, though tolerable, might fail to entirely satisfy one or more persons.

MACROSOCIETALLY DISRUPTIVE SOCIAL SITUATIONS THAT WARRANT DESTABILIZATION

The macrosocietally disruptive social situation warranting destabilization is a rather difficult and often too simplistically understood type of policy-making situation. It may have conflictive origins (e.g., a revolution or war) or predominantly consensual ones (e.g., generalized acquiescence to spending policies that bankrupt a country). In any case, it involves the serious disruption of one or more societies or large societal sectors, or serious limitations on the freedoms and well-being of their members. Now there is little doubt that certain societal sectors or societies are so objectionable, cause people such utter misery, disregard their dignity as persons to such an extent, and engage in such rampant and arbitrary oppression that their demise would be highly welcome, perhaps even needed for the flourishing of humanity among those societies or sectors. Indeed, such sectors or societies often face resistance, prompt liberation movements and wars, and are caught up in more or less societally disruptive conflicts with sectors of their own societies or with other societies. But such reactions may not occur and, for whatever reason, people may be largely acquiescent to the situation. The policy question then arises: What ought to be done about situations that involve such disruption or limitations on individual freedoms and well-being? This leads to the next hypothesis.

HYPOTHESIS IV: THE RADICAL CHANGE HYPOTHESIS

If, first, a policy-making problem or set of problems arises in a largely disruptive or oppressive situation (e.g., the problem of how to free an invaded country, how to introduce basic freedoms or a minimum of well-being for a country's oppressed citizens, or how to prevent a country's economy from collapsing);

second, the differences of opinion or conflicts of demands involved in the situation are not predominantly addressed through reliance on reason and meaningful dialogue, but instead are predominantly addressed through confrontation (e.g., armed resistance in the invasion case and armed insurrection in the oppression case) or, alternatively, through irrational consensus (e.g., acquiescence based on unreflective indifference or blind faith in the oppression or the collapsing economy case);

third, a policy, decision, or combination of these is likely to be both feasible and effective in dealing with the problem(s) through radical changes in one or more of the societies involved (e.g., within the time available, a foreign country's policy of supplying weapons or even troops to the resistance is likely to defeat the aggressors and subject them to international controls; or a foreign country's policy of supplying weapons or even military advisers to the armed insurrection forces is likely to help overthrow the oppressors and institute a new, nonoppressive power structure; or policies aimed at immediately discontinuing the economic practices leading to the country's likely economic collapse are likely to prevent this collapse while radically redistributing and perhaps increasing the population's burdens); but

fourth, the policy decision, or combination of these is also likely to lead to societal disruption or limit the freedoms or well-being of those affected in at least one of the societies involved or abroad, and at least in the short run, the disruption and limitations are as great or (quite likely much) greater than those of alternative, nonradical policies, decisions,

*or combinations of these (e.g., use of foreign embargoes in the aggres-
sion and the oppression cases, and incrementally discontinuing the said
spending policies in the economic collapse case);*

*fifth, at least some members of the society(ies) likely to be affected by
the contemplated radical changes, or their trustees or representatives
(who, in cases of war and armed insurrection, may be third parties such
as the U.N. Secretary General or its appointees), when of cool and
sound mind, free from the influence of coercion and manipulation, and
well-informed, are likely to find the policy, decision, or combination of
these intolerable, even if they also believe that radical change is needed,
then it is not permissible to make the decision or contribute to introducing the policy or combination of policies. But in order to settle on
alternatives within the time available, some combination of social
decision procedures may be used in the following order of priority:*

*First, if they are at all feasible and likely to be effective (as they may
be whenever irrational consensus predominates), such nonconfrontational social decision procedures as discussion of merits, negotiation,
consensus building, bargaining, mediation, arbitration, and simply
coping while waiting may be used.*

*Second, if the latter are not feasible or likely to be effective (e.g.,
because time is of the essence), then nonconfrontational procedures
involving pressure tactics such as publicity campaigns, letterwriting,
demonstrations, and appeals to higher authorities (including the international community) may be used.*

*Third, if none of the previous methods is feasible or likely to be
effective (e.g., because time is of the essence), then confrontational but
still nonviolent procedures such as, depending on the case, civil disobedience, outflanking or bypassing, political insulation, and various forms
of manipulation (perhaps involving traditional allies of the country
reluctant to comply or meaningfully negotiate) may be used.*

*Fourth, if none of the previous procedures is feasible or likely to be
effective (e.g., because time is of the essence), then more confrontational
procedures such as economic embargoes, freezing of a country's foreign
investments, undermining or preventing the delivery of goods and
services other than those needed to meet basic survival and health needs
to crucial social sectors or entire societies, blockades, threats of force,
and, in crisis situations, even combat may be used, so long as they are
accompanied by reasonable mediatory or other nonconfrontational
efforts aimed at stopping and diminishing the degree of confrontation
and increasing the use of procedures that primarily involve appeals to*

reason and meaningful dialogue. If none of the previous procedures is feasible or likely to be effective, then coping and waiting may still be used (as the United States did concerning Cuba after the Bay of Pigs and economic embargo failures).

On the other hand, *if the first three conditions are satisfied, but the fourth and fifth conditions are not (that is, the policy, decision or combination of these is likely to lead to less social disruption or to less limitations of freedom or well-being than the alternatives or, even if it does not, the said people are likely to find the new situation tolerable, once they experience it),*

then *it is permissible to make the decision and contribute to introducing or retaining the policy or combination of these and to employ more drastic social decision procedures, including such confrontational ones as economic embargoes and combat, but never beyond what is likely to be required in implementing the policies, decisions, or their combination, and always so as to bring about a situation in which people primarily use procedures that appeal to reason and meaningful dialogue.*

PLACING HYPOTHESIS IV IN THE APPROPRIATE PERSPECTIVE

The latter hypothesis rules out, first, all attempts at revolution or radical change that are likely to be unfeasible or ineffective. Of course, for policy-making purposes, this likelihood must be assessed in advance, not after the fact. Afterwards, no matter how instructive it might be, it would be of no use in guiding policy-making that already occurred. Given this, the 1989 Chinese students' uprising, though in retrospect a failure, would not be ruled out. At the time, it appeared likely to undermine the oppressive Deng Xiaoping and Li Peng regime and promote democracy in China.

Second, the hypothesis rules out attempts that involve or lead to situations that the victims of the objectionable sector or society would find intolerable. For example, it rules out foreign groups' protesting a country's governmental terror when this is only likely to increase and hasten executions.[21]

Third, the hypothesis rules out attempts that would require sacrifices on the part of ordinary people in societies or sectors other than the one with the objectionable features if, when meeting the conditions of the hypothesis, they would find it intolerable. Examples of this would be the policy of hijacking or bombing airplanes carrying passengers who have nothing to do with the conflict other than happening to be on an airplane that belongs to an airline from an involved country. In fact, some of these passengers may sympathize with the cause of the culprit. However, what is crucial is that many, of not all, of them would not be willing to lose their lives, liberty, or well-being for it.

Fourth, in an analogous manner, the hypothesis rules out the policy of instituting or retaining slavery, genocide, governmental terror, or economic exploitation. It also rules out attempts at taking advantage of grand opportunities at costs that, under the said conditions, those affected would find intolerable. Most importantly, it rules out bringing about radical change in one society at the cost of destabilizing another, so long as individuals likely to be affected in the latter, or their trustees or representatives, when of sound and cool mind, free from the influence of coercion and manipulation, and well-informed would find it intolerable.

This applies to reasonably good as well as to significantly objectionable societies (including those that engage in aggression or involve oppression), however distasteful our idealism may find them. First, suppose they have been defeated. Victory does not grant just any rights, but only redress rights, and these do not involve radically changing the vanquished societies. Second, as previously argued, it is both morally and politically crucial and, indeed, democratic, to rely on the judgment of those likely to be affected (including the vanquished) or, if these are unreliable, on that of their trustees or representatives. This is what the hypothesis does. Not surprisingly, in doing so, it rules out sacrificing individuals for the sake of a cause, however appealing and ideally just the latter might be.

AN OVERALL PRINCIPLE

The preceding hypotheses and main types of policy-making situations are covered by a principle that, as previously mentioned, serves to compare these types, thus making it clear that they are morally relevant. It can be formulated as follows:

HYPOTHESIS V: THE PRINCIPLE OF PRACTICAL EQUITY

If, first, a policy-making problem or set of problems arises in one or more societies;

second, a policy, decision, or combination of these is likely to be both feasible and effective in dealing with the problem(s);

third, it is also likely to lead to undesirable consequences for the society or, if more than one society is involved, for at least one of them, or to limit the freedoms and well-being of individuals; as much as, or more than, alternative policies, decisions, or combinations of these;

and fourth, the individuals likely to be affected, or their trustees or representatives, when of sound and cool mind, free from the influence of coercion and manipulation, and well-informed, are likely to find the said societal consequences or limitations on their freedoms and well-being intolerable,

then *it is not permissible to make that decision or contribute to intro-*
ducing or retaining the policy or combination of policies. But in order to
settle on alternatives within the available time, social decision proce-
dures may be used in the following order of priorities:

First, only nonconfrontational procedures, if feasible and likely to be
effective, may be employed.

Second, among confrontational procedures, only those that are non-
violent, if likely to be feasible and effective, may be used.

Third, if only violent procedures are feasible and likely to be effec-
tive, then only the least violent of these may be employed and no more
than to the extent they are necessary (an extreme case under this
category is that in which only combat and war are feasible and likely to
be effective).

Fourth, if none of the preceding procedures is feasible or likely to be
effective, then coping and waiting, perhaps accompanied by discussion
of merits, consensus building, and other feasible procedures (e.g., eco-
nomic embargoes) that may be marginally effective in the long run may
be used until the circumstances change.

Otherwise, *if the policy, decision, or combination of these is likely to be*
both feasible and effective in dealing with an existent policy-making
problem or set of problems, and the third and fourth conditions are not
satisfied,

then *it is permissible to make the decision and contribute to introducing*
or retaining the policy or combination of these.

A PRAGMATIC APPROACH TO REASONABLE
DISAGREEMENTS AMONG REASONABLE PEOPLE

One might object to this principle on the grounds that, sometimes,
ordinary people who are of sound and cool mind, free from the influence of
coercion and manipulation, and well-informed simply do not know what to
think about given policies and decisions. For example, they may not know
what to think about policies and decisions concerning a new technology
such as personal computers in the 1980s or the automobile in the early 1900s,
even if they have all the information available to decision makers at the time.

Yet, in cases such as these, although they are uncertain about the manner
in which a new technology's expansion might affect them in the future, and
partly because of this uncertainty, ordinary people are not without ideas.
They are likely to think that policies, procedures, and decisions are less
tolerable the more they preempt the possibility of future corrections. Hence,
though lacking a definitive answer about the technologies, they are likely to

have a clear and defensible answer about policy-making concerning such technologies. This answer is often likely to be: Keep options as open as circumstances permit.[22]

The same applies to those situations in which well-informed, rational people in a rational frame of mind disagree. It is in cases such as these that negotiation, social interaction accompanied by discussion of merits, and other social decision procedures are appropriate for pragmatically working out the differences. The more future options are preempted, the more this process is undermined. Hence, if public participation is, as previously argued, crucial for politically wise and morally acceptable policy-making, options should be kept as open as circumstances permit. Indeed, whatever other disagreements ordinary people have, they are often likely to agree on this.

The outcomes of such a process may not completely satisfy anyone, but a minimum standard of provisions is likely to be met. This is often all that can be accomplished in political and moral life. In faithfully reflecting this fact, the hypotheses I have proposed are central components of a satisfactory theory in the sense of this term explained at the outset.[23] With its help, one can strike a sound balance between the excesses of social order and those of social disorder. Realistically speaking, individual freedoms and well-being would be the better for it.

Dialogue

— Your hypotheses appear to involve some difficulties. For example, suppose that there is a policy-making problem and some policy, decision, or combination of these, though feasible and likely to be effective, would lead to roughly at least as much disruption or limitations on people's freedoms or well-being as the alternatives. Suppose also that those likely to be affected would find it intolerable. According to your hypotheses, the policy, decision, or combination is not permissible. However, it is permissible to engage in certain social decision procedures—at the very least, in coping, discussion of merits, and negotiation. But, in pursuing decision procedures, some decisions are involved—namely, those to engage in the social decision procedures. Do your hypotheses entail that these latter decisions are also impermissible?

— Not at all. The fact that some decisions are not permissible in the situation does not mean that no decisions are permissible in it. Indeed, the policies and decisions that are not permissible in the case you described are those that address the entire policy-making problem(s) in question. The decisions to engage in such things as discussion of merits and negotiation address a special aspect of the problem(s)—the differences of opinion or existing objections—and are permissible.

— But suppose that the procedures themselves would lead to at least as much social disruption or limitation on people's freedoms or well-being as the impermissible policies and decisions. In such a case, nothing would be permissible, not even coping, which is absurd.

— So far, you have formulated conditions under which, if the hypotheses were applicable, the said results would appear to follow. But you have offered no actual or plausible case in which such a situation would arise. Until you present such a case, your objection has no force. It is merely an abstract possibility.

— The following case should do. Suppose that there has been an earthquake in a remote region of the country, and you are in charge of a first-aid contingent sent to the area. Upon arrival, you realize that those in need of help are scattered in two separate valleys. You can reach one as easily as the other and, given the reports you have received, one group needs as much help as the other. But the needed help cannot be provided to any group if you split your contingent and resources. You must make a policy decision. If you do nothing, no one gets help. If you split your contingent, no one gets help. If you and your contingent go to one valley, no one in the other valley gets help. And it is quite unlikely that a new contingent will arrive with additional help early enough to make a difference. Now, according to your hypotheses, it is not permissible to do nothing or split your contingent, because these alternatives would limit the well-being, if not the freedoms, of those affected—in this case, the earthquake victims. Relative to these alternatives, it is permissible to go to one valley or the other. But the decision to go to one valley would limit the well-being, if not freedoms, of the victims in the other valley, and vice versa. So, relative to each other, none of these decisions is permissible. Further, any permissible procedure you use must be nonconfrontational. Coping or discussion of merits, however, will amount to doing nothing for the victims, hence are not permissible. Negotiation or bargaining is irrelevant, because no one is in a position to negotiate with you about the matter. So is mediation, for there is no happy or even unhappy medium to be reached. So is arbitration, unless you appoint yourself the situation's arbiter. But on what grounds would you base your arbitration?

— I can see the point of your case, but not its force. Though it is morally significant, it is not a policy-making case, because no policy is being made. Nor is the decision a policy-making decision. It is just an episodic decision made while simply carrying out policies already in existence and not questioned in the context. Besides, I don't think your case is realistic. Usually, in a situation like the one you described, it is feasible to send advance scouting parties to the affected areas in order to determine whether their needs for help are indeed roughly the same. Alternatively, it is often feasible for a helicopter crew to scout the areas and radio reports to the aid contingent. I bet you ten to one that, normally, they will report significant differences. Indeed, the helicopters might start delivering help, thus giving your contingent time to help the victims in one valley and then those in the other.

— But suppose that, in the case I am describing, the reports you receive indicate that the need for help is roughly the same in both valleys, and that the help the helicopters could provide is too little to make a difference.

— I must admit that your efforts at imagining a real dilemma are quite fashionable. Yet, the closer you get to attaining your purpose, the less realistic and more unusual your case becomes. Hence, its force diminishes. Besides, even if your case were a real dilemma, as well as realistic and frequent, it would not show a flaw in my hypotheses. There is one, however unsatisfactory, nonconfrontational procedure you have not mentioned: flipping a coin or something to that purpose.

— Isn't that heartless, though?

— It need not be. One might flip the coin, decide accordingly, and then be haunted by the misery and maybe death of those one did not help.

— Maybe so, but it still trivializes a morally significant decision.

— I don't see how. *Unnecessarily* flipping a coin to make decisions would do that. But given your description of the case, it or a procedure like it was necessary. If the type of case you described were common, however, the decision might be trivialized by the fact that flipping a coin to make moral decisions was an everyday affair. But the case is quite rare, if at all actual or plausible.

— However this may be, another problem with your hypotheses is that they are redundant. According to them, policies or decisions that are feasible and likely to be effective are permissible only when, in addition, they are likely to lead to less societal disruption or limitations of freedom and well-being than the alternatives *and* those likely to be affected would find it tolerable. How could they find it intolerable in such a case?

— Very simply. Though the policies and decisions may lead to less societal disruption, they may limit freedoms or well-being in a manner that those likely to be affected (or at least some of them) would find intolerable. Alternatively, the policies and decisions might lead to greater freedoms (e.g., free international trade) and well-being (e.g., extra goods or services bought with a $1,000 check from the government to each citizen) while increasing social disruption (e.g., by increasing the national deficit too much). In this case, the people might find such costly extra freedoms and well-being intolerable, for example, because their children and grandchildren, or simply future generations, would suffer as a consequence.

— Even if the policies are not redundant, they are too restrictive. Suppose that given policies or decisions would lead to societal disruption *and* limit the freedoms and well-being of those likely to be affected more than the alternatives; but all those likely to be affected would, nonetheless, find them tolerable. Why should they be impermissible?

— I'm afraid I find your case unconvincing, since the people we are talking about are supposed to be of cool and sound mind, free from the influences of coercion and manipulation, and well-informed. It is unlikely that they would tolerate being shortchanged when the policies or decisions that do it are avoidable. But even if they would tolerate the worse situation, why let it come about if one could do better? One thing is sure: They would not find *improvements* intolerable. No doubt, if those likely to be affected by a policy, decision, or combination of these are likely to find it intolerable, policymakers should not institute it, even if it appears likely to bring about improvements. But the situation described is not one in which people find intolerable what policymakers think to be better, but one in which people find tolerable what policymakers think to be a worse alternative; they would also find tolerable and welcome a better alternative. Surely policymakers would not be doing their jobs well if they stopped engaging in policy-making likely to bring about improvements just because people are content with a worse situation.

— Given your answer, I must still conclude that your hypotheses are too restrictive. They place an undue burden on policymakers by requiring them to engage in self-sacrifice for the sake of the public good.

— That is not true, because policymakers are also included among those likely to be affected by policies or decisions, including those that apply to policy-making concerning new policies or decisions and those that apply to their future implementation. Hence, if, when thinking freely, coolly, and reflectively, policymakers judged the policies or decisions intolerable (e.g., because they required severe self-sacrifice), the policies would not be permissible. Of course, appropriate social decision procedures could be used to work out alternatives.

— On another matter, rather than too restrictive, your hypotheses appear incomplete, or involve practical contradictions, or lead to an infinite regress. How are policymakers supposed to go about deciding what social decision procedure to use in order to settle differences? Would you expect them to negotiate or not? Such a thing would involve a practical contradiction, wouldn't it?

— If they negotiated whether to engage in any negotiation whatsoever, a practical contradiction would appear to be involved. They would go along with one negotiation while, in negotiating whether to engage in any, they would presumably be committed not to go along with any yet. But this is not how things actually happen. Typically, people use one procedure, such as mediation, to institute another procedure, such as negotiation, in order to settle differences. And if they use negotiation, they use it simply to settle whether to use negotiation to settle differences affecting the permissibility or effectiveness of policies or decisions about a certain subject, (e.g., about nuclear energy). There is no contradiction here, because there are two logically and chronologically separate negotiations about two different matters.

— But it leads to an infinite regress. What procedure could people use to make the decision to use mediation, in order to agree to use negotiation, in order to settle differences that affect the permissibility of, say, a given nuclear energy policy? Whatever procedure constitutes the answer, the question arises: What procedure may they use to decide to use that one? This situation recurs forever.

— It may recur in the never-never land of mere logical possibilities and possible worlds, but not in the actual world. In the latter, things start with people trying to use a variety of different social decision procedures and, as a result, they go along with some of them. My hypotheses, however, are not incomplete. They imply that this is permissible. The only constraints are on what procedures may be used given the type of policy and decision problems being faced. For example, it is impermissible to use combat in dealing with a problem primarily addressed through reliance on reason and meaningful dialogue.

— A policy-making area in which your hypotheses still strike me as too permissive or vague involves people's self-esteem and human dignity. For example, what guidance, if any, do they give us concerning policies about people's ability to undergo ten or eighteen plastic surgery procedures simply to look better, not to correct disfigurements caused by illness or accidents?

— I am glad you asked, because this case belongs in a large class that includes genetic engineering techniques used to improve an individual's features, ranging from height to memory; the ability to sell one's own organs for transplant into other people; the ability of a woman to serve as a surrogate mother for a price; and the more puzzling case of the consequences, if any, of computer developments on people's self-esteem. I discuss primarily this latter case in the next essay, but my conclusions have implications for the others.

9 Between Triviality and Worth: Computers, Education, and Self-Esteem

When I was a teenager, a musician of my acquaintance once said, upon being told that machines could create music: "That does not worry me in the least. I will worry the day they can *appreciate* music." I then thought that the ability to appreciate music or, for that matter, other forms of art or a piece of reasoning was not enough. I believed that something else, which we developed through our education in addition to appreciation skills, made us worthy in a manner that machines were not. Like many people, I used to feel secure in the thought that building design, music making, painting, financial advising, and learning and reasoning skills were strongholds of human creativity and incapable of computer emulation.

However, judging by what some artificial intelligence experts tell us, these examples are unlikely to fill the bill. They are increasingly becoming skills that machines also have or can have in the foreseeable future.[1] All are technically possible, though some may not become technical realities because of lack of money or will. Some ethically and politically significant questions nonetheless arise: Does the ever-expanding technological feasibility of computers to have skills traditionally associated with people's education jeopardize people's self-esteem? If so, what policies and decisions are permissible concerning such computer developments? Should they aim at promoting any such developments, at stopping them, or at striking some balance between them and people's self-esteem? How should this balance be determined?

These are the questions I address in this essay. In doing so, I argue for eight theses. First, there is reason to believe that the said computer developments undermine one current conception of self-esteem, namely, that associated with skills and, in particular, with those a person acquires through education. Second, however, the fears that this situation prompts appear

151

exaggerated. Third, at any rate, the skills acquired through education do not suffice as grounds of a person's worth. Fourth, a better alternative bases self-esteem on character traits such as honesty, kindness, and fairness. That is, traditional virtues are crucial and, arguably, basic grounds for self-esteem. Fifth, the problem posed by computer developments' undermining of self-esteem associated with the said skills needs to be addressed. Sixth, in general, there appears to be consensus among the public at large that computer technologies that facilitate work, including the work that goes into acquiring an education, are a good thing. Seventh, arguably, this consensus is based more on faith (whether in machines or in experts) than on fact. Eighth, in accordance with the hypotheses stated in Essay 8, policies concerning computer and related technological developments are permissible so long as they balance four things: people's current notions of self-esteem, their economic needs, those of their society, and the need to facilitate their adaptation to the wider and more basic conception of self-esteem based on good traits.

AN EDUCATION TO BE PROUD OF

One often hears people say, "You should be proud. It isn't easy to get the education you got. These days, it's unusual to find someone with the breadth and depth of education you have. That's something to be proud of." These statements indicate that a person's education is often thought to involve sound grounds for self-pride, self-respect, or self-esteem. And in talking of self-pride, self-respect, or self-esteem, people typically mean a sense of pleasure or satisfaction taken in something done, produced, or acquired by oneself, which is supposed to be to one's credit. On what grounds is acquiring an education thought to be to one's credit?

A context significantly related to that of acquiring an education is that of work done in producing goods, typically in jobs. The education one acquires partly involves acquiring the knowledge and ability needed to perform this or that job. Hence, the conditions regarded as grounds for self-esteem in acquiring an education are likely to be analogous to those regarded as grounds for self-esteem in job-related work. David Braybrooke offers a characterization of the latter, which he calls "conditions for relatively highest esteem":

> (1) Doing the work, people produce goods that serve other people by meeting their needs. (2) That people should do this work and that these goods should be produced are both indispensable in this connection. (3) Doing the work, people use skills that are exacting (both in acquisition and in performance) in ways that other people respect. (4) The work is in some sense arduous for the people doing it, and necessarily so; there is no easier way of doing it in current technology.[2]

Other conditions might be added. Braybrooke mentions a measure of actual recognition, variety, a degree of autonomy, and a chance to leave some personally distinctive impression on the good produced. One could also add the mere sense of having acquired an unusual breadth and depth of knowledge or an outstanding ability to do a variety of complex jobs. At any rate, Braybrooke does not focus on these additional conditions because he is concerned with giving "sustained attention" to needs.

In what follows, I do not focus primarily on needs, though the capacity to meet needs is a crucial way in which people and their products are valuable. Nor do I focus primarily on the listed additional conditions. Instead, I focus primarily on the second, third, and fourth conditions Braybrooke mentions and investigate their role as grounds for self-esteem in having acquired an education.

There are at least three frequently recognized grounds for having self-esteem concerning one's education. First, the person's education is thought to be and to make the person unique, nearly unique, or somehow unsubstitutable. Second, the education thus acquired is generally presumed valuable to oneself or others. Third, acquiring the education is difficult. These conditions are analogous to Braybrooke's last three conditions. One difference is that although one's education or the skills it involves may be exacting in ways other people respect, this is not required by the conditions I just listed. They require only that it be generally presumed valuable to oneself or others. I argue later that policy-making must be sensitive to the fact that people's self-esteem is often based on these conditions. However, this is not incompatible with arguing that basing self-esteem exclusively or primarily on these conditions is a mistake. Before arguing for these theses, however, let us turn to the effects of computers on education.

COMPUTERS AND EDUCATIONAL PRIDE

The previously discussed computer developments appear to undermine people's educational self-esteem to the extent that it is exclusively or primarily based on grounds of difficulty and unsubstitutability. Given such developments, eliminating such difficulty and unsubstitutability is already *technically possible* or is likely to be so in the near future.

One might be tempted to object that there is no harm in the fact that certain things would be learned more easily if the learning environment had plenty of computers and printers at the students' disposal. This might make it easier to write better looking papers or to study. What could be wrong with it? It would certainly not do away with all difficulty in learning, because there would still be many other difficult learning tasks to perform. Some would be new, such as the task of using word-processing programs.

Other tasks would be traditional ones. One would still have to spell words right, write well, think well, and use one's imagination to solve design problems or prove logical theorems.

However, as previously mentioned, computer developments are likely to make it technically possible for computers to facilitate and even perform any of the tasks just listed. Eventually, they might be capable of performing *any tasks*.[3] That is, first, computers increasingly do away with the difficulty traditionally associated with learning and displaying task-oriented skills. And second, computers are increasingly capable of taking the place of such skills. These developments are merely contingent on financial or social constraints, not on technical ones. Hence, current computer developments undermine people's self-esteem, so long as it is exclusively or primarily based on the difficulty and unsubstitutability of skills acquired through education. And they are likely to undermine it even more in the foreseeable future.[4]

As stated, this phenomenon is not peculiar to education. For example, in the context of the ideal of work and technological (not just computer) development, David Braybrooke envisions the situation as follows:

> One should not necessarily expect widespread despair, or even widespread boredom. People may well contrive to amuse themselves, and to lead congenial lives together, when they have little work to do and no opportunity to win esteem by achieving high cultural ambitions. . . . What will have been lost, with the loss of opportunities to help other people in urgent, morally primary matters, will have been so many opportunities to demonstrate sympathy, compassion, gratitude. A large part of the field of application for moral sentiments and ethics will have gone. One may anticipate, even if despair and boredom are avoided, an impoverishment of sentiments, a growth of egoism, a certain moral emptiness.[5]

I sympathize with the concern that appears to guide Braybrooke in envisioning this situation. It would indeed be a sorry success if "the elimination of work and trouble—success, supersuccess, according to the ethics of welfare—will have helped to make our situation trivial."[6] However, how likely is the trivialization of human lives he envisions? I must confess a certain skepticism about the matter and pursue it in some detail.

HABITS AND VALUES

There are at least two reasons for being skeptical of Braybrooke's vision of a generalized technological takeover. First, it is much more thorough than the current or foreseeable technical possibilities I previously described. And second, there is evidence that economic and other constraints tend to prevent technical possibilities from becoming realities.[7]

However, Braybrooke's concerns should not be taken lightly. People cannot change their ideas or attitudes overnight. This fact leads to a crucial policy-making question: What policy-making is permissible about the fact that current developments in computer technology may jeopardize people's skill-based self-esteem, *given that those who thus ground their self-esteem are not likely to abandon these grounds overnight?* In this regard, the role that Braybrooke assigns to meeting needs in this vision is significant. So is the role of satisfying crucial wants that may be simply based on customary habits. Given these factors, how defensible are the inferences Braybrooke draws?

One might think that at least one of these inferences is exaggerated. Suppose that, under highly advanced technology, one could not demonstrate sympathy or compassion by performing health care or analogous tasks because computer-guided machines performed them. One could still demonstrate sympathy or compassion concerning the circumstances that called for such care. At the very least, one could do such things as visiting people in the hospital and keeping them company. The same opportunities for doing these things today would be present then. To be sure, some ways in which one could demonstrate sympathy or compassion (e.g., a nurse's supervising the intravenous administration of a certain medicine to a patient and making the appropriate changes) would be gone. But this in no way entails that a large part of the field of application for moral sentiments and ethics would be gone. Nurses and others could still be there to offer support and reassurance.

Concerning gratitude, Braybrooke's scenario involves difficulties of a different sort. It is not clear how highly advanced technology could meet all needs or desires so that no one could demonstrate gratitude. Unless machines themselves became persons—a highly improbable, if not impossible, development—they could hardly meet people's need or desire for attention, companionship, and loyalty. And, as I have just argued, people could always provide attention and companionship, be loyal, and demonstrate gratitude for the attention and companionship others provided to them by doing the same things in return. Hence, concerning gratitude, the field of application for moral sentiments and ethics also appears significantly intact though, to be certain, changed.

Habits, however, have a way of creating values. The mere fact that people are accustomed to and expect the old, traditional ways of demonstrating sympathy and compassion makes those ways valuable. Indeed, some of them can arguably be said to be the most poignant and satisfying ways in which people demonstrate and expect sympathy and compassion. Hence, even if many other ways of demonstrating them remain available, and new ways develop, the loss of those crucial old ways will be experienced by many ordinary people as an intolerable trivialization of life.

It might be argued that these people would be carried away by sheer sentimentality and nostalgia. No doubt, this characterization may be true of some of them. There are always people given to weak emotionalism or excessive indulgence in sentiment. Others, however, would be simply giving due weight to various attachments they reasonably formed throughout their lives and judging it intolerable to have to cope with the loss. There is no denying that sentimental values would be involved in coming to this judgment. But there is no reason to dismiss them, so long as people find them crucial when judging with a cool and sound mind, free from the influences of coercion and manipulation, and on the basis of adequate information.

One might grant that those who would find the changes intolerable are not *carried away* by sheer sentimentality and nostalgia, but still argue that, for the sake of progress, all sentimental values should be put aside. But this reply involves a big leap of faith, besides being both morally insensitive and politically unwise. First, it involves a big leap of faith because progress is a vague term whose application in this case is highly controversial. And so is saying that all sentimental values should be put aside for the sake of progress. Second, the response is morally insensitive because it unjustifiably plays down the fact that the people described would find the situation intolerable. Third, the said reply is politically unwise; the prospect that many people are likely to be affected by computer developments in ways they find intolerable is not something that, from a political standpoint, one can simply disregard. They may not simply grin and bear it but, as many workers have done, seriously resist the change.[8]

In response, it might be objected that the preceding remarks presuppose that people will not adapt. But there is evidence that they will. Consider the United States between 1950 and 1990. In a few decades, people adapted to a great deal of technology and much loss of human contact and support. For example, in many places, impersonal supermarkets and department stores have replaced small local stores and the more personal local life that surrounded them. Indeed, catalog buying is doing away with the need to go to the store at all. Also, banking by computer is becoming increasingly common. In health care, many computerized devices have done away with the need for frequent human exchanges. Yet people do not seem to mind. Some rather welcome not having to talk to people they did not always, if ever, like.

This response, however, misses part of the point. The problem is twofold: Technology development may make life unjustifiably intolerable for some because it may make it easy to the point of triviality for all. First, in doing away with the need to have as many exchanges with people as before, computer technology and related developments may undermine people's ability to relate to one another. It becomes harder to demonstrate sympathy or compassion, for example, when we have increasingly less contact with one another. Second, the envisioned situation may do away with the need to make an effort to attain things that used to be hard to attain. Computers could help us attain the same things (e.g., designing buildings, making music, producing paintings, and giving financial advice) almost effortlessly.

By the way, other technologies could help do away with effort in other areas of life. Is your body looking out of shape? Why exercise to fix it? If you can afford it, have some aesthetic surgery instead! It takes less effort and, often, less pain. And when the surgery's results begin to go away, have more surgery (like car tune-ups). And if it is fine to use aesthetic surgery this way, why not get genetically engineered products implanted in our bodies so that we can grow a bit taller or improve our memory?

No doubt, aesthetic surgery is of great help in reconstructing the features of victims of accidents or fires. And some genetically engineered products may be of great help in treating growth defects or the effects of illness on memory. These applications, however, meet needs and crucial wants. In contrast, the previously mentioned applications are frivolous and trivial. They are further evidence that the technological developments just discussed may trivialize life. Indeed, they may make it so easy, boring, and shallow that people may not merely lose their self-esteem. They may begin to fight simply to escape from boredom, as they were doing in the South Seas when Captain Cook came upon the circumstances of paradise.

As indicated, however, the said computer and other technology developments are unlikely to make everyone, or even most people, lose their self-esteem by making them inessential. Nor are these developments likely to lead all, or even most people, to become so bored with life as to be driven into despair or violence. Nor are they likely to make most people, let alone everyone, shallow to the point of becoming unable to conceive that thrills do not exhaust what is valuable. Nonetheless, current computer and other technology developments may affect many people in one of these ways. Hence, as I have argued, policy-making about the said developments should be morally sensitive to these not unlikely consequences.

The consequences just described largely concern matters of character, which raise a number of questions: What is the significance of character in dealing with the matters we are discussing? Does it constitute an alternative to the difficulty and unsubstitutability of task-oriented skills used as exclusive grounds for self-esteem? Is it better? I address these questions next by focusing again on computer developments.

A MATTER OF CHARACTER

The conception of self-esteem associated exclusively or primarily with the difficulty and unsubstitutability of task-oriented skills is not uncommon.

Yet, in this extreme version, it is unsound. Instead of leading to self-esteem, it leads to the loss of self-esteem in the contemporary world. After all, if people had not based their self-esteem exclusively or primarily on these features, current computer developments would not undermine it. Such a conception is accordingly self-frustrating, and any self-frustrating conception of self-esteem should be abandoned.

It might be objected, however, that the conclusion that it should be abandoned is too facile. One needs to deal with the objection that current computer developments, not the said notion of self-esteem, ought to be abandoned. This objection, however, is merely ad hoc. First, why make it, other than because one is caught up in a conception of self-esteem based exclusively or primarily on difficulty and unsubstitutability? And second, the objection is unrealistic. Computer developments, including those that replace people such as building designers and airplane pilots, are here to stay. Why insist on making people feel hopelessly unworthy for the sake of a moral tradition? After all, it is not the only one.

Even people who base their self-esteem on the difficulty or unsubstitutability of their accomplishments often do not exclusively or primarily base their self-esteem on them. They also base it on character traits. Indeed, there are good reasons for connecting one's self-esteem to the value of one's character or character traits. Before proceeding, let us briefly characterize some notions central to this conception.

In this alternative conception, character traits are those among a person's characteristics that are to the person's credit or discredit and make the person good, bad, or objectionable. A person's character is made up of his or her character traits, and the manifestation of these is not exhausted in specific tasks.[9] The motives for performing these tasks are crucial. Among these traits are fairness, benevolence, and a sense of duty. Another, courage, was highly valued by the ancient Greeks, but it appears to have lost its moral preeminence in the largely impersonally organized twentieth-century societies. I have elsewhere argued for adding to the list a sense of humor, understood not merely as wit but also as not taking oneself too seriously.[10]

This character-based conception of self-esteem is much more impervious to the ill effects of computer developments than that based on skills. Indeed, current developments in computer technology may prove to be a blessing in disguise, for they bring out the preeminence of good character and character traits in giving worth to our lives. These character traits and the act of nurturing them through education—both in and outside school—are crucial for preserving the field of application for moral sentiments and ethics. They are also crucial for preventing our lives from becoming trivial.

These features of the character-based conception of self-esteem strengthen the view that character and character traits are sound grounds of self-esteem, and task-oriented skills by themselves are not. As previously stated, however, Braybrooke's concern should not be taken lightly. Granted that the strictly skill-based conception of self-esteem should be abandoned in favor of the character-based conception, nagging policy questions remain. What policy-making is permissible about the fact that current developments in computer technology jeopardize people's skill-based self-esteem, given that those who thus ground their self-esteem are not likely to abandon these grounds overnight?

There is already some controversy about this policy problem. Some academics, for example, resist computers in their offices and courses at all costs; others promote them with equal fervor. However, such controversy is largely circumscribed to academic circles and does not appear to have significantly disrupted the educational sector, let alone society at large. Indeed, the members of the public who have an opinion about it appear to want or, at the very least, not object to the further development and introduction of computers in education. Various reasons are offered in support of this attitude. Let us next discuss some that are relevant to the policy problem under consideration.

COMPUTERS, EDUCATION, AND JOBS

It is said in the controversy that although self-esteem is certainly a concern, so are jobs. Along these lines, discussions tend to focus exclusively on arguments in favor of rushing to introduce computers in education. It is argued, for example, that the job market is bad, the competition is tough, and the jobs will go to those who have the new computer skills already required in the market. Hence, the argument goes, since an education should put students in a position to compete in this market and to get jobs in it, computers should be used in education as widely as possible. This way, students will develop the necessary skills and therefore have a good chance of getting jobs.

There is no doubt a lot of truth and common sense in this position. It should be noted, however, that the notion of an education emphasized in it is different from the one previously discussed. Based on this conception, a student's acquisition of computer skills is primarily a ground for temporary relief from anxiety about the job market. It is not primarily a ground for self-esteem. One's supposed accomplishment, if any, is that one has acquired certain computer skills well enough and fast enough to beat the competition to a job. It goes without saying that one may lose the job to another competitor, possibly to a machine, in the foreseeable future. Although the difficulty in acquiring the skills is not yet gone, one's unsubstitutability is. And those opposing the unrestricted introduction of computers in education are unlikely to miss the opportunity to mention it.

Of course, such substitutability as a result of computers' irruption in education is no reason to disregard job competitiveness. Indeed, it would be foolish to do so. However, policymakers faced with the conflictive demands of education and jobs must face the following social fact: Giving absolute priority to market survival and the avoidance of all market risk tends to focus on the ever-present need to develop new marketable skills to the detriment of all the above discussed grounds for self-esteem. Hence, if market survival and the avoidance of all market risk are given absolute priority, such grounds for self-esteem as skill difficulty and unsubstitutability are further weakened. But, in addition, character and character traits are brushed aside. That is, all grounds for self-esteem are gone. This is a reason not to give market survival and the avoidance of all market risks absolute priority. Besides, bad job markets and tough competition do not usually rule out considerations other than market survival.[11]

The weakening of self-esteem based exclusively or primarily on difficulty and unsubstitutability might be welcomed. One might believe, as I previously argued, that they are insufficient grounds for self-esteem. Indeed, along these lines, one could hail task-oriented computer developments as a means of dramatizing the inadequacy of task-oriented skills as a ground for self-esteem and as a reason to support the character-based notion of self-esteem. Yet, as we also saw, none of the above is sufficient for disregarding the policy-making and morally significant fact that many people still base their self-esteem on the difficulty and unsubstitutability of the tasks they can perform. The policy-making question still remains. Rephrased in a more specific manner, it is this: What policies are permissible concerning this situation, given that people are not likely to abandon the said conception of self-esteem overnight?

IN SEARCH OF BALANCE

The preceding discussion points to four main concerns that should be addressed in dealing with the policy question: (1) people's current notions of self-esteem, (2) their economic needs, (3) the economic needs of their society, and (4) the need to facilitate people's adaptation to a sound conception of self-esteem, which is, as I argued, the character-based conception. Policies are permissible so long as they are sensitive to all these concerns. In particular, policymakers should not simply brush the first and fourth concerns aside. In other words, policies of neglect are unjustified, as are those that focus only on market concerns. Such policies reflect the conception that everything and everyone has a price, and the value of character does not matter. This conception is in conflict with the defensible and widely held notion of character-based self-esteem.

Also, though the strictly skill-based conception of self-esteem is flawed, the suffering and alienation people would undergo if such a conception were brashly undermined are morally significant. Hence, policies that disregard this skill-based conception for the sake of prompt computer development are unjustified. This points to the remaining concerns. Extreme economic exigencies of society would justify undermining the flawed, though not the character-based, conception of self-esteem. Fortunately, such economic exigencies are not as common as some make them out to be. However, individual economic needs are often at stake, and policies concerning computer development must take them into account.

One might be tempted simply to poll people about their opinions on the matter and pass policy accordingly, but this would be overly simplistic. Public opinion about current and foreseeable computer developments in the late twentieth century may be significantly affected by lack of information about the developments and their consequences. But suppose those polled are given the available information about these things. If asked whether they favor these developments, they might say that they are in favor of them, that they are not, or that they do not know. Some might add that they favor policy-making that keeps their options open as much as circumstances permit. After all, many people want to see whether they can adapt to the new situation.

For purposes of comparison, let us return to the case of the automobile discussed at the book's beginning. Imagine people being asked at the beginning of the twentieth century whether they favored the development and introduction of the automobile. This was supposed to be a means of transportation faster than the horse and carriage and, unlike the train, capable of being used as private transportation. Some claimed that it might significantly increase injuries and deaths from traffic-related accidents, but the technology had not been tested. What would people have said? Some might have favored it (many did). Others might have opposed it (some did). Still others might not have known what to say. And many in each group might have wanted to keep their options open.

With hindsight, we know what happened. Individually, people adapted to the automobile and the enormous number of injuries and deaths associated with it in the late twentieth century. Collectively, however, society found itself ill-adapted to the air pollution, resource depletion, energy dependency, and other consequences of using the automobile for private transportation. Yet alternatives to it have been significantly preempted by both practice and policy. None of this, however, was known at the beginning of the century. This situation is analogous to that concerning computer development today. Hence, it provides reasons to conclude that policies concerning computer development are permissible so long as they do not unjustifiably preempt viable and defensible options.

Throughout the process, research and public education concerning computers and their consequences for society and individuals are crucial. Otherwise, those involved in the policy-making process or affected by it will develop little appreciation of computers, people, and their mutual relations. In the United States, some of this has been done. There are currently fifty to sixty science, technology, and society programs in U.S. colleges and universities whose aim in part is to develop such appreciation. More of them would be of help.[12] Maybe appreciation dispositions (which are crucial to a well-balanced character, and whose display is not exhausted in narrowly specified tasks) have something to do with what makes us worthy of self-esteem after all. Maybe the musician of my acquaintance had a point.

At any rate, the consequences of new computer technologies for self-esteem cannot be soundly or easily disregarded by simply discounting self-esteem, whatever its grounds, as a thing of the past—a sort of ethical dinosaur. As Joan Didion put it in her *Slouching Towards Bethlehem*, "To protest that some fairly improbable people, some people who could not possibly respect themselves, seem to sleep easily enough is to miss the point entirely, as surely as those people miss it who think that self-respect has necessarily to do with not having safety pins in one's underwear."[13]

Dialogue

— Granted that basing one's self-esteem exclusively or primarily on uniqueness or difficulty is not sufficient, the alternative you suggest does not seem much better. As Braybrooke argues, computer developments undermine the manifestation of such good character traits as sympathy and compassion.

— They would undermine such traits if the developments were extensive. But extensive developments appear unlikely. As for current and foreseeable developments, they are not likely to undermine the manifestation of good character traits as much as they undermine the uniqueness or difficulty involved in acquiring or employing the abilities acquired through an education.

— Be that as it may, I'm unclear about the application of your hypotheses. On the one hand, you state that there is some controversy, primarily in academic circles, concerning computer developments and their social effects. On the other hand, you state that there is general consensus among the public that these developments are a good thing. How should one classify this case: as a controversy or as a case of predominant consensus?

— First, you must be clear about the scope of the policies or decisions you envision. Are they supposed to be merely local, say, confined to one academic institution? Or are they supposed to be national, say, applicable to computer developments in the United States? If the former, and if there is controversy about the matter in the academic institution in question, then you are dealing with a controversy. If the scope of the envisioned policies or decisions is national, and there is general consensus about the matter among the public, then you have good reason to classify the case as one that primarily involves consensus, not conflict. Of course, you will also have to get additional information. For example, you would need to establish whether the situation is disruptive at the macrolevel of society. Equally important would be to establish whether the freedoms and well-being of individuals are currently limited more than they would be in the situation that the envisioned policies and decisions would bring about.

— And what about the procedures to use in the policy-making process? Which ones should be used?

— My hypotheses are meant to tell you what types of procedures are permissible, and what types are not, in given types of situations. They are not, however, meant to tell you what particular procedure to use in the situation you face. To establish the latter, one needs to examine the evidence indicating what is likely to work in given circumstances. For example, if the policy-making situation involves—as it appears to involve in one of the cases just described—a controversy, then mere discussion of merits, though partly useful, will probably be insufficient. If, however, it primarily involves consensus—but this consensus is a bit thoughtless or shortsighted—then discussion of merits and education are permissible and may be crucial.

— I can see what you are saying, because the situations we are discussing point to no impending crisis. But what about nastier situations? I am still waiting to see a full-fledged case exemplifying how your hypotheses apply.

— You won't have to wait any longer. Let us move on to the next essay.

10 Like the Phoenix: Ethics, Policy-Making, and the U.S. Nuclear Energy Controversy

The U.S. nuclear energy controversy, like the phoenix, keeps on being reborn from its own ashes. Since 1945, when it all began, up to the present, the controversy has arisen in a new form each time it was thought to be buried. Why is the controversy recurrent? What are the political and ethical implications of its recurrence for technology policy-making? What specific ways of dealing with the controversy are both politically sound and morally permissible? Are science courts and technology tribunals among them? Is the legislative process a better alternative? How promising are any of these when assessed in light of the fact of issue-overload discussed at the book's outset? These are the main questions I address.

I argue for various interrelated theses. First, the recurrence of the U.S. nuclear energy controversy shows various trends. Among these, secrecy and lack of public influence on nuclear policy-making have increasingly become concerns among wide sectors of the public. Second, the fact that these and related concerns were not squarely addressed in the past by largely technocratic policy-making partly explains the recurrence of the controversy. Third, the growing public concern about secrecy and lack of public influence highlights technocratic policy-making's lack of political realism and ethical sensitivity about nuclear energy and, in fact, any socially significant technology. In other words, it makes plain the political wisdom and ethical soundness of participatory policy-making about nuclear energy and other technology matters. Fourth, along participatory lines, the science court proposal is inadequate. Fifth, the technology tribunal, though promising for some purposes, does not make enough room for the range of social decision procedures useful for dealing with technology controversies and is liable to be bogged down by issue-overload. Sixth, technology policy-making through the legislative branch of government is much more open than the

165

technology tribunal to such procedures as bargaining and negotiation and, therefore, would be better attuned to many political realities and ethical concerns. Yet, seventh, though the legislative process is less liable to yield issue-overload than the technology tribunal, it is not impervious to such an eventuality. Eighth, for technology policy-making to be successful, it needs to proceed in the spirit of compromise and diplomacy. Ninth, disjoint technology policy-making, in which a variety of channels (e.g., legislative and court-like) are tried—often independently of each other—is most likely to avoid the ever-present risk of promoting further proliferation of opinions and controversy and getting bogged down by issue-overload.

A POINT OF METHOD

In arguing for the theses, I outline the history of the controversy in the United States, especially up to 1954. In that year, with the passing of the Atomic Energy Act, the basic legal stage for the controversy in its present form was largely set.[1] This will suffice for my main purpose, which is not historical but simply to provide a developed case useful for discussing this essay's theses and clarifying the application of this book's hypotheses. In this latter regard, the said historical outline helps bring out the nuances of nuclear energy policy-making. This is the only way that the applicability of the book's hypotheses to technology policy-making, and the value of ideas such as the science court and the technology tribunal, can be realistically tested.

THE MCMAHON ACT AND ITS AFTERMATH

In the beginning, everything was in the hands of the military.[2] As soon as World War II ended, however, people came to see this military monopoly as undesirable for a variety of reasons. One was that it emphasized bomb making rather than peaceful applications of nuclear energy. Another reason was that, by means of secrecy, the military monopoly restricted the freedom of inquiry necessary for vigorous research progress. Still another reason was that the military monopoly led to administrative inefficiency. Committees for Civilian Control of Atomic Energy were formed in various U.S. cities, and the nuclear energy controversy was on its way.

After one year of postwar atomic politicking, on August 1, 1946, President Truman signed the McMahon Bill into law. It placed all policy decisions, including those concerning the production and custody of atomic weapons, in the hands of a civilian Atomic Energy Commission. If people believed that the controversy had come to an end, however, they were mistaken.

The controversy reappeared, Hydra style. It was now about two monopolies rather than one. Concerning world policy, some criticized the McMahon Act on the grounds that it was meant to fit a U.S. program that would put all fissionable materials in the hands of an international agency. But, the argument went on, the program was bound to fail because the Soviet Union flatly rejected any international control of fissionable materials. Concerning nuclear energy control in the United States, others criticized the McMahon Act on the grounds that it legalized a monopoly in the United States and hence ran counter to free enterprise.[3]

Centralization of U.S. energy production in the hands of government, though not without supporters, had become the target of criticism. The critics held that although private ownership of raw materials, fissionable materials, patents, and production plants certainly should be *controlled*, it should be permitted by the government. Otherwise, they argued, industry would find no incentive in atomic development.[4] Advocates of such centralization, President Truman included, pointed to U.S. security, or to the people's interest in general, as a fundamental interest that such centralization served to satisfy.[5]

One might think that the government's monopoly was opposed because the power companies were eager to produce electricity from privately owned nuclear fuels and power plants, but they were not. As Philip Sporn, president of the Advisory Committee on Cooperation between the Electric Power Industry and the Atomic Energy Commission said as late as December 28, 1950, the utilities were reluctant to use atomic energy. First, there were the technical obstacles involved. Second, at the time, the prospects of conventional power production were bright. And third, they thought that the operation and maintenance of a nuclear reactor would be more expensive than that of a conventional plant. This was a prophetic expectation borne out by the economic difficulties faced by the U.S. nuclear industry during the 1970s and 1980s.[6]

Today, it is almost an article of faith that only the government was interested in the development of industrial applications of nuclear energy, not industry.[7] However, though the utilities were reluctant, they were not entirely uninterested; nuclear development would have provided what they thought was a convenient and cheap fuel. Nor was the government as eager to develop nuclear power plants as it was made out to be. This is evidenced by the fact that six months after Monsanto Chemical Company made a proposal for the design, construction, and operation of an atomic power plant built by industry with its own funds, the government had allowed Monsanto to study its existing reactor projects but had not yet supported Monsanto's reactor development.[8]

Feasibility studies jointly conducted by government and industry, however, were soon to become a reality. In January 1951, the Atomic Energy Commission announced the Industrial Participation Program, under which the commission would accept "limited proposals to surveys of existing reactor data."[9] On May 16, 1951, the Atomic Energy Commission announced that it would accept four proposals submitted by eight corporations working in pairs, with each pair including at least one utility company:

1. Monsanto Chemical Company and Union Electric Company of Missouri
2. Dow Chemical Company and Detroit Edison Company
3. Commonwealth Edison Company and Public Service Company of Northern Illinois
4. Pacific Gas and Electric Company and Bechtel Corporation

This arrangement was soon to be called "the biggest monopoly in America."[10]

Talk of monopoly is strong talk. Was any interested industrial sector excluded from the Industrial Participation Program, leading it to talk of monopoly? The utilities themselves, as indicated, were only mildly interested, but the chemical companies were quite interested. In addition, the newly developed possibility of profitably collaborating with chemical companies made participation very appealing to still other companies. Monsanto's secretary, Edwin J. Putzell, Jr., explained the chemical companies' interest: They especially wanted to sell the plutonium resulting from nuclear production of electricity to the government, which needed it for military purposes. Charging for it would allow them to bring down the price of electricity, which they consumed in high quantities, and maybe make a profit on the sale of plutonium itself.[11] A lot of money was at stake. Hence, it is no wonder that those excluded from the Industrial Participation Program and technologically able to engage in the profitable arrangements it involved would talk bitterly of monopoly.

Whenever a lot of money is at stake, a big risk is involved. The arrangement between the government and the corporations was likely to work as long as the government needed to buy plutonium—a weapons material. Some government officials raised questions about this way of making the nuclear energy industry profitable.[12] The dependence of nuclear energy's peaceful applications on its military applications thus became a new element in the nuclear energy controversy.

U.S. nuclear energy development, however, went on despite the controversy and the warnings of prominent physicists. Among these were Maria Telkes of the Department of Metallurgy at MIT and Hans Thirring, Director of the Institute for Theoretical Physics at the University of Vienna. In addition, warnings were heard from members of President Truman's Materials Policy Commission itself. All these scientists and policymakers supported the development of solar rather than nuclear energy.[13] As for the public, according to a 1951 University of Michigan Survey Research Center study, it did not care. The general attitude was that the experts knew what they were doing.[14]

THE 1951 AMENDMENT

Governmental decisions are often inscrutable and perplexing. Why did the U.S. government pursue the development of nuclear reactors for electricity production despite the experts' advice to the contrary? The October 30, 1951 amendment to the 1946 Atomic Energy Act may provide an answer. It authorized the Atomic Energy Commission to release large amounts of restricted information to any friendly nation, not just to war partners, as had been the case. It also permitted private participation in the production of fissionable materials outside the United States.

Byron S. Miller, who had been counsel to the Joint Committee on Atomic Energy, hypothesized that the U.S. need for fissionable materials and any technical information it could get might have motivated the amendment.[15] Keep in mind that the amendment was passed four months after the Korean War started, when the arms race and the competition for fissionable materials throughout the world were escalating. In the United States, however, access to nuclear information and private participation were still ruled out as before. Why? The rationale was kept a secret and is hard to imagine. At any rate, a long-standing aspect of the controversy became even more controversial than before: the matter of secrecy.

To complicate things, the policy matters that concerned nuclear energy could not be squarely addressed. Secrecy about nuclear energy kept even important government officials ignorant of basic facts of nuclear life. Thomas E. Murray, a member of the Atomic Energy Commission, criticized this situation about half a year after the Korean War ended.[16] Secrecy was now being criticized from a political, not merely a research or business, standpoint. A new aspect of the controversy was emerging: The public, and certainly government officials, should be informed about matters concerning the peaceful development of nuclear energy. These should not—indeed, could not—be kept out of the ordinary world of politics.

A group of conflicting concerns was beginning to be publicly recognized. Some corporations and a few government officials were concerned with keeping nuclear energy matters out of the ordinary world of politics by means of secrecy. This concern was openly in conflict with various others, such as the public's concern with national security and enlightened publicity about nuclear matters. In fact, though not explicitly in the public's perceptions, it was also in conflict with the public's concern with safety (which would become a source of public anxiety in the mid- and late 1950s).[17] In addition, it was in conflict with the concern of policymakers who represented the public and who, together with the public, were kept in the dark about nuclear energy. This made it impossible for them to determine when U.S. security, or the safety or freedoms of U.S. inhabitants, would be endangered by nuclear policies. The generalized recognition of these conflicts, especially at the level of governmental policymakers, marked the beginning of an aspect of the nuclear energy controversy with which we are often faced today: the conflict between technocracy and democracy in nuclear policy-making.

THE NEW ATOMIC ENERGY ACT:
THE BEGINNING OF OUR TIME

A mere decision sometimes resolves a long-standing controversy, making the preceding controversy irrelevant. This seemed to have happened to the nuclear energy controversy in 1954, when President Eisenhower signed the new Atomic Energy Act. It had one main effect: The development of peaceful uses of nuclear energy was no longer kept out of the normal world of business. The Act shifted the emphasis from government research to government aid to permitted private research. It also permitted private ownership of patents, fissionable materials, and nuclear facilities under the regulation of the Atomic Energy Commission. But there was a catch: The Act gave the Commission a great deal of leeway to determine what patents, fissionable materials, and nuclear facilities could be privately owned. It also gave the Commission absolute power to decide what nuclear information could be declassified and disseminated. The only requirement was that the Commission maintain a continuous review of nuclear data in an effort to make public all those that would not endanger U.S. security. Nuclear energy was no longer left to the experts. It was now left to committees. With the enactment of the 1954 Atomic Energy Act—which, with only relatively minor modifications, is still in force—the basic legal stage for the controversy in its present form was set.[18]

FAILURES OF TECHNOCRACY

The history of the U.S. nuclear energy controversy is a history of slowly recognized conflicting concerns. These are not restricted to economic concerns; they also involve concerns about safety and security. Nor are they reduced to material concerns alone, because they also involve concerns about research and publicity. In any case, all the conflicts involve matters of secrecy, which more and more has become a crucial concern about nuclear energy policy-making.

This is a significant trend in the nuclear energy controversy, and it reached its peak not long ago. The public outcry about the Three Mile Island accident and the secretive way in which it was initially handled by the industrial groups involved and the Nuclear Regulatory Commission marked the peak of the controversy. This public outcry was repeated following the Chernobyl accident and the secretive way in which it was initially handled by Soviet bureaucrats.[19] It has finally dawned on people that experts and committee members may not know what they are doing after all, or may not be as trustworthy as they were supposed to be. The reliability, if not the good faith, of the U.S. nuclear industry and of the government officials in charge of overseeing it has become increasingly questioned.

This growth in public skepticism has resulted from technocratic policy-making and one of such policy-making's main concerns: preserving national security and keeping nuclear energy matters out of politics through secrecy. This concern conflicts with various public concerns, such as the need for safety, enlightened publicity about nuclear matters, and national security that is preserved through public participation, not mystery—through democracy, not technocracy. The feeling among wide sectors of the public has gone beyond merely wanting to be informed. Significant numbers of people now want to have influence on both nuclear and technology policy-making in general.

These conflicting concerns in the U.S. nuclear energy controversy have underlain the controversy through the years. Yet, as the preceding sections indicate, they have never been squarely addressed through participatory channels. That these conflicts are still with us explains the recurrence and intermittent virulence of the controversy. That they have never been square-ly addressed through participatory channels explains why they are still with us. And they are likely to keep on leading people to engage in the controversy unless something is done about them in a more participatory, more fully democratic way.

PUBLIC PARTICIPATION IN TECHNOLOGY POLICY-MAKING

The nuclear energy controversy points to some basic practical implications for policymakers. First, the fact that the controversy has so far been intractable is an important reason for policymakers to address the societal fact of this controversy fairly and squarely and do something about it. And second, since a concern with secrecy and the traditional centralization and attempted depoliticization of nuclear policy-making is at the core of the controversy, nuclear policy-making about nuclear energy should be more participatory, not technocratic.

There are at least three reasons for these theses. First, as the history of the controversy makes plain, it is unrealistic to expect policy-making to succeed without such participation. Instead, it is likely to lead to recurrences of the controversy that are likely to be wider in scope and increasingly disruptive, if not destabilizing, both politically and economically.

A second reason for more public participation is epistemological. Sound technology policy-making requires policymakers to know as many of the concerns involved as circumstances permit them to know. This, of course, is not to say that all concerns should always be taken into account before making policy. As argued in previous essays, lack of time and means, as well as political pressures, often make it necessary to decide before all the information is in. But there is no good reason not to acquire information that is attainable. As John Stuart Mill said:

> The only way in which a human being can make some approach to knowing the whole of a subject is by hearing what can be said about it by persons of every variety of opinion, and studying all modes in which it can be looked at by every character of mind. No wise man ever acquired his wisdom in any mode than this; nor is it in the nature of human intellect to become wise in any other.[20]

This points to a third, ethical reason for a participatory approach. Morally speaking, policy-making should be sensitive to the various concerns involved, but such sensitivity is impossible without adequate knowledge of these concerns and the reasons prompting them. The previous outline of the nuclear energy controversy's history evidences that such knowledge and sensitivity have been inadequate. Hence, greater public participation should be brought to bear in the policy-making process.

Of course, what is to be done in the United States is not the same as what should be done in other countries whose policy-making circumstances are different (indeed, it must and ought to be quite different). In any case, unless the various concerns about nuclear energy are addressed in a participatory way, policy-making will disregard circumstances that are both morally and politically central. Hence, it will be hopelessly and unjustifiably introducing policy in a political and moral vacuum.

Concerns, like ideas, have histories that give them their political and moral force. Those discussed above have the force gained through their long-standing appeal since the 1940s. Policy-making that disregards such concerns—for example, by seeking merely short-term solutions—is unlikely to succeed in addressing the recurrent nature of the nuclear energy controversy. The question is: What is likely to succeed?

ETHICS, POLITICS, AND NUCLEAR TECHNOLOGY: WHAT TYPE OF PUBLIC PARTICIPATION?

The history of the U.S. nuclear energy controversy makes it plain that policy-making about nuclear energy in this country has never been a detached activity, taking place in a political and moral vacuum. Like much policy-making about new technologies, it is subject to the demands of interest groups, the constraints of law and implementation, and criticism of the technology assessment efforts it involves. Indeed, not even technology assessment is free from these demands, constraints, and criticisms. Yet questions remain even after granting that technocratic approaches are politically unsound and morally impermissible, and that a more participatory approach to technology policy-making should be adopted. For one: What type of participation should this be?

THE SCIENCE COURT PROPOSAL

One prominent proposal regarding public participation in technology policy-making is that of the science court. It was made in "The Science Court Experiment: An Interim Report," authored by the Task Force of the Presidential Advisory Group on Anticipated Advances in Science and Technology. According to it, the court members would be competent, impartial scientists from disciplines adjacent to the subject of a particular dispute— that is, their discipline would not be involved in the dispute. The court members would hear testimony on the various sides of an issue and would report their findings on the scientific facts at issue. In addition, the court's proceedings would have three stages. First, the court would identify the scientific and technological—not the ethical, political, and policy— questions associated with an issue. Second, scientist-advocates would engage in adversary proceedings, very much like those in a court trial, presided over by the said impartial judges. Third, the judges would decide what the scientific facts concerning the issue actually are.[21]

The science court idea never went beyond the proposal stage. The Task Force was dissolved when President Carter took office. But the idea has elicited a great deal of discussion. One of the criticisms formulated against it is that of Alex Michalos. He argues that the proposal involved the untenable epistemological assumption that facts can be clearly separated from values.[22] However, he believes that this assumption does not damage the proposal, because the fact-value distinction is not crucial for the court's purposes. That is, he has no quarrel with the remaining features of the science court proposal.

K. S. Shrader-Frechette has criticized Michalos's critique because, except for the fact that it treats all findings as value laden, it leaves the basic structure of the court intact.[23] This, she argues, would lead to overemphasis on facts and domination by experts. To be sure, Michalos was aware of this objection, and he addresses it by presenting two counterarguments. First, regarding overemphasis on facts, he says that the court will not overemphasize facts because it will deal with value-laden matters. Second, about domination by experts, he says that ordinary citizens cannot be expected to pass good judgment on purely technical considerations such as the court deals with.

Shrader-Frechette questions the validity of this response on the grounds that its counterarguments undercut each other. According to her, Michalos cannot have it both ways: The considerations either are or are not purely technical. Indeed, given Michalos's view that the fact-value distinction is untenable, he cannot consistently say that any considerations are purely technical.[24] This criticism is well taken only if characterizing considerations as purely technical entails that they are purely factual. Michalos, however, might respond that the considerations are purely technical in the sense that they involve specialized knowledge, but this does not make them purely factual. They are predicated on the (hardly questionable) evaluative presupposition that public opinion is irrelevant for establishing such matters as "whether or not saccharin is carcinogenic."[25]

Without a defense along the lines just indicated, Michalos must give up the view that some considerations are purely technical. Yet, as Shrader-Frechette correctly points out, he can still say, as he does, that the court, though made up exclusively of scientists, will not overemphasize facts because it will deal with value-laden matters. In fact, he adds, other societal and governmental groups will also be dealing with the evaluative aspects of the issues treated by the court.

This leads to Shrader-Frechette's main criticism of Michalos's position. She criticizes it on the grounds that "the court likely would add merely to the proliferation of opinion on an issue, rather than to a final conclusion regarding it."[26] To avoid overemphasis on the factual aspects of issues without opening the door to the mere proliferation of opinion, Shrader-Frechette suggests a promising expansion of the court's subject matter. It would "address the major social-political-ethical-scientific facets of current controversies over technology, and not just the scientific aspects." The "court could address questions like 'how safe is safe enough?' and not merely questions like 'how safe is this particular technology?'"[27] In addition, she argues that if such an extension is reasonable, so is the inclusion of ordinary citizens among the juries. Her label for this modified version of the science court is the "technology tribunal."[28]

THE TECHNOLOGY TRIBUNAL

Shrader-Frechette's arguments in support of the technology tribunal are largely arguments in support of participatory rather than technocratic policy-making about technology. I sympathize with the participatory thrust of her position and, as the arguments I have previously offered indicate, I have no quarrel with most of them. But a question arises: Do her arguments specifically support the technology tribunal proposal, or do they simply support policy-making through the legislative branch of government?

One might object that the technology tribunal seems open to the same objection Shrader-Frechette formulated against Michalos's view. It "likely would add merely to the proliferation of opinion on an issue, rather than to a final conclusion regarding it."[29] Although the tribunal would expand the court's subject matter and membership, it would not diminish the occasions for opinions to proliferate. At best, it would make it possible for them to proliferate within the tribunal rather than in society at large.

In accordance with Shrader-Frechette's concern for achieving closure on issues, one might respond that, in any case, something would be gained from the tribunal arrangement. So long as its proceedings would come to an end through a jury's vote, a decision would be reached. And the fact that it was reached through a process that paid due attention to the views at issue would make it democratic and lend some legitimacy to the decision reached. To be sure, this does not cut down on opinion proliferation, but it shifts the emphasis from opinions to decisions. The final conclusion to be reached is a decision, not an opinion, since a decision procedure such as voting is involved.

Of course, if a final conclusion concerning an issue is supposed to be a well-established opinion shared by the tribunal members, the above suggestion will not do. But one may defend such a suggestion on the grounds that it is the decision's legitimacy, not its being based on such an agreed-upon opinion, that is politically and ethically crucial concerning technology policy-making.

There is a great deal of truth in the position just stated. In addition, it exemplifies a fact discussed in previous essays: that policy-making decisions are not simply and univocally based on individual judgments. They are reached through social decision procedures that, besides judgment and critical scrutiny, often involve a variety of social interactions, some of which make little room for judgment. Yet none of this suffices to establish the legitimacy of the technology tribunal, which is what is in question. Like the court system, the technology tribunal would contribute to issue- and, specifically, court-overload, a development likely to undermine rather than further democratic policy-making.

ISSUE-OVERLOAD AND DISJOINT POLICY-MAKING

Issue-overload is a situation in which issues are so many, complex, or intractable that they exceed, or nearly exceed, what ordinary individuals can understand and ordinary societies can handle through the courts, legislation, or executive or other institutional channels as traditionally set up. The social fact of issue-overload results not only from the number of issues or the speed with which new ones develop but also from addressing the issues through inadequate and costly institutional channels. In democracies, where public accountability is crucial, it may also result from addressing them through institutional channels that make little, if any, room for this accountability.

In general, frequent mismatches between issues and the procedures used for addressing the policy and decision problems they pose are indicators of issue-overload. When, as a consequence of these mismatches, a crucial social institution, sector, or entire society is politically undermined (e.g., through loss of public acquiescence) or economically destabilized (e.g., through costs the institution, sector, or society cannot afford), issue-overload is present.

This essay has so far evidenced how science and technology have become entangled in controversies in the United States. They have also become entangled in issue-overload through court-overload that is caused partly by the tendency to seek the resolution of scientific and technological matters through the courts. This situation has contributed to increasing public distrust of the court system. Therefore, approaches to science and technology policy-making that are patterned primarily on the court system are a bad idea. Adversarial, court-like approaches are unlikely to gain the trust of a public that distrusts the court system, since they are too much alike.

Such a court-like institution would also undermine the legislative branch of democratic governments. It would have some of the same functions this branch exercises through such channels as congressional hearings and the Office of Technology Assessment. In this regard, Shrader-Frechette points to "the difficulty faced by administrative, regulatory, and legal procedures, all of which are severely limited by the high cost of citizen participation."[30] But this limitation does not apply to the legislative branch as much as to the governmental channels involved in said procedures. Even if it did, it is a reason to concentrate funds on proven policy-making channels to further support citizen participation, not to further diffuse public funds by channeling them into additional, let alone unproven, institutions. From this standpoint, science courts and technology tribunals would be luxuries and, by diffusing public funds, would undermine democratic policy-making.

Of course, private funds could be used to support such courts. But there are additional, noneconomic reasons that the exclusive or primary use of science courts and technology tribunals would undermine democratic policy-making and, in particular, its legislative side. The reasons go back to the notion that court-like proceedings should "achieve closure on a particular controversy" and "be decisive."[31] It is questionable whether court-like procedures are decisive enough to achieve closure on a controversy. And even if they were, it is questionable that such closure would be a good thing. It would leave little if any room for the ongoing nature of policy-making dialogue from which better policies and reform develop.

This, of course, is not to say that no change in the controversies' scope or nature is possible or desirable. But changes for the better need not be, and typically are not, definitive changes.

In defense of the technology tribunal, one could try to drop the closure requirement in order to make room for the ongoing policy-making dialogue. But how? Even if such a thing were possible, it would involve straining the court-like institutions beyond or nearly beyond their capabilities. As indicated, such a mismatch between social decision procedures and the policy and decision problems they are made to address is likely to lead to issue-overload and undermine democratic policy-making.

What is the alternative? Many policy-making channels for dealing with science and technology issues are already in existence. They could be improved and, with the previously mentioned qualifications, others could be added. That is, disjoint policy-making—where the problems are addressed through different policy-making channels, at different levels, and often through mutually independent efforts—may work in many cases. Environmental policy in the United States has largely been made in such a decentralized manner during the 1970s and 1980s.[32] And, by dividing the policy-making labor, issue-overload may be diffused.

What is crucial, however, is to snap out of strictly adversarial thinking without jumping to institute additional policy-making arrangements that overload the system. The legislative process provides one viable alternative. It makes room for a wide range of social decision procedures—from discussion of merits and negotiation to bargaining and compromise. Still other channels (currently used by unions and business firms) make room for mediation, arbitration, and other social decision procedures. This largely decentralized but parsimonious approach to policy-making can be more sensitive than strict court-like approaches or, for that matter, than a simply legislative approach to the varied and ongoing nature of technology policy-making.

No doubt, the legislative process itself—or the described combination of policy-making arrangements and procedures—could lead to issue-overload and get bogged down by the sheer proliferation of opinions. This is where the hypotheses formulated previously in this book can help. When issue-overload is present or impending, time and policy-making simplification become of the essence. In such a case, procedures that are moderately confrontational but can cut through the maze (e.g., political insulation) are permissible and may be crucial to address the prospect of issue-overload.

When issue-overload is not present or impending, policies, decisions, and procedures that lead to issue-overload are neither politically sound nor morally permissible. They would lead to more social disruption or limitations on individual freedoms or well-being than more compromising alternatives. For example, neither policy-making by referendum, which has been increasingly fashionable in the United States since the 1970s, nor policies and decisions that promote referendum politics are ordinarily politically sound or morally permissible. Equally unsound and impermissible are those policies, decisions, and procedures that tend to turn legislatures into mere brokerage houses for constituencies' interests and legislators into mere brokers for interest groups. In contrast, politically sound and morally permissible policies, decisions, and procedures are those that are in accordance with a more balanced, measured, diplomatic approach. Unless policy-making proceeds along these lines, the nuclear energy controversy and technology controversies in general will keep on being reborn from their own ashes.

Dialogue

— I'm not convinced that to approach policy-making through a variety of policy-making channels avoids issue-overload any better than the alternatives.

— I have my reservations about it too, but let us review the situation. At least one of the court-like alternatives, the technology tribunal, is promising in some cases. Yet, as I mentioned, it is too inflexible and adversarial from a procedural standpoint. The legislative approach is more flexible, hence more likely to help us deal with many policy-making cases calling for something other than adversarial approaches while avoiding issue-overload. In addition, a variety of other approaches can be used to deal with still other cases. That is, in no way do I mean to say that participation should take place through the legislative branch of government alone. My point is only that other less flexible approaches should not be used to the detriment of the legislative process. But there is no doubt that there are many viable participatory approaches other than the legislative process and that, within the said constraints, they at least deserve a try. The question is which and when? The hypotheses formulated in Essay 8 provide some guidelines to answer this question.

— But couldn't we end up faced with issue-overload anyway?

— Of course. No procedural approach is foolproof against issue-overload, but as I argued in the essay, the said hypotheses also have implications about the manner in which issue-overload should be avoided or curbed. Indeed, diversifying the participatory process through various arrangements that amount to disjoint policy-making may often help curb or prevent issue-overload.

— But not always?

— Not always. There may be some matters, say, the space program, that require more steady, long-range, and unified policy-making than can be attained through a disjoint approach. Also, in crisis situations, when time is of the essence and concerted action is crucial (e.g., concerning the U.S. debt), disjoint policy-making is unlikely to work.

— Isn't that a reason in favor of technocratic rather than participatory policy-making?

— Not at all. It is simply a reason for channeling public participation in a manner that accords with the long-run perspective or urgent and coherent action the case requires, not for eliminating it.

— Even if the legislative branch is well-suited for concentrating public participation, a different problem arises. It is an information and communication problem. How can people sensibly participate in policy-making about such things as the space program and the genome project when they hardly have any idea of the technical details involved? Besides, even those who have an idea (e.g., scientists and technologists) often use concepts and methods that others (e.g., legislators) never use and can hardly translate into their language. What results could one expect from public participation by such disparate groups?

— That is a problem with no simple or easy solution. Let us turn to the next essay, which examines the problem by reference to the various constituencies it involves and affects: scientists, technologists, philosophers, and nonacademicians in various walks of life.

11 Bridging Gaps in Babel: Ethics, Technology, and Policy-Making

Controversies about new technologies are like discussions in more than one language: Everybody mispronounces something and no one entirely masters all meaning. Today, these communication failures are enhanced by the unprecedented extent and increasing pace of worldwide technological developments and their likely double-edged consequences. Modern industrial, agricultural, information, recombinant DNA, health care, nuclear, and aerospace technologies promise a confusing mixture of benefits and harms for humans and nonhumans at the individual, local, regional, national, and even global level. These mixed prospects and the controversies—so sharp and heated that they amount to issues—prompted by the technologies pose difficult and urgent policy-making problems.

These problems cover a wide variety of topics. One is the coating of crops with genetically engineered heat-producing substances to prevent the effects of frost. Another is the extent, pace, and manner of workplace robotization. Still others are the regulation of organ transplants and the placing of weather satellites in geosynchronous orbits above equatorial countries. So new and alien are these topics, and so unfamiliar and varied the languages in which they are discussed by technologists, policymakers, and philosophers, that the situation amounts to a contemporary Babel. Is ethics (the discipline, the branch of inquiry that reflects on morals and mores and seeks to develop theories for addressing problems of right and wrong, good and bad, justified and unjustified) suited for dealing with these technology policy-making problems? In particular, are the scope, methods, concepts, practices, and social organization of ethics suited for addressing such problems? What changes, if any, would be for the better? These are the main questions I address.

In addressing these questions, I argue for six interrelated theses. First, at

181

present, ethics is not well-suited for dealing with technology policy problems. Second, this is so partly because its concepts, methods, and practices are not sufficiently integrated with the concepts, methods, and practices of the technology and policy-making communities and the public at large. Third, developments toward greater integration call for changes in the practices and scope—if not also the language, concepts, and methods—of ethics, at least at the applied technology ethics level. Fourth, greater integration is desirable for all communities involved and society at large. Fifth, there is some—though not much—evidence of change toward such integration among these communities. Sixth, multioccupational approaches to the study and practice of ethics concerning technology offer promise of helping attain greater integration. Before proceeding to argue for these theses, let us clarify the notions of ethics, technology, and technology ethics that I use in the ensuing discussion and have presupposed throughout the book.

ETHICS, TECHNOLOGY, AND TECHNOLOGY ETHICS

What is ethics? The question is loaded with ambiguities. The term *ethics* may mean (1) personal ethics, or a person's morals; (2) group or conventional ethics; (3) a branch of inquiry, or moral philosophy—a critical inquiry about morals and mores; (4) an ethical theory, or a generalized device for formulating, clarifying, and dealing with problems addressed in ethics as a branch of inquiry. When the inquiry seeks to deal soundly with problems that concern matters of technology, it is technology ethics or the ethics of technology. In this essay, I focus on ethics in the branch-of-inquiry sense, especially at the applied level of technology ethics.[1]

As for the sense of *technology* in *technology ethics*, I leave the matter open and discuss a variety of developments that have a claim to being instances of technology. They have such claim if they are considered technological developments by ordinary people, scientists (e.g., anthropologists), and members of the technology community (e.g., engineers). This is a realistic approach, since if technology ethics is to be of any use in addressing problems, it is crucial to develop a conception of technology that is sensitive to the issues and the policy and decision problems they actually pose. Such a conception is not likely to be reliably formulated until the task of addressing the problems has been carried out far and comprehensively enough. As the ensuing discussion makes plain, with regard to carrying out this task, we are very much at the beginning.

With these clarifications in mind, let us first examine the predominant concepts, methods, and practices used in dealing with technology policy problems by the technology, policy-making, and philosophical communities and members of the public at large. The degree of integration between these concepts, methods, and practices will evidence the extent to which ethics can (or cannot) currently help address the problems.

A FRAGMENTED WORLD

MORAL PHILOSOPHERS AND EXPERTS:
A COMMUNICATION GAP

Sylvia Doughty Fries has studied the congressional testimony of 130 "expert" witnesses—most of them influential in the natural and social sciences and engineering in academia and, to a lesser extent, in industry and government—on a series of bills intended to create what eventually became the Office of Technology Assessment. She interpreted the record of their testimony as evidence that the witnesses conceived of technology as expertise or intelligence whose societal predominance was imminent. Many witnesses even saw technology as expertise with "exceptional authority over the definition of 'good' government."[2] This latter claim, Fries argues, jeopardizes a basic presupposition of democratic politics: that a responsible citizenry is a preeminent condition of a free society. My aim here, however, is not to examine this thesis, which is, no doubt, significant. Rather, it is to examine the usefulness of moral philosophy for addressing technology policy problems such as that posed by the said conflict between democracy and technology as expertise. How unique, extensive, and useful are the conceptual and methodological contributions ethics can make?

Philosophers in applied ethics tend to believe that the contributions of ethics can be unique or extensive and, in any case, useful. Ethics can provide greater conceptual clarity, help avoid logical fallacies, convey a better understanding of moral theories and concepts, and prompt critical examination of alternative ethical arguments. And, presumably, these things are likely to help nonphilosophers find better ways of addressing technology topics and problems than they would by ignoring these elements of ethical evaluation.[3]

Now, it is true that ethics practitioners can make these contributions to technology policy-making discussions. But the skills involved in making them are not the prerogative of philosophers, as many technology assessors would be quick to point out. In all fairness, it should be mentioned that some philosophers, for example, Annette Baier and Kai Nielsen, have also acknowledged this point.[4]

In response, one could argue that the point just made establishes only that philosophers are not the only ones capable of making such contributions. It does not establish that philosophers cannot make such contributions better and more extensively than many or even most nonphilosophers. The uniqueness of philosophy's contributions may be gone, but not its usefulness.

However, this usefulness may not be as clear as some might think. For example, why would a better understanding of moral theories and concepts be likely to help nonphilosophers find better ways of addressing technology topics and problems? Whether it does will depend on both how good the theories are and how extensive the understanding of the theories is among assessors. If this understanding is limited, shared by only a few, and influences their analysis, the policy result may be worse, not better. Jon Elster illustrates this type of situation with the following story:

> Once upon a time, two boys found a cake. One of them said, "Splendid! I will eat the cake." The other one said, "No, that is not fair! We found the cake together, and we should share and share alike, half for you and half for me." The first boy said, "No, I should have the whole cake!" Along came an adult who said, "Gentlemen, you shouldn't fight about this: you should compromise. Give him three quarters of the cake."[5]

One could object that the particular solution suggested here, and therefore the principle of compromise, is inadequate and the adult should learn more ethical theory. However, by the very manner in which negotiations aimed at issuing technology policy-making work, compromise is to be reached from the positions advanced. Suppose that, as in the example, only a minority advances a position partly based on crucial elements of moral evaluation, such as taking the good of others into account for its own sake. Not merely compromise but, indeed, arbitration, mediation, and other social decision procedures may then lead to a worse situation than the one that would be reached had all participants advanced less morally imbued positions.

In response, one could argue that the above situation would develop if, as in the previous case, the theories used were simplistic or their users did not understand them well enough. Sometimes, one might explain, adequate ethical theories make it permissible to negotiate with the immediate overriding aim of maximizing the satisfaction of one's own or one's own constituencies' or organizations' interests. This is so when other negotiating parties do it too. Ethical studies of state-of-nature situations characteristically argue for this position.[6]

Such an objection, however, would miss the point. The point is *not* that there are no theories of ethics better suited for dealing with ethical problems concerning technology policy. After all, I have outlined one such theory in the preceding essays. Rather, the point concerns sufficiently widespread understanding and communication. If ethics is to help make better, rather than worse, technology policy (and, indeed, any policy), the understanding of ethical theories must be significantly deep or widespread among technology practitioners and policymakers. Otherwise, as previously argued, there may be situations in which a little knowledge is worse than none at all.

Situations of this type undermine ethics' usefulness in the technology community. As I argue next, its usefulness is also undermined in the policy-making community and among members of the public at large.

MORAL PHILOSOPHERS, POLICYMAKERS, AND THE PUBLIC

Ethical theory illiteracy is widespread not merely in the technology and policy-making communities but among members of the public. Indeed, it is at least as widespread as technology illiteracy among members of the public and, to a lesser extent, the philosophy community.[7] This is not to place the blame on members of these groups for not knowing such things. Illiteracy concerning technology or ethical theory is partly a result of the high complexity and specialization of certain subjects, which has become rampant in the twentieth century. And this development is beyond any one individual's control.

Should one then turn one's back on ethics? Not at all. But the question arises: Is ethics now in a position to contribute enough knowledge of ethical theories, concepts, and methods so that no ill comes from inadequate enlightenment? In addressing this question, I next examine predominant conceptions of technology and attitudes about technological developments and philosophical attempts at integration. They provide evidence for the claim that ethics' concepts, methods, and practices significantly lack integration with the concepts, methods, and practices used in the everyday world in which technology policy problems actually arise. Indeed, they provide evidence for the lack of integration between all the groups involved—not just the philosophical community on the one hand and the technological and policy-making communities, as well as the general public, on the other.

The witnesses in the previously mentioned study do not exhaust the conceptions of technology that have a bearing on the manner in which technology policy problems are addressed. Public conceptions also matter. Some were already common in the nineteenth century. Nonexperts, and even some experts, reflect these conceptions when they think of technology as inventions, devices, or gadgets. Others, more in accord with the seventeenth-century conception, think of technology as the practical arts. Still others think of it as applied science, a notion that has a family resemblance to conceptions of the arts held by Plato, Aristotle, and some Hellenistic writers.[8] This notion is seriously set in question by the current development of superconductors, where technology is taking place before there is any science available to explain it and apply it to the data.[9] And all these conceptions are different from, if not in conflict with, technology as expertise, the notion predominant among the previously mentioned witnesses. To this, one must add a frequent distrust and even fear of some new technologies and technology takeover (discussed in Essay 9) and the fact that workers and unions have a dislike, distrust, and sometimes fear of information systems that they see as threatening their jobs, job status, job-related human companionship, and self-image.[10]

These often conflicting conceptions of, and responses to, new technology contribute to pose the policy and decision problems technology ethics is meant to help address. There have been philosophical contributions toward an approach that articulates ethical, political, and other aspects of problems,[11] and the present book is meant to be a further contribution toward such an approach. But the generalization of this approach has not yet come about. Nor has this work been significantly integrated with discussions in the technology or policy-making communities. It remains highly specialized—however interdisciplinary—and significantly restricted to the world of academia.

As previously indicated, this lack of integration partly results from the degree of complexity and specialization of certain subjects. In turn, such complexity and specialization simply reflect the increasing complexity of technological developments, contemporary governments, and contemporary individual and social life. This complexity is an obstacle to both the public's and the policymakers' understanding of what is at issue—so much so that, in the United States, it led to the creation of the congressional Office of Technology Assessment.[12] That such an office had to be created evidences lack of conceptual and methodological integration not just between the specialized communities involved but also between these and the policy-making community. Today's social world is fragmented—a contemporary Babel.

Nielsen alludes to this fragmentation when he refers to the different jargons of philosophers, lawyers, economists, and others.[13] The fragmentation, however, does not amount simply, as Nielsen's statement appears to imply, to a linguistic or at most conceptual difference. It concerns practices in accordance with which these concepts and methods are used and specialized languages developed. I have provided ample evidence for this sort of fragmentation elsewhere.[14] Here, the point I want to stress concerns familiarity, which practices tend to enhance or hinder. Ethical theory considerations are familiar primarily, if not exclusively, to academic philosophers. They are not familiar to members of the technology or policy-making communities or, for that matter, to the general public.

A MANY-WAY STREET

The sort of situation just described also concerns philosophers' familiarity with the problems as perceived in the technology community. As Carl Mitcham put it, they "still have some way to go to deal with the world as the technical community actually experiences it."[15] This lack of familiarity is not just a matter of methods, such as cost-benefit analysis, or concepts, such as technology management. It also includes matters of practice: what courses of action are, as a rule, perceived as feasible; what economic, political, or other constraints on action are perceived as significant; what considerations are unreflectively perceived as irrelevant or secondary; and what hypotheses are taken for granted in each group.

In addition, this situation is not peculiar to the relation between the philosophy and technology communities. Think of the long-standing and quite accurate objections by policymakers and members of the general public concerning moral philosophers' (or, for that matter, technology practitioners') lack of familiarity with the actual world of politics or business.[16] In short, different, significantly disjoint concepts, methods, and practices are at work in the ways in which the technology, policy-making, and philosophical communities and the general public address ethical problems concerning technology policy.

SOCIAL FRAGMENTATION AS A SOURCE OF CURRENT LIMITATIONS IN ETHICS

The preceding discussion supports this essay's first two theses. For, first, the previously described fragmentation makes it difficult to communicate ethics' contributions in a way that the technology and policy-making communities and the public can readily understand and apply. Second, it is questionable that technology ethics currently has much to offer beyond what logic can offer. The previously described fragmentation hinders ethics from using enough and sufficiently articulated knowledge of the manner in which the technology and policy-making communities experience technology policy and decision problems. This undermines ethics' ability to make substantial, hence significantly useful contributions for dealing with technology policy-making problems. Third, this difficulty in using sufficiently articulated knowledge hinders the testing of ethical theories in actual policy-making situations. All in all, under the previously discussed fragmentation, ethics develops largely in a political and technological vacuum, which makes it of little use of for addressing actual technology policy-making problems.

Can ethics change so as to overcome these limitations? There seem to be no conceptual or methodological obstacles to such change. But the question arises: Is ethics institutionally set up to work toward integration, to fill the gaps between the groups caught in today's Babel? Let us turn to this question.

THE INSTITUTIONAL VIABILITY OF TECHNOLOGY ETHICS: SOME NEEDED CHANGES

Some philosophers have argued for the need to test the applicability of moral theories in the actual contexts in which ethical problems arise. Along these lines, Annette Baier says:

We philosophers, by having given thought, may have help to give, but only if we are willing to investigate (or subcontract the investigation of) the actual results of trying to live by the principles that commend themselves to us in our armchairs and debating halls.[17]

This is true. Suppose, however, that the previously discussed conceptual, methodological, and practical integration never comes to pass. It will then be quite unlikely that such investigation can take place, that its results can be effectively understood and communicated, and that the contributions of the theories surviving the investigation can be put to work.

To be sure, moral philosophers could still play consulting or advisory roles in other professions. Indeed, the very fact that they play these roles now, when they did not a few decades ago, is evidence of change toward greater practical, if not conceptual, and methodological integration between the groups involved. However, the question is whether they play relevant or necessary roles *as philosophers*. In this regard, Arthur Caplan describes one of his contributions to hospital practice (he suggested that physicians making rounds wait until patients have finished using a bedpan before they and their attendants gaze upon the patients), and notes that a Ph.D. in philosophy is hardly necessary to make this suggestion.[18]

One could respond that moral philosophy would nonetheless benefit from moral philosophers engaging in consulting or advisory activities outside academia. At least, as Annette Baier says, it "might help us to escape from the arrogance of solitary intellect which has condemned much moral theory to sustained self-delusions concerning its subject matter, its methods, and its authority."[19]

I have no doubt that this would benefit moral philosophy. But why would it benefit other communities involved, or society at large? One reason is pragmatic. Most people, busy pursuing the pressing concerns of their everyday lives, must often put complex, sometimes highly theoretical, ethical problems aside. One of these problems is that of running society by appeal to reliable theories that encompass and integrate technological, economic, political, and ethical concepts and methods. Otherwise, technology policies and decisions will be based only on such methods as muddling through, poking in the dark, and trial and error. And in today's complex and rapidly evolving technological world, these methods are too ad hoc to deal with technology policy problems effectively and sensitively. Traditionally, moral philosophy, in contrast with other branches of inquiry such as economics and political science, has formulated such comprehensive theories. This makes it especially fit for contributing the needed theories, *so long as it bridges the testing gap by becoming empirical.* If it does, the technological and policy-making communities, and the general public, would benefit.

Bridging the testing gap in the manner suggested, however, requires (in accordance with the essay's third thesis) an expansion of the scope and practices of technology ethics beyond not just the discipline but academia. Otherwise, the theories—tested only by philosophers' armchair appeals to their individual thought experiments or arguments, or by their discussions with other philosophers in the rarefied halls of academia—remain mere sets of hypotheses. Some of the changes internal to philosophy that the preceding discussion entails have been mentioned, for example, by Kai Nielsen. He writes:

> I want to suggest that there may be a way that philosophy might transform itself in a way that would answer to our unschooled reflective hopes. It would involve (a) giving up all pretensions to autonomy and instead interlocking philosophy fully with the human sciences and (b) taking the resolution of the problems of human life to be very centrally a part of philosophy's reasons for being.[20]

As far as it goes, this is sound doctrine. Yet, given the preceding discussion's partial conclusions, it does not go far enough. If, as in Nielsen's vision, the problems of human life are to become central, the suggested interlocking must involve not just the social sciences but the nonacademic world as well. In addition, as I argue next, this interlocking that encompasses the nonacademic world is unlikely (because the methodological and conceptual integration of the groups involved is unlikely), so long as the social organization of moral philosophy—in particular, of technology ethics— remains unchanged.

TOWARD A MULTIOCCUPATIONAL APPROACH

The interlocking between philosophy, the human sciences, and the public requires changes in the social organization of ethics. It requires at least an expansion of its activities outside of the discipline itself and, indeed, outside of academia. This requirement, however, is in conflict with some of the institutional constraints produced by the support systems of ethics (e.g., philosophy departments and ethics journals) and by the analogous support systems of the other branches of inquiry involved. They sometimes seem to boil down to mere conflicts of academic turf. Other times, they are a matter of allocating resources on the basis of criteria developed from a traditional, merely disciplinary, perhaps not even applied approach to academia. Still other times, the conflicts appear to be also, or mainly, a matter of disciplinary loyalties. And they may also result purely and simply from the difficulty of conceiving of technology policy problems by means of concepts and methods other than those of one's own discipline. If the previously discussed integration is to be attained, and moral philosophy as envisioned by Annette Baier or Kai Nielsen is to develop, all these things must change.

To argue for these changes is not to say that basic research in ethics and the current organization of such research must change. Nor is it to say that everyone doing applied ethics or, more narrowly, technology ethics must start doing things differently. Rather, it is to say that technology ethics—and, perhaps, applied ethics generally—must undergo some changes—at least some extensions—as a collective enterprise. Indeed, the needed changes are significantly theoretical and include a conceptually integrated formulation, clarification, and evaluation of policy and decision alternatives in dealing with technology policy problems. This must be a collective result from a collective, multioccupational, activity—not the privileged subject of any one philosophy researcher, technology practitioner, or policymaker. Nor can it be the privileged subject of any one discipline, profession, or occupation.

The fact that technology policy is not the privileged subject of any such sector points to a second reason that the previously discussed integration is unlikely unless the social organization of technology ethics changes. To proceed toward such integration, it is necessary to combine *in actual practice* the perspectives of academicians studying ethics and technology, policymakers, practitioners of technology—from engineers to health care and agricultural technologists—and the general public.

Granted, some if not all of the problems cannot even be formulated without the methods of the disciplines involved. Think, for example, of global environmental problems such as those posed by atmospheric carbon dioxide and chlorofluorocarbons. In order to help make sound technology policy, these methods cannot be applied only within the narrow scope of each discipline or, indeed, within the mainstream of existing interdisciplinary approaches, which combine disciplines but do not ordinarily include nonacademic participants. Nor can only policymakers be included in addition to academics. Ethical problems concerning technology policy arise and are directly felt outside the scope of academia and policy-making alone. They are felt in hospitals, factories, technology-related firms, and society at large. Hence, without somehow including all these constituencies, they are unlikely to be addressed in a manner sensitive to all concerns involved. Some of these concerns may fall through the conceptual and methodological cracks reflected in the languages of ethics, or of some combination of academic disciplines alone, or merely of politics, or of the technology community, or of all these but not the general public.

If the problems are real, however, they will be addressed, well or not, by people anyway, with or without the help of aloof academicians or busy technologists. But there is good reason to believe that policymakers—

however involved in the process—or the general public—however literate it may become about technology—will not have enough time or perhaps sufficient wisdom to make all other contributions unnecessary. The essay's fourth thesis follows.

What forms should the multioccupational approach take? Some have been tried on a limited basis in health care ethics, for example, through hospitals' ethics committees (which supports the fifth thesis). Though still largely under scrutiny, they can provide the beginnings of a model for addressing ethical problems concerning technology in areas other than health care. The multioccupational approach, however, need not be implemented through technology ethics committees alone. For example, the technology tribunal discussed in Essay 10 may be more appropriate in certain circumstances.

In any case, the development of such committees in health care offers instructive evidence of likely conflicts as well as ways of dealing with them. They concern the process of selecting participants; the perceived incompatibilities between disciplinary loyalties or personal styles; academicians' fears of being co-opted by representatives of government, industry, or labor; their uneasiness about becoming entangled in conflicts between government, industry, or labor factions; and the unwillingness on the part of practitioners to subject their practices to academic or public judgment.[21]

Such conflicts have occurred and should be expected. Ethical inquiry, especially in the highly institutionalized environment in which it is pursued today, is not an apolitical, let alone neutral, activity. In this politically charged environment, squarely acknowledging and addressing such conflicts is crucial if we are to have any chance of dealing sensitively and effectively with the pressing problems posed by technological developments in our turbulent times.

Another positive feature of the multioccupational approach is that, if adopted, philosophers will not have to choose, as Annette Baier puts it, "between being pretend accountants, pretend lawyers, pretend revolutionaries, failed priests, and unsuccessful comics."[22] This also goes for other disciplines if their practitioners by and large lack live contact with the business, political, technological, and, in general, social world. At any rate, in accordance with the essay's sixth thesis, multioccupational approaches would help moral philosophy develop the earthiness that Hume recommended for philosophers and tried to develop himself by becoming a real diplomat and historian, and that Dewey attempted to develop in the twentieth century.[23]

In the earthier multioccupational approach, philosophers join—partly as philosophers and on an equal footing with academicians and nonacademicians—in policy- and decision-making outside academia. No doubt, adopting such an approach will involve many changes, not the least of which is the development, by way of support systems, of multioccupational technology ethics committees, centers, and programs. In this area, almost everything, including a thorough discussion of this very suggestion, is still to be done. The science, technology, and society centers developed worldwide constitute a precedent (although I must admit, a somewhat faltering one), mostly at the merely interdisciplinary, largely academic level.[24] Would moving beyond this boundary, into the nonacademic word, jeopardize technology ethics? The ensuing discussion addresses this question.

BETWEEN KNOWLEDGE AND IDEOLOGY

Some may think that multioccupational approaches will not work in many technology-related environments or will compromise the disciplines or academia. In response, one can say, first, that whether it will work is not an a priori but an empirical matter. Second, one can point out that the reticence and skepticism about moving beyond disciplinary, let alone academic, boundaries have typically come from academia, not from nonacademic environments. Third, one can offer a pragmatic argument: Though there is no guarantee that the suggestion will work, if we believe that it will not work, its chances of working are minimal or nil. In addition, the alternative for technology ethics (and perhaps for many other applied ethics branches of inquiry) is to fade away, ending perhaps in academic extinction and no doubt in its failure to carry out one of its central functions: to help deal soundly with ethical problems as they arise in the actual world.[25]

There are, of course, risks in taking this line, and it should not be taken incautiously. Technology ethics could lead to the development of a social elite, technology ethicists, who might come to be seen by themselves and others as moral experts: individuals with special insight into right, wrong, good, bad, justified, and unjustified on matters of technology. Such a development would undermine morality. It would tend to disqualify necessary persons from fully engaging in critical scrutiny concerning ethical problems and issues. This, in addition, could compound the undermining of morality if, as a result, some constituencies treated these professionals as high priests of morality, or if the professionals became corporate or technocratic rubber-stampers.

A related danger is that the theories developed in technology ethics and moral philosophy in general would be mere ideologies of technology ethicists and given societal sectors. However, the danger can be curtailed if moral philosophy becomes interlocked with the social sciences and the reflections of common life *without exceptions or exclusions*. This will provide a scientific as well as ordinary basis for assessing the extent to which the theories, and the explanations and descriptions they involve, are true rather than mere ideological distortions.

No doubt, after all is said and done, multioccupational approaches to technology ethics may have to be discarded. But at this point in the development of ethics, they deserve a good try. They are promising, and the need to bridge the gaps between crucial policy-making groups in our fragmented world is urgent. If they are not bridged, technology ethics and, indeed, human societies may not amount to more than the remains of Babel: ruins witnessing humans' failure to rise above their fragmented times.

Dialogue

— I cannot but feel dizzy as a result of the multiple ways in which policy-making problems could be addressed. I understand that this goes along with your support of disjoint policy-making for certain purposes. Yet I'm afraid that such an approach will lead to more, not less, social fragmentation, which is one thing your multioccupational approach is supposed to help us curb. It will do so through the sheer multiplication of ethics committees, science courts, technology tribunals, technology committees, and whatnot. People involved in one of these groups are unlikely to be able to be involved in many more. As a result, the languages, concepts, methods, and practices shared by the members of one group may well become quite different from those shared by members of other groups. How would this be an improvement?

— First, if the groups' members are from a wide variety of relevant professions, jobs, political constituencies, and policy-making organizations, then each group is likely to receive roughly the same overall input. Besides, I never said that members of one group should not try to communicate with those of another. They could.

— Yes. But would they be more likely to succeed than under the current circumstances?

— One should not minimize the fact that the people we are talking about, given the multioccupational membership of each committee, would share roughly the same input and would have engaged in critical scrutiny about it within their groups. As a result, they would be likely to communicate with members of other groups much more easily than in the present circumstances, even if these other people have different social backgrounds. Through the process, a common ground is likely to have been found or, to some extent, created.

— Yet how much of a common ground would have been produced? Would it be enough to have a common plan? If not, how could policymakers mount a coherent attack on a problem?

— There is no certainty that, invariably, there will be enough common ground to deal with a problem in such a manner. But, as I argued previously, this is a virtue, not a defect of the proposed approach, so long as there is no impending crisis and time does not become of the essence. Remember that the disjoint approach I am proposing need not—indeed, is unlikely to—work in such extreme situations. But if there is time and no impending crisis, what would be the advantage of policies or decisions that are coherent but fail to preserve significant public insights and responses by disregarding them for the sake of coherence? As I argued concerning rational choice, social choice, and related theories at the book's outset, such approaches are both politically unwise and immoral.

— Is your position, then, that appeals to reason and meaningful dialogue are required so long as there is no crisis, but as soon as there is one, anything goes? In other words, do you agree that all is fair in love and war?

— That is not my position at all. Even within crisis or near crisis situations, there is a great deal that appeals to reason and meaningful dialogue can accomplish. What happens is that, in such situations, the scope of application of such appeals and dialogue is significantly restricted.

— How does that work?

— I think it will be best for me to give you an example. It will be, like some that I have already given you, an extended example. This is the overall purpose of my next essay.

12 Between Negotiation and Combat: Ethics, Politics, and Regional Wars in a Fluid World Order

Against nearly all expectations, the cold war appears to have ended sometime around 1990. Yet, despite initial optimism, world peace is not on the horizon, as Iraq's August 2, 1990, invasion and annexation of Kuwait made plain.[1] The cold war world order is unraveling, facilitating a variety of regional, nationalistically charged, and internationally significant conflicts. Most dramatic among these are events in Eastern Europe: the rebellion of Lithuania, Estonia, Latvia, Ukraine, and Georgia against the ex-Soviet Union; the generalized democratization of Eastern Europe; the advent of a unified Germany; and the unraveling of Yugoslavia and consequent war in the region.[2] What role should negotiation, bargaining, and other social decision procedures, including combat, play in dealing with these conflicts? This is the main question I address.

I focus on the changing international situation in the 1980s and 1990s and the type of international conflicts that characterize it. One such conflict is the 1990–91 Persian Gulf crisis, which I use as a case exemplifying and giving support to the four theses I present. First, from a historical and political standpoint, the 1990–91 Persian Gulf crisis evidences not just the unraveling of the cold war order or its effects on the ex-Soviet Union and its client states (Iraq was, to some extent, one of them) but also the fluid state of international order in the Western world. Second, from a moral standpoint, a country or group of countries with the moral and political authority—and the power—to redress the wrongs of international aggression by using military force still has an obligation to seek meaningful negotiations aimed at resolving the conflict. That is, the negotiations to be sought should address

196

the interests and demands involved as fairly and comprehensively as circumstances (e.g., time, knowledge, and available resources) permit. Third, this obligation is present throughout the entire conflict, though its discharge does not invariably require that the country cease hostilities to seek meaningful negotiations. Fourth, military responses to aggression are justified only if, as far as circumstances permit, they are likely to avoid harming civilians of any country, creating political or economic instability in nonaggressor countries, and bringing about any conditions that would further undermine world peace.

The moral and political significance of all these theses in the latter part of the twentieth century is a matter of political prudence and moral sensitivity. From a political standpoint, the efforts made toward attaining a meaningfully negotiated solution throughout a conflict—not just in the conflict's aftermath, but during the conflict as well—are crucial to whether or not world peace is further undermined. And from a moral standpoint, the failure to seek a meaningful negotiated solution is simply to be unduly nonchalant and insensitive about the injuries and loss of lives combat involves.

A POST–COLD WAR MANIFESTATION OF THE FLUID STATE OF INTERNATIONAL ORDER IN THE WEST

The cold war world order was largely based on a balance of power between the Western allies led by the United States and the Eastern bloc countries led by the Soviet Union. In such a context, regional armed confrontations took two main forms: those that directly involved a superpower, such as the United States in Korea and Vietnam and the Soviet Union in Afghanistan; and those that involved only a superpower's regional allies or groups. For example, Iraq was a U.S. regional ally during the Iraq-Iran war; Cuba was a Soviet ally in the armed conflict in Angola. These allies fought their wars with the support of unweakened superpowers whose interests they furthered.[3]

Given this characterization, at least four features of the 1990–91 Persian Gulf crisis provide evidence of a different and quite fluid international order in the Western world. First, the economically weakened condition of one of the Western superpowers, the United States, facilitated it. Second, the United States' policy inadequacies, largely developed in cold war circumstances, also fueled the conflict. Third, the countries most prominently involved in the conflict (the United States and Iraq) were recent allies. Fourth, a third world country challenged one of the leading world powers on largely nationalistic—not superpower—political grounds, raising the prospect of radical changes in the Middle East balance of power and the Western world. Let us see what evidence there is for saying that these features were present.

First, at the beginning of the crisis, the United States, however strong, was economically weaker than in previous decades. Various facts evidenced this weakness. Its national deficit had reached nearly inconceivable proportions. Corporate profits had been declining since the fourth quarter of 1988. Almost half of its states reported revenue collections equal to or below the inflation rate. The auto and housing markets were depressed. In addition, foreign oil was more crucial to the soundness of its economy than ever before. Indeed, during the first six months of 1990, 49.9 percent of the oil used in the United States was imported, in contrast with 36 percent in 1973 and 45 percent in 1979. To be sure, only 3 to 4 percent of this amount came from Iraq. But 9 percent of worldwide oil production came from Iraq and Kuwait together. And this amount was greater than the 7 percent supply drop the International Energy Agency traditionally used as a trigger to schedule a coordinated drawdown to curb skyrocketing international oil prices and prevent serious shortages. In any case, to face up to such shortages, the United States now had a Strategic Petroleum Reserve created in response to the 1973–74 oil embargo. This reserve was supposed to provide supplies for up to ninety days in case of an emergency.[4]

Second, U.S. foreign policy in the Middle East, developed during the cold war, had focused on the conflicts between Israel and the Arab countries considered as a unit. This was totally inadequate for realistically addressing the conflict between Iraq and Kuwait. In addition, once the crisis erupted, the United States' traditional foreign policy in the region reasserted itself. The United States refused to link Iraq's withdrawal from Kuwait to the promise of a conference on the Middle East that would address the Palestinian question. It also refused to take the position that it might consider such a conference if Iraq withdrew from Kuwait. In addition, as I discuss later, it refused to take any favorable stand on promises from other countries—the ex-Soviet Union for one—that they would make strong efforts toward arranging such a conference if Iraq withdrew from Kuwait.[5]

Third, the central countries in conflict, Iraq and the United States, were recent allies. In fact, in accordance with cold war rules, the United States had supported and contributed to arm Iraq in its 1980s war against Iran.[6]

Fourth, a third world country challenged one of the leading world powers on largely nationalistic grounds, raising the prospect of radical changes in the Middle East balance of power and in the Western world. That superpower politics was not significantly involved is confirmed by the November 18, 1990, Paris Conference on Security and Cooperation in Europe. It made plain that the cold war had ended and superpower politics was nonexistent. Primarily mediatory behavior by the Soviets during the conflict further confirmed it.[7]

Iraq's grounds for engaging in the conflict were not prompted by superpower politics but were largely nationalistic. This does not rule out the existence of other grounds, however. For one, Iraq charged that Kuwait had stolen billions of dollars worth of oil from fields on the Iraq-Kuwait border during the war with Iran. Also, just before its invasion of Kuwait, Iraq made territorial claims on Bubyian and Warba, two islands in the Persian Gulf. But despite all this, wider nationalistic grounds appeared to be involved. After all, Saddam Hussein had campaigned to restore Babylon to its former glory, and he continuously alluded to Nebuchadnezzar, the sixth-century B.C. ruler whose empire stretched from India to Palestine. All this points to an overall nationalistic attempt at making Baghdad the center of political and cultural influence in the Arab world.[8]

THE POLITICS OF SELF-DECEPTION

It is hardly questionable that Iraq's policies aimed at cultural and political hegemony belong with the politics of self-deception. No doubt, its eight-year war against Iran and its eventual victory meant that the skill and strength of its military were not to be discounted. But having developed one of the most powerful military forces in the world was only a minor step toward hegemony in the Arab world, given that Egypt and Syria were no minor powers. At any rate, such hegemonic dreams are significant because they affected Iraq's ability and willingness to negotiate.

In a somewhat analogous manner, the United States' approach to the crisis had some signs of self-deception, partly based on the assumption that the old world order had broken down only in the Eastern bloc. This is not to say that a pax Americana was expected, but a new and better world order in which the United States and other Western democracies would play a leading role was thought to be just around the corner before the Persian Gulf conflict. President Bush mentioned it in his August 8 address about the conflict, and again during his January 16 announcement that the war had begun.[9] This self-delusion partly explains the United States' increasingly and narrowly aggressive stand.

This stand, however, is also partly explained by a psychological assumption that it apparently involved. It appears to have been assumed that if Saddam Hussein were faced with a sufficiently serious military threat, he would back off. After all, he wanted to survive. Evidence that this assumption was at work is provided by the recurrent explanation President Bush gave of Hussein's failure to comply with the various United Nations resolutions: that Hussein had not got the message, or that he had not understood the consequences of failing to comply. In fact, this assumption was apparently shared by those who argued that economic sanctions should be given more time to work. Both sides of the policy debate appeared to hold the belief that, when faced with extreme hardship—whether military or economic—Hussein would (1) give up so as not to suffer defeat and possibly death, (2) give up so that his people would not have to suffer to the bitter end, or (3) be ousted by powerful groups unwilling to undergo such suffering.

Expecting things to work out this way was also self-delusional. First, it assumed that Saddam Hussein or some powerful group in Iraq would simply want to avoid suffering, defeat, or death. But this had been declared a holy war by Hussein himself, so he does not seem to have been all that concerned with mere survival. A more plausible interpretation is that he wanted to either survive in a manner that gave him a sense of dignity in the Arab world or die with dignity. Many Iraqis who had the power to overthrow him probably felt the same way: They would rather suffer, even die, with dignity in the eyes of other Arabs than give up. As it was clearly stated by the P.L.O representative to Great Britain on January 19, ideas cannot be killed; they survive the destruction of institutions upholding them.[10]

Second, the significance that Saddam Hussein attached to dealing with the conflict in a manner that attained him dignity in the Arab world was connected with strategic matters. To survive with such dignity, or at least keep his version of the Arab cause alive, Saddam Hussein only needed to stand up to the United States and its Persian Gulf coalition. As evidenced by the aftermath of Arafat's defeat in Lebanon, defeated leaders are unlikely to lose their political power in Arab nations. Instead, they may gain stature in the eyes of their people. Hence, even if defeated, Saddam Hussein would have achieved his purpose had he survived and had his forces withstood the attack for any length of time. If he died, his cause would have gained, not lost, momentum among his followers.

It took very little for Saddam Hussein to enhance his ascendance and promote his cause through martyrdom. He was likely to be able to withstand the attack for a while and survive it, hence achieving Arab dignity. In other words, Saddam Hussein had the political upper hand. A sheer show of force or economic sanctions aimed only at his early unconditional withdrawal were bound to fail. In fact, they made meaningful negotiations aimed at averting the war impossible. Was U.S. public opinion supportive of this approach? What was the role of third countries in dealing with the crisis?

PUBLIC OPINION, A CHANGING WORLD ORDER, AND THE 1990–91 PERSIAN GULF CRISIS

During the Persian Gulf crisis, such countries as France, other members of the European Community, and the Soviet Union provided a moderating influence, as did the United Nations. To be sure, soon after the Iraqi invasion of Kuwait, the UN Security Council unanimously condemned

Iraq, calling for the immediate and unconditional withdrawal of its troops. Soon afterwards, it approved mandatory sanctions under Chapter 7 of the United Nations Charter, and it kept on passing various pressure-building resolutions. The twelfth and most crucial of these resolutions authorized member states to use all necessary means to implement the previous eleven resolutions and restore peace and security in the area, unless Iraq complied with the resolutions by midnight, January 15, 1991. In addition, it called for the restoration of the Kuwait monarchy.

The resolution, however, said nothing about Iraq's meeting these conditions in exchange for nothing. This left the door open for a consideration of the territorial and economic claims it made in connection with the invasion. It also left the door open for a conference, the promise of a conference, or the promise that some country, for example the Soviet Union, would make a serious effort to arrange a conference about the Middle East conflicts, including the Palestinian question.[11]

As for the U.S. Congress, it was sensitive to public attitudes about the conflict and played a crucial role in slowing down the momentum toward war that had built up by November's end. Indeed, January's congressional support for the president's plan to use military force was hardly unanimous. And the swing votes were largely predicated on the belief that such support of military force would offer the best chance of avoiding war by leading Saddam Hussein to negotiate.[12]

Yet, until a few days after the war had begun, the strongest moderating influence came from public opinion. Significant sectors of the public tended to think of the conflict as a mere fight over oil. Although this was not the whole truth, it led many to question the wisdom of attacking Iraq rather than sticking to the original U.S. objective of simply defending Saudi Arabia against Iraq's threat of invasion. By January 13, 1991, the mood was ambivalent, uncertain, and confused—not all-out in favor of war. This changed when the war began. On January 16, polls indicated that about 73 percent of the U.S. population supported it. On January 18, after the initial exhilaration about the apparent success of the air bombardment, about 86 percent supported the war. In addition, 34 percent supported the further objective that Saddam Hussein leave power altogether.[13]

Despite all this, comparing Saddam Hussein to Hitler or portraying Iraq as a threat to the Western world simply did not work on the U.S. public. People knew that the old world order was gone, and they did not quite trust the executive's application of cold war thinking to this new situation. Nor was the public moved by references to a new world order. Though the cold war world order was gone, no detectable new world order was in place or clearly in the making. In this regard, the politics of self-deception may have found more appeal among some U.S. policymakers than among the public.

This is puzzling, since policymakers were continuously faced with rapid changes in the world order and the United States' position in it.

UNEXPECTED INTERNATIONAL IMPLICATIONS

The 1990–91 Persian Gulf crisis brought about an unexpected rearrangement of international forces. The United States became an ally of Syria and an enemy of Iraq. Great Britain restored ties with Iran. The United States brought the ex-Soviet Union into Middle East discussions. This rearrangement of international forces made the Persian Gulf crisis sharply different from the Korean War, when, after North Korea invaded South Korea, the United Nations also authorized U.S. military intervention. Back then, the United States was politically in control of the process that led to the said authorization; in 1990, the United States was significantly led by the international situation to seek UN support, and received it at great cost. This contrast is evidence that the Persian Gulf crisis was a manifestation of the old world order breakdown in the West.[14] In addition, the specter of nuclear war also loomed—though meekly—on the horizon.[15] This completes the evidence for my first thesis: From a historical and political standpoint, the 1990–91 Persian Gulf crisis evidences not just the unraveling of the cold war order or its effects on the ex-Soviet Union, but also the fluid state of international order in the Western world.

What the preceding discussion does not clarify is why policymakers, most notably President Bush, were inclined to think of the situation as an incipient new world order. Given that they have kept on mentioning it since then, it does not appear to have been simply something they said to gather public support against Saddam Hussein's designs. Yet the evidence did not—nor does it now—indicate a new world order, but simply a fluid situation following the end of the cold war.

Arguably, however, the international situation was an opportunity, a grand opportunity, to make an ideal world of peace a reality. Given this, the perception of a new world order threatened by Saddam Hussein's designs may be best understood as an instance of what William James called "the will to believe." Some, perhaps many, in the U.S. leadership pragmatically believed that a new world order—or at least Western world stability and the United States' and its allies' position in it—was being defended. If they did not believe that, such a new world order had no chance of becoming a reality, and Western world stability would be more undermined than it already was.[16] Were they justified in holding such a belief? Addressing this question sets the stage for a discussion of the remaining theses.

ESCALATION STAGES AND POLICY-MAKING OPTIONS

THE DAMAGE CONTROL STAGE

The start of a war, at least of a contemporary war, does not ordinarily lead to an immediate escalation of the war. For example, in discussing the 1982 South Atlantic war between Argentina and Great Britain (arguably an early manifestation of the cold war order breakdown in the West), Virginia Gamba describes this warfare stage as follows:

> [A]fter crisis interaction between two states—and the failure of crisis management—open warfare starts. Nevertheless, the early stages of a war are fought with moderation and a desire to limit damage. There is still room for negotiation, at least whilst the remnants of deterrence continue to exist. This rationale places emphasis on the control of escalation so that events in the battleground do not overtake any possibilities of a peaceful settlement. At times, when credibility is exceptionally low, a period of open albeit limited warfare tends to encourage rather than prevent a negotiated settlement.
>
> Both parties to a dispute tend to be as cautious about the use of force as they were competitive about the risks they could take during the crisis management.[17]

Open warfare in the Persian Gulf began on January 16, 1991. The coalition's announced strategy was to cause such widespread damage to Iraq's forces that the very possibility of going through this first stage was minimal. This, plus the planned continuous nature of the attack and its initial success—only two coalition planes and their crews were lost, while Iraq's forces were largely paralyzed—made it practically impossible to slow down to evaluate the effects of the initial armed engagements.[18]

One can argue that the search for meaningful negotiations and mediation is possible at any stage. The ex-Soviet Union pressed its own plan on Iraq hours after the UN deadline had passed. It called for Iraq's immediate withdrawal from Kuwait in exchange for the promise that the Soviet Union would make a serious effort to arrange a Middle East peace conference to address regional stability and the Palestinian question. Iraq had apparently been given evidence of international support for the Soviet effort, were it to take place in exchange for Iraq's withdrawal.[19] Yet the successful opening attack created a momemtum toward war that made negotiations unlikely. In fact, on January 17 at around noon, various policymakers at the United Nations announced that the current situation was not one for negotiations.[20]

This, plus the war momentum, plus Iraq's January 18 and 19 missile attacks against Israel's population centers in Tel Aviv and Haifa suggested that, short of Iraqi capitulation, the war would quickly move into a second stage. Such a development would have played into Saddam Hussein's hands.

It would have achieved militarily what he had unsuccessfully tried to achieve politically: a recognition by all participants that the Palestinian question and conflicts with Israel were linked to the Persian Gulf crisis. Yet Israel decided not to retaliate. This behavior was not simply due to the fact that President Bush and Prime Minister Major had urged Israel to show restraint and statesmanship. It was also in Israel's interest not to undermine the coalition. To reduce the risk of further casualties, the United States sent crews to Israel to manage the Patriot missiles capable of neutralizing further attacks. Although Israel had received the missiles in September, its crews were still being trained in Texas.[21] These factors tended to undercut the move toward the second stage. But the question was pressing itself: What roles could negotiation and mediation have in it?

THE LOCAL WARFARE STAGE

The local warfare stage goes beyond damage control. All-out warfare starts, and ground troops play a much more central role than at the opening stage. (So far in the Persian Gulf crisis, however, ground forces were not significantly, if at all, involved in combat.) But even at the local warfare stage, despite the increasingly serious nature of the armed conflict, reason and meaningful dialogue have some role to play through third parties. Such third parties may be able to formulate policy-making options for ending the war. If no such mediation effort is successful, it becomes difficult to avoid the next stage, where the international community at large is affected.

Fears of serious effects on the international community were present early in the Persian Gulf war. If attacked by the United States, Iraq was determined to attack Israel, which would in turn retaliate. If Israel retaliated, Israeli planes might fly over Jordan, which had announced that it would shoot them down. Another likely consequence of Israel's entering the war was that Syria would switch sides. Syria was supporting but was not part of the coalition. Kuwait and Saudi Arabia were unlikely to leave the coalition, and Egypt's President Mubarek vowed that Egypt would stay in it, as did Egypt's ambassador to the United Nations.[22] Yet if things were not contained, there was no telling what other international rearrangements could come about.

The initial crippling of Iraq's offensive facilities put many of these fears at least temporarily to rest, but other complications remained. For one, Soviet military actions in Lithuania shortly before the United Nations' January 15 deadline for Iraq's withdrawal from Kuwait raised doubts about the integrity of the United Nations' anti-Iraq support.[23] This would have been clearly jeopardized if the United States had pressed for sanctions against the ex-Soviet Union. Such a development would have moved the war closer to the next stage. The question arises: What could be achieved through mediation and negotiation at such a stage?

THE WORLD IMBALANCE STAGE

The developments just described make it plain that a crisis such as that in the Persian Gulf can easily escalate in an internationally unsettling manner. In fact, it is questionable whether, at this stage, further war can attain more than negotiation can. For example, even if the fighting had been brought to an end, the territorial and international power conflicts that led to the crisis would not have been resolved. The balance of power in the area, which had been destroyed by Iraq's defeat of Iran, would not have been restored.

In addition, other problems were likely to be added to those posed by the said conflicts. For example, once the war was over, what force should remain in the area? Should it include mainly Arabs? Should it include U.S. forces? For how long? And how should Iraq's development after the war be regulated. Many regional and some world powers were likely to oppose the slightest possibility that Iraq recover the way Egypt did after its late 1960s defeat by Israel, and the way Syria did after its 1982 defeat by Israel.

These were sobering thoughts. Also sobering was the fact that the participants most directly involved in the crisis, Iraq and the United States, were least likely to have the ability to bring it to an end through negotiation. Here, more than at any of the previous crisis stages, the role of third countries and the United Nations was crucial. And so was their role in the postcrisis stages. Yet why should the United States and other coalition members, or Iraq, have paid attention to them? This question involves the essay's remaining theses.

ETHICAL AND PRUDENTIAL IMPLICATIONS OF THE CONFLICT

The remaining theses are ethical and prudential. They focus on the role of various social decision procedures—from negotiation to combat—in dealing with international conflicts. In order to address the matter, I begin by examining the procedures' actual role in the conflict.

NEGOTIATION, THREATS OF COMBAT,
AND ACTUAL COMBAT: A BALANCING ACT

The tendency to seek a military solution has a way of preempting negotiated options. This is what some perceived and feared concerning the Persian Gulf crisis after November 8. At that time, President Bush announced that he was nearly doubling the U.S. force in the gulf and took a more aggressive posture. This move was considered questionable by those who thought that economic sanctions were working, given that only four months had gone by, and twelve to eighteen months were necessary for them to have their supposed effect.[24] Being skeptical about the success of economic sanctions alone, and concerned with bringing about a new world order, the Bush administration sought a quick end to the conflict.

This tendency to seek and expect a rapid military solution often results largely from short-term thinking. It may also be yet another instance of the politics of self-deception, which has invariably led to predictions of rapid victory in the United States or other societies with a higher reliance on technology and faith in it than their opponents. In Korea, General Mac-Arthur predicted (and soon corrected his prediction) that the troops would be home by Christmas 1950. The war ended in 1953. President Johnson predicted that the war in Vietnam would be over in late 1966. It took six more years for U.S. troops to leave Vietnam.[25] And though the first rounds of the 1991 Persian Gulf war pointed to an early end of that conflict, only faith could lead one to be sure of that outcome.

At any rate, the expectation of rapid victory, no doubt borne out by the initial coalition success, had behavioral consequences. It led policymakers to seek a rapid victory, especially when they were moved by the perceived (arguably rightly perceived) justice of their cause. Such perceived just causes have a tendency to desensitize policymakers to the lives lost and the suffering undergone by those who must fight the war for the cause. Whatever the motivation driving toward a primarily military and rapid solution, the crucial policy question was pertinent then and always remains: When, if at all, is military action justified in dealing with the problem posed by a conflict such as that in the Persian Gulf? To answer it, one must consider the long-term as well as the short-term consequences, for the survivors will have to live with the new situation a war invariably creates.

OLD THINKING IN NEW TIMES?

The cold war is over, but cold war thinking and institutions are not. This discrepancy needs to be addressed. First, there is some evidence that the United Nations' mechanisms for collective security and peaceful change are ineffective. This is so even though, in handling Iraq's invasion of Kuwait, the United States sought and was granted the authority by the United Nations to use military force. Thus seeking UN approval was a step in the direction of establishing a new world order, though not necessarily a peaceful one. It did not address the tendency Anthony C. Arendt describes as "the legitimation of force based on the 'justice' of the cause."[26] In this regard, though there seems to be no wholesale "retrogression to the pre-League of Nations regime of self-help," the very legal and moral principles to be used in the new international situation are at issue.[27] And judging by the position of the United States and other nations concerning the Persian Gulf crisis, little trust is placed on options other than the use of military force.

Second, it is crucial to address this aspect of cold war thinking and institutions, especially when it comes to sovereignty claims. For, after all

is said and done, conflicts such as that between Iraq and Kuwait are significantly, though not only, about sovereignty. And as long as military solutions are more trusted than others, sovereignty conflicts can and will lead to
war, however much one postpones addressing the sovereignty questions.

Addressing this matter is crucial because a number of unsettled sovereignty disputes concerning land boundaries exist. For example, there are such
disputes between China and members of the ex-Soviet Union, Chad and
Libya, Iran and Iraq, Sudan and Ethiopia, India and China, Vietnam and
China, Venezuela and Guyana, and Peru and Ecuador. There is also the
Falklands/Malvinas conflict, which led to the 1982 South Atlantic war
between Argentina and Great Britain (arguably, an early manifestation of
the cold war order breakdown in the West) and is still unsolved. Of particular relevance to this are the sovereignty disputes involving coastlines between Colombia and Nicaragua, the United Arab Emirates and Iran, Japan
and the ex-Soviet Union, and South Korea and Japan.[28]

Third, as the previous discussion makes plain, there is always a risk of
superpower involvement in such disputes.[29] And this leads to a fourth
reason: The use of nuclear weapons is not unlikely in such confrontations;
indeed, smaller nations may be more likely to use nuclear weapons than
superpowers.[30] Regarding this point, it has been claimed that, during the
1982 South Atlantic war, Great Britain had prepared for a nuclear attack if it
became necessary.[31] To this, one should add that Argentina is reputed to
have some sort of nuclear capability and has neither signed the Nuclear
Nonproliferation Treaty nor ratified the Tlatelolco Treaty, which establishes
a nuclear weapon free zone in Latin America.[32] At any rate, if a regional war
like those under discussion gets too drawn out and costly, there is no reason
to believe that none of the countries involved will use nuclear weapons.
Finally, a fifth reason is that even if nuclear weapons are not used, nearly as
devastating chemical, biological, and so-called conventional weapons are
likely to be used. They are so devastating that, during the Persian Gulf crisis,
about one million civilian casualties were expected during the first days of
the war.[33]

THE OBLIGATION TO SEEK A NEGOTIATED PEACE

Even if the situation just described provides good grounds for resolving
conflicts such as the 1990–91 Persian Gulf crisis through new principles,
what principles could be invoked? There is evidence that new principles may
be gaining force in the community of nations. One is that even though states
subject to foreign aggression have a right to defend themselves, they also
have an obligation to make a reasonable effort to find a peaceful resolution of
the conflict. Indeed, in the unlikely context of defending a country's right
not to end hostilities, David C. Gompert suggests this view:

Provided that they are making a reasonable effort to find a peaceful solution, countries that have been attacked must be spared the onus of refusing to end hostilities.[34]

No doubt, one can disagree with Gompert's wholesale defense of a country's refusal to end hostilities. His position is too simplistic. Of prime importance is how continuing hostilities will affect world peace and the peaceful resolution of the conflict. But it is hard to disagree with another aspect of his view: that a country has an obligation to make a reasonable effort to find a peaceful resolution of the conflict, no matter what stage the conflict has reached.

To take the position just stated is not to deny that, in crises involving aggression or the threat of aggression, responding through exclusive reliance on negotiations is pointless. Rather, this position acknowledges the pointlessness without falling into the trap of thinking that *any* reliance on negotiations is pointless. This position is politically realistic, yet sensitive to the requirements of morality. It is politically realistic because it makes it possible to address situations, such as that in the Persian Gulf, in which territorial and economic claims appear to be driven by hegemonic aims. The implication of the position just advanced is that, at some stage, the use of military force is permissible in trying to redress the wrongs of aggression. Yet the position is sensitive to the requirements of morality because it says that reasonable peace-seeking efforts are never pointless and always required.

Indeed, such is the view reflected by the November 29, 1990, United Nations resolution. It authorized all member states to use "all necessary means" to uphold previous United Nations resolutions condemning Iraq's invasion and calling for the restoration of the Kuwait government.[35] However, as many involved in passing the resolution rushed to indicate, the role of negotiation was not ruled out by the moral and political authority to use military force. This was further confirmed by last-minute attempts by then UN Secretary General Javier Pérez de Cuéllar and the French government.[36]

The preceding discussion may lead some to ask the question that arose during the Persian Gulf crisis: Are the efforts significant enough? This question, however, is incomplete. The full question to ask is: Are the efforts significant enough, *given the nature of the conflict, the likely consequences of war, and the feasible social decision procedures open to those involved?* As previously indicated, in addressing this question, moral concerns other than the justice of a cause are relevant. Predominant among these are concerns with the lives and suffering of those who would have to fight a war, as well as the concern with world peace. Indeed, depending on the cause of war, however just it may be, those other moral concerns may override it.

In addition, when it comes to world peace, prudential concerns often go hand in hand with moral concerns and give them political significance. At any rate, as Haim Ramon, a Knesset member, said in 1988 about the various Middle East armed confrontations: "Maybe each of the sides will be one hundred percent right; but both of the sides will be one hundred percent dead."[37]

We are now in a position to infer theses two through four in this essay, which are in accordance with the hypotheses formulated in Essay 8. They are the following: Second, from a moral standpoint, a country or group of countries with the moral and political authority—and the power—to redress the wrongs of international aggression by using military force still has an obligation to seek meaningful negotiations aimed at resolving the conflict. That is, the negotiations to be sought should address the interests and demands involved as fairly and comprehensively as circumstances (e.g., time, knowledge, and available resources) permit. Third, this obligation is present throughout the entire conflict, though its discharge does not invariably require that the country cease hostilities to seek meaningful negotiations. Fourth, military responses to aggression are justified only if, as far as circumstances permit, they are likely to avoid harming civilians of any country, creating political or economic instability in nonaggressor countries, and bringing about any conditions that would further undermine world peace.

As stated at this essay's outset, the moral and political significance of all these theses in the latter part of the twentieth century is a matter of political prudence and moral sensitivity. From a political standpoint, the efforts made to attain a meaningfully negotiated solution throughout a conflict are crucial to whether or not world peace is further undermined. They are crucial not just in the conflict's aftermath, but during the conflict itself. And from a moral standpoint, the failure to seek a meaningful negotiated solution is simply to be unduly nonchalant and therefore insensitive about the injuries and loss of lives that combat involves. In a nutshell, these reasons lead to the conclusion that, in the latter part of the twentieth century, seeking negotiated solutions to regional conflicts is a matter of political prudence and moral sensitivity.

PROACTIVE POLITICS

The preceding discussion indicates the need for a new type of thinking in international affairs. It must be proactive, aimed at preventing crises rather than simply reacting to them. And when crises start, in accordance with the book's hypotheses, it must aim at using as little force as necessary to bring about a situation in which other, less confrontational social decision procedures have a good chance of success. This applies to conflicts such as the

Persian Gulf war, and reasonable efforts along the lines just mentioned should be made to find solutions to them. Some approaches suggest themselves. For example, precedents, if not models, for addressing the conflicts peacefully can be found in the 1984 agreement between Great Britain and China about Hong Kong, in the 1984 agreement between Argentina and Chile about the Beagle Channel, and in agreements that have withstood the test of time reasonably well, such as the Spitsbergen/Svalbard, Antarctic, and Torres Strait treaties.[38] The question arises, however: What do current conditions permit in dealing with conflicts? The answer, I am afraid, calls for caution and patience. Whatever the resolution of conflicts turns out to be, there is reason to believe that it will not be reached easily or soon. The simple fact of the matter is that, in contrast with light rays, policy-making, especially in conflictive situations, does not proceed in a straight line.

Dialogue

— You have paid no attention to the role of prior injustices in dealing with confrontations. In fact, you pay little if any attention to it throughout the book. This, I believe, is a weakness in your approach.

— I have not talked *directly* about prior injustices, but the approach I outline does not disregard them. It relies on what people are likely to find intolerable when they are of sound mind, free from the effects of coercion and manipulation, not carried away by passion and emotion, and well-informed. Now, normally, a policy's or a decision's failure to take past injustices into account will be found intolerable by those people. In the case of the Middle East conflicts, for example, just as in many of the other regional conflicts I mentioned in the essay, questions of sovereignty are crucial and are often tied to prior injustices. They may be tied to injustices previously committed by aggressor countries or colonial powers. These injustices will be reflected in the judgments of people who meet the said conditions.

— Yet, your saying "normally" suggests that some policies or decisions may be permissible even though they disregard past injustices altogether. In accordance with your hypotheses, policies that are feasible and likely to be effective are permissible so long as people who have the characteristics you mentioned are not likely to mind and the policies and decisions are likely to limit freedoms and well-being less than the alternatives. This is perfectly compatible with disregarding past injustices. Being from a country where the dirty war led to so many human-rights violations, you will be able to understand the example I have in mind. Those violations included many killings. The victims are dead. In some cases, their children were adopted by the killers. Indeed, there appear to have been cases in which, presumably for the sake of their grandchildren

211

and out of a desire to see them, the grandparents became friends with their children's killers rather than denouncing them. If you ask these people, they will not object to policies that let the killers literally get away with murder.

— First, the people you describe are unlikely to meet the characteristics they must meet for their judgment to count. Aren't they being carried away by passion and emotion, at the very least, by the desperate love for their grandchildren? In addition, they are not the only ones likely to be affected by the policies or decisions. Normally, these will include victims who managed to survive, or relatives of those killed who want justice done, or still other people who think that the injustices should be addressed even if the victims are gone and their descendants do not care.

— But couldn't all these people fail to find certain policies and decisions intolerable, despite the fact that some injustices would not be redressed?

— Under extreme conditions, they could. For example, faced with the prospect of their country falling apart in a bloody war driven by the desire to redress those wrongs, they may, on balance, conclude that they should regrettably put those matters aside and get on with life. But bear in mind that *they*—the victims and those whose concerns for the victims of past injustices would be affected by the policies or decisions—would reach this judgment. And if *they* reached such a judgment, who could reasonably claim to be in a better position to judge the matter? It is a virtue of my approach that it is sensitive to the nuances in the example you gave.

— Your approach may reasonably take into account past injustices, but how can it be sensitive to future generations?

— Just as I said it could be sensitive to children and nonhumans: through third parties who act as their trustees.

— That's an odd idea. How can anyone be the trustee of people who do not yet exist?

— We know that, barring quite far-fetched unpredictables, there will be future generations so long as we take care of the planet.

— Granted, but that's too general. What can your approach tell us, for example, concerning population policies. Who is likely to be affected by the policies?

— Those affected would be those born under the policies, plus those living at policy-making time who would have their societies, individual freedoms, or well-being affected by the policies.

— Do you mean to imply that those who, because of the policies, would not be born would not be among those affected by the policies?

— Should they be included simply because the policies presumably lead to their not being born? I must confess that I find your suggestion quite unconvincing. For one: How can a totally and irretrievably imaginary person (that is, one who, by assumption, never existed and never will exist) be affected by an actual policy at all? At most, the policy may affect people who could be, but never will be, parents of such a person.

— I see your point. However, even if we can assess policies and decisions only by reference to those likely to be affected by them, how reliable are our predictions when we are dealing with future generations?

— They become less reliable the further into the future those generations are supposed to exist. However, we can still make some reasonable generalizations about them. They will need at least such things as clean, uncontaminated land, water, and air; fertile soils; predictable weather patterns (hence, a preserved rain forest to regulate them); viable societies; a certain freedom of choice concerning their own lives and future; and a modicum of human companionship. These are not minor things and, in connection with the hypotheses I formulated, lead to a variety of practical injunctions.

— You seem quite sure that your hypotheses will do the job.

— I am as sure as the reasons I gave throughout the book permit. Yet my approach entails that the hypotheses should be tested further. In particular, they should go through a process of social testing, that is, of critical scrutiny and limited interactions with the hypotheses' implications in actual social life. Like policy-making itself, its study in ethics and sociopolitical philosophy is an ongoing process in which a theory sometimes turns out to have unforeseen or even unforeseeable practical implications. And after all, as the saying goes, the proof of the pudding is in the eating.

Notes

PREFACE

1. Lewis Anthony Dexter, "Intra-Agency Politics: Conflict and Contravention in Administrative Entities." *Journal of Theoretical Politics* 2: 151–72 (1990).
2. David Braybrooke, *Meeting Needs* (Princeton, N. J.: Princeton University Press, 1987).
3. David Braybrooke, *Ethics in the World of Business* (Totowa, N. J.: Rowman & Allanheld, 1983), pp. 55–56, 480.

ESSAY 1. ISSUES AND ISSUE-OVERLOAD

Some of the ideas in this essay were included in a paper presented at the Philosophy Colloquium, Department of Philosophy, Central Connecticut State University, on April 18, 1990.

1. For recent characterizations of issues, see the discussion below, entitled Levels of Policy and Decision Problems.
2. Some of these procedures are described in Brian Barry, *Political Argument* (London: Routledge and Kegan Paul, 1976), pp. 84–93. Manipulation in politics is discussed in Robert E. Goodin, *Manipulatory Politics* (New Haven and London: Yale University Press, 1980). Policy insulation is discussed by Patrick W. Hamlett, "A Typology of Technological Policymaking in the U.S. Congress," *Technology and Human Values* 8 (2): 33–40 (Spring 1983); also included in my *Contemporary Moral Controversies in Technology* (New York and London: Oxford University Press, 1987), pp. 313–22.
3. This method, and its tradition in studies of social process, are described in the Appendix to Lewis Anthony Dexter, "Intra-Agency Politics: Conflict and Contravention in Administrative Entities," *Journal of Theoretical Politics* 2: 151–72 (1990).
4. Daniel C. Dennett, "The Moral First Aid Manual," in Sterling M. McMurrin (ed.), *The Tanner Lectures on Human Values, VIII* (Salt Lake City, Utah, and Cambridge, England: University of Utah Press, Cambridge University Press, 1988), pp. 119–47.
5. Eugene Kennedy, "The Looming 80's," *New York Times Magazine*, December 2, 1979. Quoted in Jethro K. Lieberman, *The Litigious Society* (New York: Basic, 1981), p. vii.
6. David L. Bazelon, "Governing Technology: Values, Choices, and Scientific Progress," *Technology and Society* 5: 17–18 (1983); also in my *Contemporary Moral Controversies in Technology*, pp. 134–35.
7. Dennett, "The Moral First Aid Manual," p. 123. For a brief discussion of Dennett's position as it compares with related recent discussions in ethical theory, see my review of Sterling M. McMurrin, ed., *The Tanner Lectures on Human Values, VIII*, in *History of European Ideas* 10 (4): 484–85 (1989).
8. Dennett, "The Moral First Aid Manual," p. 124.

9. Ibid., p. 138.
10. Ibid., p. 144.
11. Ibid.
12. Ibid.
13. Ibid., p. 123.
14. For an additional discussion of this point, see my *Contemporary Moral Controversies in Technology* and *Contemporary Moral Controversies in Business* (New York and London: Oxford University Press, 1989).
15. For the questions the taxonomy should help ask, see Frank Fischer, *Politics, Values, and Public Policy: The Problem of Methodology* (Boulder, Colo.: Westview Press, 1980), pp. 205–14.
16. Dennett, "The Moral First Aid Manual," p. 131.
17. See, for example, David Braybrooke, *Traffic Congestion Goes through the Issue Machine* (London and Boston: Routledge and Kegan Paul, 1974), p. 1. See also David Braybrooke, "Policy Formation with Issue-Processing and Transformation of Issues," in C. A. Hooker, J. J. Leach, and E. F. McClennen (eds.), *Foundations and Applications of Decision Theory* (Dordrecht, Holland: Reidel Publishing Co., 1978); and David Braybrooke and Charles E. Lindblom, *A Strategy of Decision* (New York: Free Press, 1963, 1970), pp. 84–86, 98–99, 194–97.
18. Marcus G. Singer, "Moral Issues and Social Problems: The Moral Relevance of Moral Philosophy," *Philosophy* 60: 12–13 (1985). For the development of Singer's notion of moral issues and social problems, see also his *Morals and Values* (New York: Charles Scribner's Sons, 1977), pp. 5–6. This distinction also appears in Singer's "Is Ethics a Science? Ought It to Be?" Zygon 15 (1): 37–38 (March 1980), where it is characterized in almost the same terms as in *Morals and Values*.
19. Singer, "Moral Issues and Social Problems," pp. 12–13.
20. Jürgen Habermas, "Morality and the Law," in Sterling M. McMurrin (ed.), *The Tanner Lectures on Human Values, VIII* (Salt Lake City, Utah, and Cambridge, England: University of Utah Press, Cambridge University Press, 1988), p. 243.
21. Jon Elster, "The Market and the Forum: Three Varieties of Political Theory," in Jon Elster and Aanund Hylland (eds.), *Foundations of Social Choice Theory* (Cambridge, England: Cambridge University Press, 1986), p. 103.
22. Ibid., p. 114.
23. Ibid., pp. 114–20.
24. Ibid., p. 128.
25. This is not to say that this type of theory applies only to cases of social conflict. Nor is it to say that no other questions should be asked about issues. It is simply to say what type of emphasis is needed in the case of issues. For policy and decision questions to ask, see Fischer, *Politics, Values, and Public Policy*.
26. I have provided evidence in support of this hypothesis elsewhere. See *Contemporary Moral Controversies in Technology*, p. 6, and *Contemporary Moral Controversies in Business*, p. 6. These books' selections constitute and refer to evidence that confirms the range hypothesis and disconfirms alternative, more simplistic hypotheses. This evidence also serves to confirm the balance hypothesis.

ESSAY 2. SOCIAL TRAPS

This essay is based on an article of the same title that appeared in *Epistemologia: Italian Journal for the Philosophy of Science* (1991).

1. There is a wide literature on social traps. See, for example, J. Plall, "Social Traps," *American Psychologist* 28: 642–51 (1973); K. C. Brechner, "An Experimental Analysis of Social Traps," *Journal of Experimental Social Psychology* 13: 552–64 (1977); J. G. Cross and M. J. Guyer, *Social Traps* (Ann Arbor: University of Michigan Press, 1980); B. Bueno de Mesquita, *The War Trap* (New Haven, Conn.: Yale University Press, 1981); D. A. Schroeder and D. E. Johnson, "Utilization of Information in a Social Trap," *Psychological Reports* 50: 107–13 (1982); and Robert Costanza, "The Nuclear Arms Race and the Theory of Social Traps," *Journal of Peace Research* 21: 79–86 (1984).
2. For a somewhat different taxonomy of social traps, see Cross and Guyer, *Social Traps*. For the elements of still another, see Jon Elster, *The Cement of Society* (Cambridge, England, and New York: Cambridge University Press, 1989), pp. 12–16.
3. For a somewhat similar characterization of rational choice, see Jon Elster, *Rational Choice* (New York: New York University Press, 1986), pp. 1, 4.
4. See Giandomenico Majone, *Evidence, Argument, and Persuasion in the Policy Process* (New Haven, Conn.: Yale University Press, 1989), p. 13; and Mario Bunge, "Game Theory Is Not a Useful Tool for the Political Scientist," *Epistemologia XII* 1989: 195–212, and *Cahiers d'épistémologie*, No. 9015 (Montréal: Université de Québec á Montréal, October 1990).
5. Cited in Edith Stokey and Richard Zeckhauser, *A Primer for Policy Analysis* (New York: W. W. Norton, 1978), p. 22. This is not a fluke. Besides Charles J. Hitch and Roland McKean, *The Economics of Defense in the Nuclear Age* (Cambridge, Mass.: Harvard University Press, 1962), see also Alain C. Enthoven and K. Wayne Smith, *How Much Is Enough?* (New York: Harper & Row, 1971), and E. S. Quade, *Analysis for Public Decision* (Amsterdam: North Holland, 1982). For a current discussion of these developments, see Majone, *Evidence, Argument, and Persuasion*.
6. Judith Shklar, "Decisionism," in C. J. Friedrich (ed.), *Nomos*, vol. 7, *Rational Decision* (New York: Atherton, 1964), pp. 3–17.
7. Majone, *Evidence, Argument, and Persuasion*, p. 15.
8. Bunge, "Game Theory," pp. 2, 17.
9. Ruth Leger Sivard, *World Military and Social Expenditures* (Washington, D. C.: World Priorities, Inc., 1985), pp. 20–21.
10. Ibid., pp. 10–11.
11. Molly Moore, "Iraq Amassing Biological Armaments," *The Hartford Courant*, September 29, 1990, pp. A1, A6. See also Douglas Frantz and Melissa Healy, "Iraq Has Next Worst Thing to Nuclear Weapons, Pentagon Says," from the *Los Angeles Times*, reproduced in *The Hartford Courant*, October 5, 1990, p. A13.
12. Ibid. There were overtones of this problem in Sen. Joseph. R. Biden Jr.'s heated exchange with U.S. Secretary of State George P. Shultz about U.S. sanctions against South Africa. See John F. Fitzgerald, "Sanctions Plan Stirs Discord," *The Hartford Courant*, July 24, 1986, pp. A1, A18.
13. Jackson Diehl, "Gorbachev's Visit to Germany Highlights East Bloc Contrasts," *The Hartford Courant*, April 23, 1986, p. A19.

14. An example of this situation can be found in Rosemary Chalk, "Commentary on the NAS Report," *Science, Technology and Human Values* 8(1): 21–24 (Winter 1983). This article can also be found in my *Contemporary Moral Controversies in Technology*, pp. 268–72; a discussion of the article is included on pp. 241–42.
15. Combined Wire Services, "Iraq Replaces Kuwaiti Rulers," *The Hartford Courant*, August 3, 1990, pp. A1, A6, A7.
16. Moore, "Iraq Amassing Biological Armaments"; Frantz and Healy, "Iraq Has Next Worst Thing." See also Combined Wire Services, "Bush Warns Iraq May Get Nuclear Weapons," *The Hartford Courant*, November 23, 1990, pp. A1, A8.
17. Jeff Sallot, "The Dreaded Mistake," *Toronto Globe and Mail*, August 8, 1987, pp. D1, D8.
18. A careful discussion of this interpretation can be found in Allan Rosas. "The Militarization of Space and International Law," *Journal of Peace Research* 20 (4): 357–64 (1983). This article is also included in my *Contemporary Moral Controversies in Technology*, pp. 183–90; a discussion of the article appears on pp. 93–95.
19. David Lauter and Norman Kempster, "Bush Urges Army Treaty for Europe," *The Hartford Courant*, May 4, 1990, pp. A1, A4.
20. Sallot, "The Dreaded Mistake."
21. Bunge, "Game Theory," p. 3. This is also the case if one uses the dollar auction game model. See Costanza, "Nuclear Arms Race," pp. 80–82.
22. Elster, *Rational Choice*, p. 2.
23. This was a central tension affecting U.S. citizens during the Vietnam War.
24. Hannah Arendt, "What Was Authority?" in Carl Friedrich (ed.), *Authority* (Cambridge, Mass.: Harvard University Press, 1966), p. xi.
25. For a good discussion of this, see Joseph Margolis, "The Peculiarities of Nuclear Thinking," in Avner Cohen and Steven Lee (eds.), *Nuclear Weapons and the Future of Humanity* (Totowa, N. J.: Rowman & Allanheld, 1986), pp. 153–68. For nuclear thinking in the 1980s, see Colin S. Gray and Keith Payne, "Victory is Possible," *Foreign Policy* 59: 14–27 (1980), and Colin S. Gray, "Nuclear Strategy: The Case for a Theory of Victory," *International Security* 4 (1): 54–87 (1979). See also Ian Clark, *Limited Nuclear War* (Princeton, N. J.: Princeton University Press, 1982). The peace movement in both the West and the East provides evidence of the erosion of states' authority on foreign policy.
26. Gorbachev's policies have opened up new options in this regard, and now intellectuals in the ex-Soviet republics and other members of the public are beginning to take advantage of them. Only the future will tell what comes of it.
27. Amartya K. Sen, "Rational Fools: A Critique of the Behavioral Foundations of Economic Theory," *Philosophy and Public Affairs* 6: 317–344 (Summer 1977).
28. For a discussion of how the process of forming a political judgment undermines decisionism, see Majone, *Evidence, Argument, and Persuasion*, p. 17.

ESSAY 3. SOCIAL CHOICE THEORY

This essay is based on a paper of the same title published in *Epistemologia: Italian Journal for the Philosophy of Science* (1992).
1. Amartya Sen, "Foundations of Social Choice Theory: An Epilogue," in Jon Elster and Aanund Hylland (eds.), *Foundations of Social Choice Theory* (Cam-

bridge, England, and New York: Cambridge Universtiy Press, 1989), p. 213.
2. Jon Elster, "The Market and the Forum: Three Varieties of Political Theory," in Elster and Hylland, *Foundations*, pp. 103–32; Brian Barry, "Lady Chatterley's Lover and Doctor Fischer's Bomb Party: Liberalism, Pareto Optimality, and the Problem of Objectionable Preferences," in Elster and Hylland, *Foundations*, pp. 11–44.
3. Sen, "Foundations of Social Choice Theory," p. 236.
4. Ibid., p. 216.
5. For a somewhat similar characterization of rational choice, see Jon Elster, *Rational Choice* (New York: New York University Press, 1986), pp. 1, 4.
6. Judith Shklar, "Decisionism," in C. J. Friedrich (ed.), *Nomos, vol. 7, Rational Decision* (New York: Atherton, 1964), pp. 3–17.
7. Giandomenico Majone, *Evidence, Argument, and Persuasion in the Policy Process* (New Haven, Conn.: Yale University Press, 1989), p. 15.
8. Amartya K. Sen, "Rational Fools: A Critique of the Behavioral Foundations of Economic Theory," *Philosophy and Public Affairs* 6: 317–44 (Summer 1977).
9. Aanund Hylland, "The Purpose and Significance of Social Choice Theory: Some General Remarks and an Application to the 'Lady Chatterley Problem,'" in Elster and Hylland, *Foundations*, p. 63.
10. Ibid.
11. For an insightful discussion of these processes, see Charles E. Lindblom and David K. Cohen, *Usable Knowledge: Social Science and Social Problem Solving* (New Haven, Conn.: Yale University Press, 1979), especially Chapter 2, "The Relation of Professional Social Inquiry to Other Inputs into Social Problem Solving."
12. For a discussion of how the process of forming a political judgment undermines decisionism, see Majone, *Evidence, Argument, and Persuasion*, p. 17. For a parallel discussion concerning rational choice, decision, and game theories, see Essay 2.
13. See, for example, "Gorbachev to Shuffle Leadership," *The Hartford Courant*, November 17, 1990, pp. A1, A8.
14. Ibid.
15. William Edward Hartpole Lecky, *The Map of Life* (London: Longmans, Green, and Co., 1921), p. 191. See also Majone, *Evidence, Argument, and Persuasion*, p. 17.
16. Herbert Simon, *Models of Man* (New York: Wiley, 1961), pp. 70–71, 253. See also David Braybrooke, *Meeting Needs* (Princeton, N. J.: Princeton University Press, 1987), pp. 204–10, especially pp. 208–9.
17. Elster, *Rational Choice*, p. 25.
18. Ibid., p. 26.
19. Ibid.
20. See Pierre Moessinger, *La psychologie morale* (Paris: Presses Universitaires de France, 1989); "Perfect Justice Procedures," and "La théorie du choix rationnel: critique d'une explication," *Information sur les sciences sociales* 31 (1): 87–111 (1992).
21. There is a great deal of empirical work being done. See, for example, A. Abbott, "Professional Ethics," *American Journal of Sociology* 88: 855–85 (1983); P. Besnard, *L'anomie* (Paris: Presses Universitaires de France, 1987); David W. Brown, *Cooperation among Strangers* (Dayton, Ohio: Kettering Foundation, 1992); R. J. Edelman, *The Psychology of Embarrassment* (New York: Wiley,

1987). See also the empirical studies included in my *Contemporary Moral Controversies in Business* (New York and London: Oxford University Press, 1989) and, to a lesser extent, in my *Contemporary Moral Controversies in Technology* (New York and London: Oxford University Press, 1987).

ESSAY 4. INFORMING THE PUBLIC

An initial version of this essay appeared in *Philosophy in Context* 20: 1–21 (1990).

1. This appeared in *The Hartford Courant* during the mid-1980s.
2. Herbert Brucker, "What's Wrong with Objectivity," *Saturday Review*, October 11, 1969, p. 79.
3. J. L. Mackie, *Inventing Right and Wrong* (New York: Penguin, 1977), p. 236.
4. Ibid., p. 146.
5. Brucker, "What's Wrong," pp. 78–79.
6. Ronald D. Milo, *Immorality* (Princeton, N. J.: Princeton University Press, 1984), p. 215.
7. Virginia Held has discussed how moral theories are politically tested in "The Political 'Testing' of Moral Theories," in Peter A. French, Theodore E. Uehling, Jr., and Howard K. Wettstein (eds.), *Midwest Studies in Philosophy* 7: 343–63 (1982). However, her account is rather subjectivistic. The notion of objectivity as social testing that I use includes, but is not reduced to, the political testing of moral theories.
8. Brucker, "What's Wrong," p. 77.
9. Ibid. See also Gary Atkins, "In Search of New Objectivity," in Leonard L. Sellers and William L. Rivers (eds.), *Mass Media Issues* (Englewood Cliffs, N. J.: Prentice Hall, 1977), p. 26.
10. Conrad C. Fink, *Media Ethics* (New York: McGraw-Hill, 1988), p. 20.
11. Atkins, "In Search," p. 34.
12. Various TV programs, for example, "Nightline," carried discussions on this topic. A very good discussion of it can be found in Alvin Rosenfeld, "The Jewish Reporter and the Code of Objectivity," *The National Jewish Monthly*, June 1975, pp. 22–25. For parallel discussions concerning the 1982 South Atlantic war between Argentina and Great Britain, see Valerie Adams, *The Media and the Falklands Campaign* (New York: Macmillan, 1987). See also R. Neil Matheson's review of this book and of Daniel C. Hallin, *The Uncensored Press: The Media and Vietnam* (New York: Oxford University Press, 1987), in *Toronto Globe and Mail*, April 11, 1987, p. C11. For coverage and discussions of the Munich Olympic game massacre of Israeli athletes, see Serge Groussard, *The Blood of Israel*, translated by Harold J. Salemson (New York: William Morrow and Co, 1975); Elie Wiesel's review of this book in *The New York Times Book Review*, June 8, 1975, pp. 4–5; and the exchange that followed between Paul Good and Elie Wiesel in the letters to the editor section of a closely following issue of the same publication.
13. Arthur Edward Rose, *Slanted News* (Boston: Beacon Press, 1957), pp. 1–2, 45.
14. Ibid., pp. 3, 57, 123–24.
15. Ibid., pp. 4–5.
16. Fink, *Media Ethics*, p. 21.
17. Ibid.
18. Ibid.

19. Ibid., p. 22.
20. Ibid.
21. Thomas Nagel, *Mortal Questions* (Cambridge, England, New York: Cambridge University Press, 1979), p. 206.
22. For evidence of the linguistic, conceptual, methodological, and related forms of fragmentation between these groups, as well as for an initial attempt at bridging the gaps, see my *Contemporary Moral Controversies in Technology* (New York and London: Oxford University Press, 1987), and *Contemporary Moral Controversies in Business* (New York and London: Oxford University Press, 1989).
23. Nagel, *Mortal Questions*, p. 213. Alasdair MacIntyre has advanced, perhaps more poignantly and usefully than others, a similar view in *After Virtue* (Notre Dame, Ind.: Notre Dame University Press, 1981). He also advanced it in a modified, more defensible version, in "Relativism, Power, and Philosophy," in Kenneth Baynes, James Bohman, and Thomas McCarthy (eds.), *After Philosophy* (Cambridge, Mass.: MIT Press, 1987), pp. 385–411.
24. This and related arguments are discussed in Marcus G. Singer, *Generalization in Ethics* (New York: Atheneum, 1961), pp. 321–22.
25. An analogous argument about the truth of ethical judgments is formulated in Marcus G. Singer, "Some Preliminary Observations on Truth in Ethics," *Philosophy in Context* 16: 11–16 (1986).
26. For a discussion of social decision procedures and their ethical significance, see Brian Barry, *Political Argument* (London: Routledge and Kegan Paul, 1976), pp. 84–93.
27. This position has a precedent in the work of John Dewey, especially in "The Construction of Good," in *The Quest for Certainty* (New York: Capricorn, 1960), pp. 254–86. A seminal philosophical discussion of objectivity in this sense can be found in Charles Sanders Peirce, "The Fixation of Belief," *Popular Science Monthly*, November 1877, pp. 1–15. For a current edition including Peirce's later revisions and comments, see Philip P. Wiener (ed.), *Charles Sanders Peirce: Selected Writings* (New York: Dover, 1958), pp. 91–112.
28. Elie Wiesel, review of *The Blood of Israel*, *The New York Times Book Review*, July 8, 1975, p. 5.
29. Concerning this point, see W. K. Clifford, "The Ethics of Belief," *Contemporary Review* (January 1877), later reprinted in his *Lectures and Essays* and, more recently, in Marcus G. Singer and Robert R. Ammerman (eds.), *Introductory Readings in Philosophy* (New York: Scribner's, 1974) pp. 115–21; E. D. Klemke, A. David Kline, and Robert Hollinger, *Philosophy: The Basic Issues* (New York: St. Martin's Press, 1986), pp. 53–58; and my *Through Time and Culture* (Englewood Cliffs, N. J.: Prentice Hall, 1993). The classic criticism of Clifford's position is the work just mentioned in the paper's main text: William James, "The Will to Believe." A recent publication of this piece can be found in William James, *The Will to Believe and Other Essays in Popular Philosophy* (New York: Dover, 1956), pp. 1–31.

ESSAY 5. CRITICAL INTERACTION

This essay is based on an article of the same title published in *International Journal of Social and Moral Studies* 6 (2) (Summer 1991).

1. An attempt to address this antinomy can be found in R. M. Hare's work,

especially in *Freedom and Reason* (New York: Oxford University Press, 1963), p. 3. It is also discussed throughout the book.

2. An incisive critique of Hare's position is advanced by Marcus G. Singer in "Freedom from Reason," *Philosophical Review* 89:253–61 (April 1970).

3. Virginia Held, in "The Political 'Testing' of Moral Theories," *Midwest Studies in Philosophy* 7:354 (1982).

4. Ibid.

5. Ibid., p. 344.

6. Such reasons would point to various testing conditions, depending on the circumstances and on what is under scrutiny. A list of such conditions appears in Ibid., pp. 344–45. The argument just given holds even if Held's expressions, "we ought to shape the world in accordance with our choices" and "we ought to impose our choices on what prescriptions and judgments to consider valid on the world," are not judgments but expressions of prescriptions advanced as a matter of choice. Based on Held's account, they are just as well based on an arbitrary choice or a blind act of the will. This rules out critical scrutiny and so the testing of moral theories.

7. This accordance with actual moral thinking is one of the various criteria relevant for assessing moral theories. For a fuller discussion of these criteria, see my *Contemporary Moral Controversies in Technology*, Introduction to Part III.

8. *Random House Dictionary of the English Language* (New York: Random House, 1966), s.v. "approve." This distinction is not peculiar to English. One can also find it, for example, in Spanish. In this language, one can say, in the judgment sense, "El aprueba de la politica gubernamental," and in the decision sense, one can say, "El Senado aprobó prontamente el proyecto de ley."

   For purposes of this inquiry, I do not dwell on the distinction between an evaluation and a judgment of value. Let us keep in mind, however, that an evaluation one reaches is treated here as identical to a judgment of value but different from an evaluation undertaken, which is an activity aimed at reaching such judgments. Of course, not all judgments of value are moral judgments: The judgment that thick-crust pizza is better than thin-crust pizza is not. The present account, however, does not deal only with moral judgments about actions. An account that does is Marcus G. Singer, *Generalization in Ethics* (New York: Atheneum, 1961), pp. 34–35. Also, a discussion of political evaluation roughly compatible with the account I am developing can be found in Brian Barry, *Political Argument* (London: Routledge and Kegan Paul, 1976), pp. 1–15. And for a discussion of value judgments, see W. D. Lamont, *The Value Judgment* (Edinburgh: Edinburgh University Press, 1955), pp. xi, xii, 295.

9. *Random House Dictionary*, s.v. "approve."

10. Ibid., s.v. "disapprove."

11. Ibid.

12. The judgment-decision distinction carries over from the verbs to their corresponding nouns. See Ibid., s.v. "approval" and, though somewhat less clearly, s.v. "disapproval."

13. Ibid., s.v. "assess," "estimate."

14. Ibid., s.v. "assess," "decision." Even this term wavers between a creation and a discovery sense.

15. J. L. Mackie, *Inventing Right and Wrong* (New York: Penguin Books Ltd., 1977), pp. 106, 123.

16. Ibid., p. 236.

17. Ibid., p. 106.
18. Ibid., p. 146.
19. Ibid., p. 148.
20. Ibid.
21. Ibid., p. 35.
22. Ibid., p. 148.
23. Ibid., p. 238.
24. Ibid., p. 102.

ESSAY 6. PHILOSOPHY AS DIPLOMACY

Parts of this essay were presented at the Philosophy Colloquium, Department of Philosophy, Central Connecticut State University, April 18, 1990.

1. This characterization is attributed to Isaac Goldberg in Robert Andrews, ed., *The Concise Columbia Dictionary of Quotations* (New York: Columbia University Press, 1989), p. 70.
2. Sir Harold Nicolson, *Diplomacy*, 3d ed. (London, Oxford, and New York: Oxford University Press, 1963), pp. 3–4.
3. José Calvet De Magalhães, *The Pure Concept of Diplomacy* (New York; Westport, Conn., and London: Greenwood Press, 1988), p. 4.
4. Ibid., p. 59.
5. Ibid.
6. Ibid., p. 57
7. James Der Derian, *On Diplomacy* (Oxford: Basil Blackwell Ltd., 1987), p. 203.
8. For accounts of these and related events, see F. F. Piven and R. A. Cloward, *Poor People's Movements* (New York: Vintage Books, 1979), p. 238. See also W. Brink and L. Harris, *The Negro Revolution in America* (New York: Simon and Schuster, 1964), p. 40.
9. From a political science perspective, some of the points I am making have been made by Giandomenico Majone, *Evidence, Argument, and Persuasion in the Policy Process* (New Haven, Conn.: Yale University Press, 1989), especially in the chapters entitled "Policy Analysis and Public Deliberation" and "Analysis as Argument." See also Benjamin Barber, *The Conquest of Politics* (Princeton, N.J.: Princeton University Press, 1988), especially the last chapter, "Political Judgment: Philosophy as Practice."
10. For a discussion of this notion, see my *Contemporary Moral Controversies in Technology*, pp. 3–4, and *Contemporary Moral Controversies in Business* pp. 3–4.
11. There are plenty of cases in which participants adopt this approach. For example, see the following from *The Hartford Courant*: Associated Press, "U.N. to Meet on Population; U.S. Criticized," August 5, 1984, p. A5; "U.N. Conference Says Population Remains Challenge, Proposes Policies to Control It," August 15, 1984, p. D7; T. R. Reid, "Nuclear Wastes Prompt Uproar in Canyonlands," October 14, 1984, p. A13; "Toxic Dump Site Choices Challenged," May 20, 1986, p. A10; Miranda S. Spivack, "Settlement Caps Bhopal Court Fight," February 15, 1989, pp. A1, A6; W. Joseph Campbell, "For Victims, the Ordeal Still Goes On," February 15, 1989, pp. A1, A6; "Bhopal Disaster Survivors Say Union Carbide Settlement Too Small," February 16, 1989, p. A28; and W. Joseph Campbell, "Bhopal Blame Still Unclear," February 19, 1989, pp. A1,

A29. From the *New Haven Register*, see Virginia Morris, "Yale Researchers in Thick of Debate on Fetal Tissue Work," September 16, 1988, pp. 3, 6; Virginia Morris, "Research Using Fetal Tissue Should Proceed, Panel Says," September 17, 1988, p. 3; Virginia Morris, "Debate Over Fetal Tissue Could Become Academic," September 20, 1988, pp. 3, 6; Paul Marx, "Political Decisions Shouldn't Block the Use of Fetal Tissue to Treat Diseases," October 17, 1988, p. 11; Associated Press, "Animal-Rights Activist Held in Bomb Attempt," November 12, 1988, p. 1; Beth Burrell, "Norwalk Bombing Attempt Dismays Animal Activists," November 16, 1988, p. 6; Associated Press, "Abortion Pill May Return if Outcry Desists," October 28, 1988; Virginia Morris, "Abortion Pill Could Save Lives, Yale Doctor Says," October 29, 1988, pp. 3–4; and Ellen Goodman, "RU-486 Pill Signals End of Abortion Fight," November 4, 1988, p. 15. See also J. Dusheck, "Protesters Prompt Halt in Animal Research," *Science News* 128:53 (July 27, 1985).

12. Immanuel Kant, *Foundations of the Metaphysics of Morals*, edited by Robert Paul Wolff (Indianapolis and New York: Bobbs-Merrill, 1969), p. 36.

13. Ibid., pp. 36–39.

14. Philippa Foot, "Hypothetical Imperatives," *Philosophical Review* 81:312 (1972).

15. Lawrence C. Becker, "The Finality of Moral Judgments," *Philosophical Review* 82:366–67 (1973).

16. Foot, "Hypothetical Imperatives," p. 315.

17. This position is analogous to that taken by Marcus G. Singer in "Moral Issues and Social Problems: The Moral Relevance of Moral Philosophy," *Philosophy* 60:10–16 (1985). For the development of Singer's notion of moral issues and social problems, see also his *Morals and Values* (New York: Charles Scribner's Sons, 1977), pp. 5–6. This distinction also appears in Singer's "Is Ethics a Science? Ought It to Be?" *Zygon* 15(1):37–38 (March 1980).

ESSAY 7. A DELICATE BALANCE

1. Auguste Comte, *System of Positive Polity*, vol. 2 (New York: Burt Franklin, 1968), pp. 244, 247.

2. Karl Marx and Friedrich Engels, "The German Ideology," in Lewis S. Feuer (ed.), *Marx & Engels* (Garden City, N.Y.: Anchor, 1959), p. 255.

3. This method, and its tradition in studies of social process, is described in the Appendix to Lewis Anthony Dexter, "Intra-Agency Politics: Conflict and Contravention in Administrative Entities," *Journal of Theoretical Politics* 2:151–72 (1990).

4. Ralf Dahrendorf, "Out of Utopia: Toward a Reorientation of Sociological Analysis," *American Journal of Sociology*, September 1958, pp. 126–27.

5. Edward Shils, "The Calling of Society," in Talcott Parsons, Edward Shils, Kaspar D. Naegele, and Jesse R. Pitts (eds.), *Theories of Society* (New York: Free Press, 1965), pp. 1405–8.

6. Robin Williams, "Some Further Comments on Chronic Controversy," *American Journal of Sociology*, May 1966, p. 722.

7. Robert K. Merton, *Social Theory and Social Structure* (New York: Free Press, 1968), p. 176.

8. Thomas J. Bernard, *The Consensus-Conflict Debate* (New York: Columbia University Press, 1983), p. 2.

9. Dexter, "Intra-Agency Politics," p. 151.
10. Dahrendorf, "Out of Utopia," pp. 126–27.
11. See Joseph A. Schumpeter, *Capitalism, Socialism and Democracy*, 3d. ed. (New York: Harper & Row, 1950), especially chs. 13, 22.
12. Bernard, *Consensus-Conflict Debate*, p. 5.
13. Ibid., pp. 5–6.
14. See, for example, Laurence H. Meyer, *Macroeconomics* (Cincinnati: South-Western Publishing, 1980), pp. 3–5.
15. See Laird Addis, "The Individual and the Marxist Philosophy of History," *Philosophy of Science* 33:101–17 (1966).
16. See A. Pablo Iannone, *Contemporary Moral Controversies in Technology* (New York and London: Oxford University Press, 1987), p. viii.
17. Thomas Hobbes, "Leviathan," in D. D. Raphael (ed.), *British Moralists 1650–1880*, vol. I (Oxford: Clarendon Press, 1969), pp. 34–38.
18. Jon Elster, *The Cement of Society* (Cambridge, England: Cambridge University Press, 1989), pp. 2–11.
19. Hobbes, "Leviathan," p. 37.
20. From Associated Press, "U.N. to Meet on Population; U.S. Criticized," *The Hartford Courant*, August 5, 1984, p. A5.
21. From the *Los Angeles Times*, "U.N. Conference Says Population Remains Challenge, Proposes Policies to Control It," *The Hartford Courant*, August 15, 1984, p. D7.
22. T. R. Reid, "Nuclear Wastes Prompt Uproar in Canyonlands," *The Hartford Courant*, October 14, 1984, p. A13.
23. *The Hartford Courant*, December 20, 1984, p. A11, and, from Combined Wire Services, "Toxic Dump Site Choices Challenged," *The Hartford Courant*, May 20, 1986, p. A10. In 1990, the uproar was in Nevada. See Associated Press, "Disposal Sites for Nuclear Waste Remain Elusive," *The Hartford Courant*, January 1, 1990, p. A4.
24. J. Dusheck, "Protesters Prompt Halt in Animal Research," *Science News* 128:53 (July 27, 1985).
25. Associated Press, "Animal-Rights Activist Held in Bomb Attempt," *New Haven Register*, November 12, 1988, p. 1, and Beth Burrell, "Norwalk Bombing Attempt Dismays Animal Activists," *New Haven Register*, November 16, 1988, p. 6.
26. The crisis, which occurred at the end of President Carter's term, was widely covered in all the media.
27. See *The Hartford Courant*: Miranda S. Spivack, "Settlement Caps Bhopal Court Fight," February 15, 1989, pp. A1, A6; W. Joseph Campbell, "For Victims, the Ordeal Still Goes On," February 15, 1989, pp. A1, A6; Associated Press, "Bhopal Disaster Survivors Say Union Carbide Settlement Too Small," February 16, 1989, p. A28; W. Joseph Campbell, "Bhopal Blame Still Unclear," February 19, 1989, pp. A1, A29; Associated Press, "Judge in Bhopal Case Threatens to Quit," March 4, 1989, p. A10; Associated Press, "Gas Victims Attack Carbide Offices," March 9, 1989, p. A17.
28. For an account of these developments, see *Nunca Más*, by the Comisión Nacional Sobre la Desaparición de Personas (Buenos Aires: Editorial Universitaria de Buenos Aires, 1985). See also *Anexos*, by the Comisión Nacional Sobre la Desaparición de Personas (Buenos Aires: Editorial Universitaria de Buenos Aires, 1985).

29. Concerning the ongoing political moves at the time the ozone-layer plan was discussed, see Richard A. Kerr, "Arctic Ozone Is Poised for Fall," *Science*, February 24, 1989, pp. 1007–8; Jim Detjen, "Artic Ozone Threatened, Scientists Say," *The Hartford Courant*, February 18, 1989, pp. A1, A14; Michael Weisskopf, "Bush Pushes Chemical Plan," *The Hartford Courant*, March 4, 1989, pp. A1, A5; and, from the *Chicago Tribune*, "World Divided on Ozone-Layer Plan," *The Hartford Courant*, March 8, 1989, p. A9.

   As for the politics involved in signing the Rio Treaty, see Eugene Robinson and Michael Weisskopf, "Germans Take Lead in Global Warming Plan," *The Hartford Courant*, June 9, 1992, pp. A1, A5; Sam Dillon, "Europe Snubs U.S. Views at Earth Summit," *The Hartford Courant*, June 10, 1992, pp. A1, A5; and Combined Wire Services, "Earth Summit Ends on Note of Optimism," *The Hartford Courant*, June 15, 1992, pp. A1, A5. For preceding discussions in the U.S. scientific community of a greenhouse policy (a sticking point that isolated the United States during the 1992 Rio meetings), see Claudine Schneider, "Preventing Climate Change," *Issues in Science and Technology*, Summer 1989, pp. 55–62; D. Allan Bromley, "The Making of a Greenhouse Policy," *Issues in Science and Technology*, Fall 1990, pp. 55–61; Charles N. Herrick, "Science and Climate Policy: A History Lesson," *Issues in Science and Technology*, Winter 1991–1992, pp. 56–57; and Rosina Bierbaum and Robert M. Friedman, "The Road to Reduced Carbon Emissions," *Issues in Science and Technology*, Winter 1991–1992, pp. 58–65.

30. Owen Ullmann, "Modest Agreements Mask Differences," *The Hartford Courant*, July 12, 1990, pp. A1, A6; David Lightman, "U.S. Assumes Lesser Role," *The Hartford Courant*, July 12, 1990, pp. A1, A6.

31. Virginia Morris, "Yale Researchers in Thick of Debate on Fetal Tissue Work," *New Haven Register*, September 16, 1988, pp. 3, 6; Virginia Morris, "Research Using Fetal Tissue Should Proceed, Panel Says," *New Haven Register*, September 17, 1988, p. 3; Virginia Morris, "Debate Over Fetal Tissue Could Become Academic," *New Haven Register*, September 20, 1988, pp. 3, 6; Paul Marx, "Political Decisions Shouldn't Block the Use of Fetal Tissue to Treat Diseases," *New Haven Register*, October 17, 1988, p. 11. For later developments in the fetal tissue research controversy, see Combined Wire Services, "House Backs Research with Fetal Tissue," *The Hartford Courant*, May 29, 1992, pp. A1, A10.

32. See note 27 above.

ESSAY 8. PRACTICAL EQUITY

1. See, for example, James S. Fishkin's use of these features to characterize ideal society in his *Tyranny and Legitimacy: A Critique of Political Theories* (Baltimore and London: Johns Hopkins University Press, 1979), p. 37.

2. The terms *macrosocietal* and *microsocietal* are used here as they are used in economics. See, for example, Laurence H. Meyer, *Macroeconomics* (Cincinnati: South-Western Publishing, 1980), pp. 3–5.

3. Herbert Simon, *Models of Man* (New York: Wiley, 1961), pp. 70–71, 253. See also David Braybrooke, *Meeting Needs* (Princeton, N.J.: Princeton University Press, 1987), pp. 204–10, especially pp. 208–9.

4. See *The Random House Dictionary of the English Language* (New York: Random House, 1970), s.v. "equity."

5. See David Braybrooke, *Meeting Needs* (Princeton, N.J.: Princeton University Press, 1987), pp. 264–76.
6. For an account of severe deprivations, see James S. Fishkin, *Tyranny and Legitimacy: A Critique of Political Theories* (Baltimore and London: Johns Hopkins University Press, 1979), pp. 26–43.
7. For the relevance of precedents in issue processing, see David Braybrooke, *Traffic Congestion Goes through the Issue Machine* (London and Boston: Routledge and Kegan Paul, 1974), pp. 44–49.
8. A seminal work leading to discussions of the connection, if any, between facts and values is David Hume, *A Treatise of Human Nature* (Oxford: Oxford University Press, 1967 [1888]), pp. 469–76.
9. There is a suggestion of this type of argument in John Stuart Mill, "Utilitarianism," in Max Lerner (ed.), *Essential Works of John Stuart Mill* (New York and London: Bantam Books, 1965), pp. 192, 220–26). For abduction, see Charles Sanders Peirce, "Abduction and Induction," in Justus Buchler (ed.), *Philosophical Writings of Peirce* (New York: Dover Publications, 1955), pp. 150–56.
10. Joseph A. Schumpeter, *Capitalism, Socialism and Democracy*, 3d. ed. (New York: Harper & Row, 1950), pp. 240–42.
11. Fishkin, *Tyranny and Legitimacy*, pp. 65–72. The quotation appears on pp. 68–69.
12. Immanuel Kant, *Foundations of the Metaphysics of Morals*, Robert Paul Wolff (ed.) (Indianapolis and New York: Bobbs-Merrill, 1969), p. 44.
13. For an analysis of moral rules, laws, and principles, see Marcus G. Singer, *Generalization in Ethics* (New York: Atheneum, 1961), ch. 5.
14. John Rawls, *A Theory of Justice* (Cambridge, Mass.: Harvard University Press, 1971). See also T. M. Scanlon, "The Significance of Choice," in Sterling M. McMurrin (ed.), *The Tanner Lectures on Human Values, VIII* (Salt Lake City, Cambridge: University of Utah Press, Cambridge University Press, 1988), p. 166.
15. This is L. Kohlberg's position in *The Philosophy of Moral Development* (San Francisco: Harper & Row, 1981).
16. Jürgen Habermas, "Morality and the Law," in McMurrin (ed.), *The Tanner Lectures, VIII*, p. 243.
17. For an excellent discussion of this topic, see Amitai Etzioni, *The Moral Dimension: Toward a New Economics* (New York: Free Press, 1988).
18. I have discussed what this involves in my *Contemporary Moral Controversies in Technology* (New York and London: Oxford University Press, 1987) pp. 49–51.
19. See Combined Wire Services, "U.N. Imposes Embargo on Iraq," *The Hartford Courant*, August 7, 1990, pp. A1, A4.
20. See Ellen Warren, "Bush, Gorbachev United Against Iraq," *The Hartford Courant*, August 7, 1990, pp. A1, A4.
21. This may be what the Bush administration had in mind when the president declined to comment on the initial executions in China after the 1989 student uprising. See "Bush Avoids Criticizing China after Executions," *The Hartford Courant*, June 22, 1989. A similar point was made about the 1978 efforts by Amnesty International, the Inter-American Commission on Human Rights, and those foreign governments considering a boycott of the 1978 World Cup unless the then Argentine government either returned those people who had been taken out of society or let their whereabouts be known. It was argued that this speeded up executions rather than curbing them.

22. For a discussion of this point, see my *Contemporary Moral Controversies in Technology*, Introduction to Part II.
23. See note 3 above.

ESSAY 9. BETWEEN TRIVIALITY AND WORTH

A previous version of this essay was read at the Central Connecticut State University symposium, Visions of Computers in University Life: Effects and Assessments, March 1, 1985.

1. Artificial intelligence developments are taking place at a very fast pace. These often involve developments in mathematics that are part of the enterprise of creating new forms of artificial intelligence. Sometimes, however, new forms of artificial intelligence are made possible by developments in mathematics prompted by other concerns. For some introductory information about these matters, see Ivars Peterson, "Send This Computer to Kindergarten," *Science News*, July 7, 1984, pp. 10–11; Dietrick E. Thomson, "Making Music-Fractally," *Science News*, March 22, 1980, pp. 187, 190; Janet Raloff, "Computing for Art's Sake," *Science News*, November 20, 1982, pp. 328–31, "Approaching the Age of Reason," *Science News*, May 26, 1984, pp. 330–32, "Swift Mechanical Logic," *Science News*, June 2, 1984, pp. 346–47, and "In Search of Gigalips Architectures," *Science News*, June 16, 1984, pp. 378–81; Margaret A. Boden, "Impacts of Artificial Intelligence," *Futures*, February 1984, pp. 60–69; Joel Shurkin, "Can Computers Speak and Understand Natural Languages?" *The Stanford Observer*, January 1986, pp. 1, 9; and, concerning fractals, Benoit B. Mandelbrot, *The Fractal Geometry of Nature* (New York and San Francisco: W. H. Freeman, 1983).
2. David Braybrooke, "Work: A Cultural Ideal Ever More in Jeopardy," in Peter A. French, Theodore E. Uehling, Jr., and Howard K. Wettstein (eds.) *Midwest Studies in Philosophy* 7:322 (1982).
3. Concerning these new tasks, Professor María C. Lugones mentioned during a phone conversation with me that, at Carleton College, where she teaches, the academic level of the philosophy papers written by students dropped as soon as the papers began to look better with the help of personal computers. As far as I know, there has been no systematic study of the extent of this effect, nor of whether it is temporary.
4. About educational effects, see Bertram Bruce, "Taking Control of Educational Technology," *Science for the People*, March/April 1985, pp. 37–40; Marcia Boruta and Hugh Mehan, "Computers in the Classroom: Stratifier or Equalizer?" *Science for the People*, March/April 1985, pp. 41–44; and M. A. Boden, "Educational Implications of Artificial Intelligence," in W. Maxwell (ed.), *Thinking: The New Frontier* (Pittsburgh: Franklin Press, 1983).
5. Braybrooke, "Work," p. 335.
6. Ibid., p. 339.
7. See, for example, Richard E. Walton, "Social Choice in the Development of Advanced Information Technology," *Technology in Society* 1982:41–49. This article also appeared in *Human Relations*, December 1982, pp. 1073–84, and was reprinted in my *Contemporary Moral Controversies in Technology* (New York and London: Oxford University Press, 1987), pp. 112–18.
8. See, for example, Sar A. Levitan and Clifford M. Johnson, "The Future of Work:

Does It Belong to Us or to the Robots?" *Monthly Labor Review* 105:10–14 (September 1982). For the concerns raised, see Thomas L. Weekley, "Workers, Unions, and Industrial Robotics," *Annals of the American Academy of Political and Social Science* 470:146–51 (November 1983). These articles also appeared in my *Contemporary Moral Controversies in Technology*, pp. 107–11.

9. Much has been written on this subject. See, for example, A. Pablo Iannone, "Character Traits," Ph.D. thesis, University of Wisconsin-Madison, 1975, pp. 313–22. See also Yves R. Simon, *The Definition of Moral Virtue* (New York: Fordham University Press, 1986); Robert B. Krushwitz and Robert C. Roberts, *The Virtues* (Belmont, Calif.: Wadsworth, 1987).

10. Iannone, "Character Traits," ch. 3.

11. For a discussion of this point and evidence supporting it, see my *Contemporary Moral Controversies in Business* (New York and London: Oxford University Press, 1989), especially Part I.

12. A short but useful discussion of the reasons in favor of science, technology and society programs, the nature of these programs, the obstacles they have met, and the conditions for their sound development can be found in Rustum Roy, "Technological Literacy: An Uphill Battle," *Technology Review*, November-December 1983, pp. 18–19, and reprinted in my *Contemporary Moral Controversies in Technology*, pp. 323–25.

13. Joan Didion, "On Self-Respect," in *Slouching Towards Bethlehem* (New York: Farrar, Straus and Giroux, 1968), p. 147.

ESSAY 10. LIKE THE PHOENIX

1. No doubt, nuclear regulation went on after 1954, but it was largely focused on working out the details of the 1954 Atomic Energy Act. An important item in this process was the 1962 Report to the President. See George T. Mazuzan and J. Samuel Walker, *Controlling the Atom: The Beginnings of Nuclear Regulation, 1946–1962* (Berkeley: University of California Press, 1985), pp. 407–26; Steven L. DelSesto, *Science, Politics, and Controversy: Civilian Nuclear Power in the United States, 1946–1974* (Boulder, Colo.: Westview Press, 1979), pp. 76–115.

2. Editorial, *Bulletin of the Atomic Scientists*, August 1946, p. 1. See also DelSesto, *Science, Politics, and Controversy*, pp. 9–17.

3. For analyses of the Act and its effects, see DelSesto, *Science, Politics, and Controversy*, pp. 17–31, and Mazuzan and Walker, *Controlling the Atom*, pp. 1–11.

4. Karl Cohen, "A Re-Examination of the McMahon Act," *Bulletin of the Atomic Scientists*, January 1948, pp. 7, 9, 10. See also Thomas E. Dewey, "The Challenge of the Atomic Age," October 1948, pp. 296–97.

5. Brian McMahon, "Author of Atomic Energy Act Comments on Governor Dewey's Speech," *Bulletin of the Atomic Scientists*, October 1948, p. 298. See also editorial, *Bulletin of the Atomic Scientists*, February 1948, p. 64; President Truman, "President Truman Answers Dewey," November 1948), p. 326; DelSesto, *Science, Politics, and Controversy*, pp. 39–40; Mazuzan and Walker, *Controlling the Atom*, pp. 13–19.

6. Philip Sporn, "How Can Private Industry Best Participate in the Development of Atomic Energy?" *Bulletin of the Atomic Scientists*, February 1951, p. 48. See also note 18 below.

7. See, for example, Ralph Nader and John Abbotts, *The Menace of Atomic Energy*

(New York and London: W. W. Norton, 1979), pp. 26–27.

8. DelSesto, *Science, Politics, and Controversy*, pp. 50–51, and Mazuzan and Walker, *Controlling the Atom*, pp. 18–19.

9. Mazuzan and Walker, *Controlling the Atom*, p. 19.

10. Editorial, "Atomic Power and Private Enterprise. A Summary of the Joint Committee Report," *Bulletin of the Atomic Scientists*, May 1953, pp. 135–36. See also Abba P. Lerner, "Should We Break Our Biggest Monopoly?" *Bulletin of the Atomic Scientists*, May 1953, p. 110, and Mazuzan and Walker, *Controlling the Atom*, pp. 20–22.

11. Edwin J. Putzell, Jr., "The Prospects for Industry," *Bulletin of the Atomic Scientists*, November 1952, p. 288.

12. Eugene M. Zuckert, "Policy Problems in the Development of Civilian Nuclear Power," *Bulletin of the Atomic Scientists*, November 1952, p. 278.

13. Maria Telkes, "Future Uses of Solar Energy," *Bulletin of the Atomic Scientists*, August 1951, p. 219; Hans Thirring, "Is It Wise to Use Uranium for Power?" *Bulletin of the Atomic Scientists*, August 1952, p. 206; and Materials Policy Commission, *Resources for Freedom*, vol. 4 (Washington, D.C., 1952), p. 220.

14. Charles A. Metzner and Julia B. Kessler, "What Are the People Thinking?" *Bulletin of the Atomic Scientists*, November 1951, p. 341.

15. Byron S. Miller, "Atomic Energy Act: Second Stage," *Bulletin of the Atomic Scientists*, January 1952, pp. 14–16.

16. Thomas E. Murray, "Don't Leave Atomic Energy to the Experts," *Bulletin of the Atomic Scientists*, February 1954, pp. 48–50.

17. Mazuzan and Walker, *Controlling the Atom*, p. 41.

18. Adrian Kuyper, "A Look at the New Atomic Energy Act," *Bulletin of the Atomic Scientists*, December 1954, pp. 390–92.

19. The Nuclear Regulatory Commission is the successor of the Atomic Energy Commission instituted under President Nixon's administration. For a detailed study of the U.S. nuclear energy controversy that extends up to the mid-1970s, see DelSesto, *Science, Politics, and Controversy*. For a variety of documents concerning nuclear power in the United States from early twentieth-century visionary works to 1980s position papers, see Philip L. Cantelon, Richard G. Hewlett, and Robert C. Williams, *The American Atom* (Philadelphia: University of Pennsylvania Press, 1984). As regards the aftermath of the Three Mile Island accident, see "The Three Mile Island Accident," *Science News* 115:227–28 (April 7, 1979); "In the Wake of Three Mile Island," *Science News* 115:292 (May 5, 1979); David F. Salisbury, "Kemeny: A Nuclear 'Reprieve'," *The Christian Science Monitor*, October 31, 1979, pp. A1, A6; "Why Kemeny Seeks Nuclear Agency Reform," *Christian Science Monitor*, November 1, 1979, pp. A1, A7; and "Nuclear Probe's Findings a Political Hot Potato," *Christian Science Monitor*, November 2, 1979, p. A5; editorial staff, "Carter Acts on TMI: A Flood of Changes," *Science News* 116:405–6 (December 15, 1979); and "'Hot' Water Cleanup Begins at TMI," *Science News* 120:247 (October 17, 1981). As regards the Chernobyl accident, see, for example, Arthur H. Purcell, "Chernobyl— Proof of Nuclear Pessimists' Worst Fears," *The Hartford Courant*, May 2, 1986, p. B11. For worldwide developments, see Bertrand Goldschmidt, *The Atomic Complex*, (La Grange Park, Ill.: American Nuclear Society, 1982). For European developments, see Dorothy Nelkin and Michael Pollak, *The Atom Besieged* (Cambridge, Mass., and London: MIT Press, 1982); Dorothy Nelkin. *The Languages of Risk* (Beverly Hills and London: Sage, 1985).

20. John Stuart Mill, "Of the Liberty of Thought and Discussion," ch. 2 in *On Liberty* in *Essential Works of John Stuart Mill*, Max Lerner (ed.) (New York and London: Bantam Books, 1965), p. 272. Quite appropriately, this passage was cited by Barry M. Casper, "Technology Policy and Democracy," *Science* 194:32 (October 1, 1976).

21. Task Force of the Presidential Advisory Group on Anticipated Advances in Science and Technology, "The Science Court Experiment: An Interim Report," *Science* 193:653–56 (August 20, 1976).

22. Alex C. Michalos, "A Reconsideration of the Idea of a Science Court," in P. T. Durbin (ed.), *Research in Philosophy and Technology*, vol. 3 (Greenwich, Conn.: JAI Press, 1980), pp. 14, 26.

23. K. S. Shrader-Frechette, *Science Policy, Ethics, and Economic Methodology* (Dordrecht and Boston: Reidel, 1985), p. 291.

24. Ibid., pp. 291–92.

25. Michalos, "A Reconsideration," p. 26.

26. Shrader-Frechette, *Science Policy*, p. 293.

27. Ibid.

28. Ibid., p. 294.

29. Ibid.

30. Ibid., p. 311.

31. Ibid., pp. 291, 311.

32. The seminal work for this strategy is David Braybrooke and Charles E. Lindblom, *A Strategy of Decision: Policy Evaluation as a Social Process* (New York: Free Press, 1963). The social fragmentation or disjoint nature of policy analysis and evaluation is discussed especially on pp. 104–6. The strategy they propose, however, is incremental; the one I am proposing need not be so. For a more recent discussion of decentralized policy-making and its forms as contrasted with centralized policy-making and its forms, see Patrick W. Hamlett, "A Typology of Decisionmaking in the U.S. Congress," *Technology and Human Values* 8(2):33–40 (Spring 1983). This article is also included in my *Contemporary Moral Controversies in Technology* (New York and London: Oxford University Press, 1987), pp. 313–22, and is discussed on pp. 305–8 of the same book.

Essay 11. Bridging Gaps in Babel

This is a modified version of papers read at Central Connecticut State University as part of the Every Monday series, on November 3, 1986, and at Dalhousie University as part of the Department of Philosophy Summer Series, on July 10, 1987. I am grateful for the intellectually stimulating questions asked and comments made during the discussions that ensued after the readings.

1. A succinct discussion of the senses of the term *ethics* that draws distinctions akin to those in this essay can be found in Marcus G. Singer, *Morals and Values* (New York: Charles Scribner's Sons, 1977), p. 11. Singer's distinctions, however, rely on the notion of a code of conduct, not on the idea of a person's or group's beliefs and presuppositions about right and wrong, good and bad, justified and unjustified—a wider perspective capable of explaining a code of conduct. A more developed version of Singer's distinction, this time in terms of rules, principles, or standards of conduct involved in ideas of right and wrong, can be

found in his presidential address delivered before the eighty-fourth annual meeting of the Western (now Central) Division of the American Philosophical Association, St. Louis, Missouri, May 2, 1986, entitled "The Ideal of a Rational Morality" and published in the American Philosophical Association's *Proceedings and Addresses* 60(1):15–38 (September 1986), especially pp. 16–21.

2. Sylvia Doughty Fries, "Expertise against Politics: Technology as Ideology on Capitol Hill, 1966–1972," *Science, Technology, and Human Values* 8(2):6–15 (Spring 1983).

3. For example, Kristin S. Shrader-Frechette, to whose philosophical position I am quite sympathetic, makes what I believe are overly optimistic remarks of this sort in *Science, Policy, Ethics, and Economic Methodology* (Dordrecht: Reidel, 1985), p. 20.

4. See Annette Baier, *Postures of the Mind* (Minneapolis: University of Minnesota Press, 1985), p. 244, and Kai Nielsen, "Philosophy as Critical Theory," *Proceedings and Addresses of the American Philosophical Association* 61:96–97 (September 1987).

5. Jon Elster, "The Market and the Forum: Three Varieties of Political Theory," in Jon Elster and Aanund Hylland (eds.), *Foundations of Social Choice Theory* (Cambridge, England, and New York: Cambridge University Press, 1989), p. 115.

6. See, for example, Kurt Baier, *The Moral Point of View*, abr. ed. (Ithaca, N.Y.: Cornell University Press, 1965), ch. 6 passim, and Marcus G. Singer, *Generalization in Ethics* (New York: Atheneum, 1961), pp. 190–92, 331–32. See also Norman C. Gillespie, "The Business of Ethics," University of Michigan Business Review 26(6):1–4 (November 1975).

7. For discussions of these topics, see Rustum Roy, "Technological Literacy: An Uphill Battle," *Technology Review*, November-December 1983, pp. 18–19, and "Science for Public Consumption: More than We Can Chew?" *Technology Review*, April 1983, pp. 1–13.

8. See, for example, Plato, *Phaedo* 90b; Aristotle, *Rhetorica* 1.1.2 and 1.2.4; Sextus Empiricus, *Against the Mathematicians* 11.40, and *Pyrronian Questions* 2.205, 247; Cicero, *Letters to Atticus* 4.46; Plutarch, *Moralia* 514a.

9. For accounts of high-temperature superconductivity developments, see I. Peterson, "New Heights in Superconductivity," *Science News*, January 10, 1987, p. 23; S. Weisburd, "Superconductive Barriers Surpassed," *Science News*, February 21, 1987, p. 116; K. Hartley, "No Resistance to Superconductivity," *Science News*, August 8, 1987, pp. 84–85; K. Hartley, "High-Temperature Superconductivity: What's Here, What's Near and What's Unclear," *Science News*, August 15, 1987, pp. 106–7, 109; K. Hartley, "High-Powered Discussions on High-Temperature Superconductivity," *Science News*, December 5, 1987, p. 359; and, for attempts at commercializing high-temperature superconductivity, Dorothy Robin, W. Wendell Fletcher, and John A. Alic, "Bringing Superconductivity to Market," *Issues in Science and Technology*, Winter 1988–89, pp. 38–45.

10. Some of these points are discussed, for example, in Sar A. Levitan and Clifford M. Johnson, "The Future of Work: Does It Belong to Us or to the Robots?" *Monthly Labor Review* 105:10–14 (September 1982), and in Thomas L. Weekley, "Workers, Unions, and Industrial Robotics," *Annals of the American Academy of Political and Social Science* 470:146–51 (November 1983).

11. David Braybrooke, *Traffic Congestion Goes through the Issue Machine* (London

and Boston: Routledge and Kegan Paul, 1974), and *Meeting Needs* (Princeton, N.J.: Princeton University Press, 1987); Kristin Shrader-Frechette, *Nuclear Power and Public Policy* (Dordrecht and Boston: Reidel, 1980), *Science Policy, Ethics, and Economic Methodology* (Dordrecht and Boston: Reidel, 1985), and *Risk Analysis and Scientific Method* (Dordrecht and Boston: Reidel, 1985); Dorothy Nelkin, *The Languages of Risk* (Beverly Hills and London: Sage, 1985); Jon Elster and Aanund Hylland, *Foundations of Social Choice Theory* (Cambridge, England, and New York: Cambridge University Press, 1986); Mark Sagoff, *The Economy of the Earth* (Cambridge, England, and New York: Cambridge University Press, 1988); Jon Elster, *The Cement of Society* (Cambridge, England, and New York: Cambridge University Press, 1989).

12. Fries, "Expertise against Politics."
13. Nielsen, "Philosophy as Critical Theory."
14. See *Contemporary Moral Controversies in Technology* and the review of this book by Dana R. Flint, *Ethics* 99(1):215 (October 1988).
15. This was stated in Carl Mitcham's review of my *Contemporary Moral Controversies in Technology* that appeared in *Canadian Philosophical Reviews* 7(8):312 (August 1987).
16. For evidence attesting to the truth of this, see my *Contemporary Moral Controversies in Technology* and *Contemporary Moral Controversies in Business.*
17. A. Baier, *Postures of Mind*, pp. 243–44.
18. Arthur L. Caplan, "Can Applied Ethics Be Effective in Health Care, and Should It Strive to Be? *Ethics* 93:311–12 (1983).
19. A. Baier, *Postures of Mind*, p. 244.
20. Nielsen, "Philosophy as Critical Theory," p. 98.
21. The relevant literature is overflowing with evidence for the types of conflicts described. Concerning health care ethics committees, see, for example, David Hellerstein, "Overdosing on Medical Technology," *Technology Review*, August-September 1983, pp. 13–17. Concerning recombinant DNA technology, see the arguments for full disclosure and public participation in the policy-making process in David L. Bazelon, "Governing Technology: Values, Choices, and Scientific Progress," *Technology in Society* 5:15–25 (1983). For whatever it is worth, my modest experience in academia—in philosophy, interdisciplinary studies, the development of interdisciplinary courses, curricula, and workshops—and outside of academia—in various business environments in the United States and abroad—corroborates the existence of the conflicts just mentioned, the viability of the multioccupational approach, and the central role that negotiation and other social decision procedures must play.
22. A. Baier, *Postures of Mind*, p. 241.
23. David Hume, *A Treatise of Human Nature*, L. A. Selby-Bigge and P. H. Hiddich (eds.) (Oxford: Clarendon Press, 1978), p. 262. For a discussion of this point, see A. Baier, *Postures of Mind*, pp. 237–244. Dewey's position in this regard is formulated in each of his works. See, for example, John Dewey, *Reconstruction in Philosophy* (Boston: Beacon Press, 1957), *The Quest for Certainty* (New York: G.P. Putnam and Sons, 1960), and John Dewey and James H. Tufts, *Ethics* (New York: Henry Holt, 1918), pt. III.
24. For a discussion of the difficulties some of these programs faced, see Roy, "Technological Literacy." A few years after Roy wrote this piece, MIT announced a curriculum restructure that points in the direction I am suggesting, at least within an academic setting. See "Sweeping Reform of Undergraduate

Education, Changes in Admissions Are Presented at MIT," *The Chronicle of Higher Education* 33(8):1 (October 22, 1986).
25. For a related discussion concerning business ethics, see Robert Allan Cooke, "Business Ethics at the Crossroads," *Journal of Business Ethics* 5(3):260 (June 1986).

ESSAY 12. BETWEEN NEGOTIATION AND COMBAT

1. Combined Wire Services, "Iraq Replaces Kuwaiti Rulers," *The Hartford Courant*, August 3, 1990, pp. A1, A6, A7.
2. For an early discussion of some of the forces at work in these developments, see Willy Brandt et al., *North-South* (Cambridge, Mass.: MIT Press, 1980). For 1989 and 1990 reports, see Rudolf Walter Leonhart, "Regionalism Rising," from *Die Zeit*, in *World Press Review*, December 1990, p. 18. See also Combined Wire Services, "300,000 Rally in Prague for Reforms," *The Hartford Courant*, November 24, 1989, pp. A1, A14; Conor Daly, "In Czechoslovakia, 'Normalcy' Continued Right to the End," *The Hartford Courant*, November 28, 1989, p. B13; Mike Leary, "Krenz Quits as President of East Germany," *The Hartford Courant*, December 7, 1989, pp. A1, A17; Combined Wire Services, "Ousted Romanian Dictator Executed," *The Hartford Courant*, December 26, 1989, pp. A1, A12; Combined Wire Services, "Gorbachev Confronts Lithuanians," *The Hartford Courant*, January 12, 1990, pp. A1, A10; Michael Parks, "Soviet Strife Nears Brink of Civil War," *The Hartford Courant*, January 17, 1990, pp. A1, A4; Ann Imse, "Soviet Party Cedes Monopoly," *The Hartford Courant*, February 8, 1990, pp. A1, A14; Combined Wire Services, "Communists Embrace New Principles," *The Hartford Courant*, February 13, 1990, pp. A1, A9; Combined Wire Services, "Estonians Renounce Soviet Law," *The Hartford Courant*, March 31, 1990, pp. A1, A5; John Thor Dahlburg, "Lithuania Backtracks on Independence." *The Hartford Courant*, June 30, 1990, pp. A1, A9; and Peter Slevin, "Germany Again One Nation," *The Hartford Courant*, October 3, 1990, pp. A1, A16. For a sense of the unraveling of Yugoslavia and its aftermath, see Associated Press, "12 Die in Shelling as Serbs Advance in Bosnia," *The Hartford Courant*, July 27, 1992, p. A8.
3. Evidence of the nature of these military activities is commonplace. The perceived implications of regional armed conflicts for the blocs engaged in the cold war were made plain by U.S. Secretary of State Haig when, on BBC's "Panorama" in April 1984, he commented on the 1982 South Atlantic war between Argentina and Great Britain: "Clearly, I think I shared the concern of the Prime Minister, that this was more than simply a local dispute in the South Atlantic. We had just experienced a decade of the consequences of Western passivity in Angola, Ethiopia, South Yemen, and Afghanistan." Cited in Virginia Gamba, *The Falklands/Malvinas War* (Boston: Allen & Unwin, 1987), p. 151.
4. George F. Will, "The Real Principle behind U.S. Actions in Arabia," *The Hartford Courant*, August 10, 1990, p. C13; David Lightman, "Conflict May Push Gasoline Prices Up," *The Hartford Courant*, August 3, 1990, pp. A1, A7; and Matt Yancey, "Higher Oil Production Might Not Stop Price Rise," *The Hartford Courant*, August 10, 1990, p. A12.
5. John M. Goshko, "France Offers Gulf Peace Plan," *The Hartford Courant*, January 15, 1991, pp. A1–A8.

6. Ruth Sinai, "U.S. Exports May Have Helped Iraq, Syria, Build Up Arsenals," *The Hartford Courant*, December 7, 1990, p. A8.
7. Associated Press, "Threat of Fighting in Gulf Dampens Summit Celebrating End of Cold War," *The Hartford Courant*, November 18, 1990, p. A3.
8. Juan O. Tamayo, "Iraq's Ultimate Goal Remains a Mystery," *The Hartford Courant*, August 3, 1990, pp. A1, A6.
9. President Bush's Address on the Iraq Crisis, *The Hartford Courant*, August 9, 1990, p. B13; Jack Nelson, "U.S. Led Warplanes Bomb Iraqi Targets," *The Hartford Courant*, January 17, 1991, pp. A1, A6, A7.
10. Said during a CBS noon report on January 19, 1991.
11. See, for example, Charles Green and David Hess, "Trip to Underline U.S. Resolve in Gulf," *The Hartford Courant*, December 1, 1990, pp. A1, A8.
12. Owen Ullman and Aaron Epstein, "Democrats Say War Would Need Consent," *The Hartford Courant*, December 5, 1990, pp. A1, A12; and John A. MacDonald, "Baker Asks for Support on Iraq Policy," *The Hartford Courant*, December 6, 1990, pp. A1, A12. See also David Hess and R. A. Zaldivar, "Bush Says War Not Inevitable," *The Hartford Courant*, January 13, 1991, pp. A1, A8; David Lightman, "Debate over Crisis Somber," *The Hartford Courant*, January 13, 1991, pp. A1, A9; and Lyle Denniston, "Bush Says Crucial Moment Reached Iraq's Decision," *The Hartford Courant*, January 13, 1991, p. A8.
13. Charles Krauthammer, "In War Americans Want What Rational People Want: The Impossible," *The Hartford Courant*, January 13, 1991, p. B3.
14. Andrew Maykuth, "Vote Is Only Second Such in History," *The Hartford Courant*, November 30, 1990, pp. A1, A7; Michael Getler, "Decision Is Turning Point in Gulf Crisis," *The Hartford Courant*, November 30, 1990, pp. A1, A10. As indicated by these reports, besides having difficulty marshaling UN support for the resolution, the United States was not placed in command of all the forces.
15. Combined Wire Services, "Bush Warns Iraq May Get Nuclear Arms," *The Hartford Courant*, November 23, 1990, pp. A1, A8.
16. William James, "The Will to Believe," in his *The Will to Believe and Other Essays in Popular Philosophy* (New York: Dover, 1956), pp. 1–31.
17. Gamba, *The Falklands*, p. 165.
18. Mark Thomson, "Missiles Likely to Strike First," *The Hartford Courant*, January 13, 1990, pp. A1, A6.
19. Announced on the Hartford-New Haven area ABC TV channel during a January 16, 1991, crisis update, at 10 a.m.
20. Quoted during the ABC coverage of the war in the Hartford-New Haven area.
21. Martin Mertzer and John Donnelley, "Iraq Launches Missiles against Israeli Targets," *The Hartford Courant*, January 18, 1991, pp. A1, A18, and ABC reports on January 19, 1990.
22. On ABC, Egypt's ambassador said on January 18: "You just don't have to worry."
23. Combined Wire Services, "Bush Decries Attacks," *The Hartford Courant*, January 14, 1991, pp. A1, A7.
24. John A. MacDonald, "Baker Asks for Support on Iran Policy," *The Hartford Courant*, December 6, 1990, pp. A1, A12.
25. David Jacobson, "Conflict May Not Be Short," *The Hartford Courant*, January 16, 1991, pp. A1, A6.
26. Anthony C. Arendt discusses this matter concerning another Western conflict, the 1982 war between Argentina and Great Britain, in "The Falklands War and

the Failure of the International Legal Order," in Alberto R. Coll and Anthony C. Arend (eds.), *The Falklands War* (Boston: Allen & Unwin, 1985), pp. 54 (regarding collective security), 59 (regarding peaceful change mechanism).

27. Ibid., p. 61.
28. David A. Colson, "The Falkland Islands Crisis and the Management of Boundary Disputes," in Coll and Arend, *The Falklands War*, pp. 212–13.
29. Alberto L. Coll, "Lessons for the Future," in Coll and Arend, *The Falklands War*, p. 241.
30. This is the topic of a research idea that Lewis A. Dexter developed in conversation with David Riesman at Harvard, soon after his April visit with us in Connecticut, and described in the June 10, 1989, correspondence I received from him.
31. Associated Press, "British Nuclear Attack Plan Claimed," *The Hartford Courant*, August 23, 1984, p. A25.
32. Editorial comment, "Buenos Aires and the Bomb," *The Guardian*, May 2, 1982, p. 10; John R. Redick, "Latin America and the Bomb," *The Christian Science Monitor*, October 20, 1982, p. 23; Milton Benjamin, "U.S. Lets Argentina Buy Nuclear Matter," *The Hartford Courant*, August 18, 1983, p. A7; and James Brooke, "Argentine Accident Raises Questions about Third-World Nuclear Standards," *The Hartford Courant*, December 14, 1983, p. A13.
33. Lucille Renwick and Kathleen Megan, "1 Million Civilians Could Die in War, Doctor Says," *The Hartford Courant*, January 14, 1991, pp. C1, C7.
34. David C. Gompert, "American Diplomacy and the Haig Mission: An Insider's Perspective," in Coll and Arend, *The Falklands War*, p. 114.
35. Andrew Maykuth, "Vote Is Only Second Such in Its History," *The Hartford Courant*, November 30, 1990, pp. A1, A7.
36. Daniel Williams, "U.N. Chief Ends Iraq Visit," *The Hartford Courant*, January 14, 1991, pp. A1, A6.
37. This statement was made by Mr. Ramon on June 1, 1988, on "Nightline," a program televised throughout the United States.
38. Colson, "Falkland Islands Crisis," pp. 214–22. See also from the *Los Angeles Times*, "Britain, China Prepare to Initial Agreement on 1997 Transfer of Hong Kong," *The Hartford Courant*, September 20, 1984, p. A16; Courant's Wire Services, "Accord Reached on Hong Kong," *The Hartford Courant*, September 19, 1984, p. A2; and Associated Press, "Argentina, Chile to Sign Channel Pact," *The Hartford Courant*, October 5, 1984, p. A21. An example of an attempt at proactive diplomacy in a near crisis situation is the U.N.'s decision to send troops to Macedonia in order to prevent it from being invaded by Serbia once this country is finished with so-called "ethnic cleansing" in Bosnia, See from the *Los Angeles Times*, "U.N. Force to Go to Macedonia," *The Hartford Courant*, Saturday, December 12, 1992, p. A3.

Selected Bibliography

Abbot, A. "Professional Ethics." *American Journal of Sociology* 88:855–85 (1983).

Ackerman, R. W. *The Social Challenge to Business.* Cambridge: Harvard University Press, 1975.

Adams, Valerie. *The Media and the Falklands Campaign.* New York: Macmillan, 1987.

Addis, Laird. "The Individual and the Marxist Philosophy of History." *Philosophy of Science* 33:101–17 (1966).

Aftergood, Steven. "The Perils of Government Secrecy." *Issues in Science and Technology.* Summer 1992, 81–88.

Aiken, William, and Hugh La Follette, eds. *World Hunger and Moral Obligation.* Englewood Cliffs, N.J.: Prentice-Hall, 1977.

American Public Power Association. "The Case for Public Power." *Bulletin of the Atomic Scientists.* May 1953, p. 134.

Anderson, James E. *Public Policy-Making.* New York: Holt, Rinehart and Winston, 1979.

Anderson, James E., et al. *Public Policy and Politics in America.* Belmont, Calif.: Duxbury/Wadsworth, 1978.

Andrews, Kenneth R. *The Concept of Corporate Strategy.* Homewood, Ill.: Dow Jones-Irwin, 1980.

Aram, John D., ed. *Managing Business and Public Policy.* White Plains, N.Y.: Pitman, 1986.

Arendt, Hannah. "What Was Authority?" In Carl Friedrich (ed.). *Authority.* Cambridge: Harvard University Press, 1966.

Arrow, Kenneth Joseph. *Social Choice and Individual Values.* 2d ed. New York: John Wiley and Sons, 1963.

Atkins, Gary. "In Search of New Objectivity." In Leonard L. Sellers and William L. Rivers, eds. *Mass Media Issues.* Englewood Cliffs, N.J.: Prentice-Hall, 1977.

Bachelard, Gaston. *Essai sur la Connaissance Approchée.* Paris: Vrin, 1969.

Baier, Annette. *Postures of the Mind.* Minneapolis: University of Minnesota Press, 1985.

Baier, Kurt. *The Moral Point of View*, abr. ed. New York: Random House, 1965.

Banfield, Edward. *Political Influence.* New York: Free Press, 1961.

Baram, Michael S. "Technology Assessment and Social Control." *Science* 180:465–73 (1973).

Barber, Benjamin. *The Conquest of Politics.* Princeton, N.J.: Princeton University Press, 1988.

Barbour, Ian G. *Technology, Environment, and Human Values.* New York: Praeger Publishers, 1980.

Barry, Brian. *Political Argument.* London: Routledge and Kegan Paul, 1965.

Barry, Brian, and Russell Hardin. *Rational Man and Irrational Society? An Introduction and Sourcebook.* Beverly Hills, Calif.: Sage, 1982.

Baum, Robert J., and Albert Flores, eds. *Ethical Problems in Engineering.* New York: Center for the Study of Human Dimensions of Science and Technology, 1978.

Bazelon, David L. "Governing Technology: Values, Choices, and Scientific Progress." *Technology and Society* 5:15–25 (1983).

Beauchamp, Tom L., and Norman Bowie, eds. *Ethical Theory and Business.* 3d ed. Englewood Cliffs, N.J.: Prentice-Hall, 1988.

Becker, Lawrence C. "The Finality of Moral Judgments." *Philosophical Review* 82:364–70 (1973).

Beiner, Ronald. *Political Judgment.* Chicago: University of Chicago Press, 1983.

Bentham, Jeremy. "The Principles of Morals and Legislation." In Mary Warnock, ed. *Utilitarianism, On Liberty, Essay on Bentham, Together with Selected Writings of Jeremy Bentham and John Austin.* Cleveland and New York: Meridian, 1968.

Berlin, Sir Isaiah. *On the Pursuit of the Ideal.* Turin, Italy: Fondazione Giovanni Agnelli, 1988.

Bernard, Thomas J. *The Consensus-Conflict Debate.* New York: Columbia University Press, 1983.

Berry, Wendell. *The Unsettling of America. Culture and Agriculture.* New York: Avon, 1977.

Besnard, P. *L'anomie.* Paris: Presses Universitaires de France, 1987.

Bierbaum, Rosina, and Robert M. Friedman. "The Road to Reduced Carbon Emissions." *Issues in Science and Technology.* Winter 1991–92, pp. 58–65.

Bluestone, Barry, and Bennet Harrison. *The Deindustrialization of America.* New York: Basic, 1982.

Boden, Margaret A. "Educational Implications of Artificial Intelligence." In W. Maxwell, ed. *Thinking: The New Frontier.* Pittsburgh: Franklin Press, 1983.

———. "Impacts of Artificial Intelligence." *Futures.* February 1984, pp. 60–69.

Boruta, Marcia, and Hugh Mehan. "Computers in the Classroom: Stratifier or Equalizer?" *Science for the People.* March/April 1985, pp. 41–44.

Bosselman, F., et al. *The Taking Issue.* Washington, D.C.: U.S. Government Printing Office, 1971.

Bottomore, Tom. *Crisis and Contention in Sociology.* Beverly Hills and London: Sage, 1975.

Bouwsma, William J. "Politics in the Age of the Renaissance." Joseph Rotschild, David Sidorsky, and Bernard Wishy, eds. *Chapters in Western Civilization.* New York: Columbia University Press, 1961.

Bozeman, Barry. *Public Management and Policy Analysis.* New York: St. Martin's Press, 1979.

Brandt, Willy, et al. *North-South: A Programme for Survival.* Cambridge: MIT Press, 1980.

Braybrooke, David, ed. *Ethics in the World of Business.* Totowa, N.J.: Rowman & Allanheld, 1983.

———. *Meeting Needs.* Princeton, N.J.: Princeton University Press, 1987.

———. "Policy Formation with Issue-Processing and Transformation of Issues." In G. A. Hooker, J. J. Leach, and E. F. McClennen, eds. *Foundations and Applications of Decision Theory.* Dordrecht, Holland: Reidel, 1978.

———. *Studies in Moral Philosophy.* Oxford: Blackwell, 1968.

———. *Three Tests for Democracy: Personal Rights, Human Welfare, Collective Preference.* New York: Random House, 1968.

———. *Traffic Congestion Goes through the Issue Machine.* London and Boston: Routledge and Kegan Paul, 1974.

———. "Work: A Cultural Ideal Ever More in Jeopardy." In Peter A. French, Theodore E. Uehling, Jr., and Howard K. Wettstein, eds. *Midwest Studies in Philosophy,* 7:321–341 (1982).

Braybrooke, David, and Charles E. Lindblom. *A Strategy of Decision: Policy Evaluation as a Social Process.* New York: Free Press, 1963.

Brechner, K. C. "An Experimental Analysis of Social Traps." *Journal of Experimental Social Psychology* 13:552–64 (1977).

Brink, W., and L. Harris. *The Negro Revolution in America.* New York: Simon and Schuster, 1964.

Bromberg, Joan Lisa. *Fusion: Science, Politics, and the Invention of a New Energy Source.* Cambridge: MIT, 1982.

Bromley, D. Allan. "The Making of a Greenhouse Policy." *Issues in Science and Technology.* Fall 1990, pp. 55–61.

Brown, David W. *Cooperation among Strangers*. Dayton, Ohio: Kettering Foundation, 1992.

Bruce, Bertram. "Taking Control of Educational Technology." *Science for the People*. March/April 1985, pp. 37–40.

Brucker, Herbert. "What's Wrong with Objectivity." *Saturday Review*. October 11, 1969, pp. 77–79.

Bryerton, Gene. *Nuclear Dilemma*. New York: Friends of the Earth/Ballantine Books, 1970.

Buchanan, Allen. *Ethics, Efficiency, and the Market*. Totowa, N.J.: Rowman & Allanheld, 1985.

Buchholz, Eugene, ed. *Business Environments and Public Policy*. Englewood Cliffs, N.J.: Prentice-Hall, 1986.

Bueno de Mesquita, B. *The War Trap*. New Haven, Conn.: Yale University Press, 1981.

Bunge, Mario. "Game Theory Is Not a Useful Tool for the Political Scientist." *Epistemologia XII* 1989:195–212, and *Cahiers d'épistémologie*, No. 9015. Montréal: Université de Québec à Montréal. October 1990.

———. *The Myth of Simplicity*. Englewood Cliffs, N.J.: Prentice-Hall, 1963.

———. *Racionalidad y realismo*. Madrid: Alianza Universidad, 1985.

———. *Seudociencia e ideologia*. Madrid: Alianza Editorial, 1985.

———. *Treatise on Basic Philosophy*, Vol. 8. *Ethics: The Good and the Right*. Dordrecht, Boston, Lancaster: Reidel, 1989.

Burckhardt, Jakob. *The Civilization of the Renaissance in Italy*. Oxford: Phaidon, 1981.

———. *Griechische Kulturgesichte*. Vols. I-V. Berlin and Stuttgart: M. Spenmann, 1898–1902.

Burke, Edmund. *The Works of Edmund Burke*. Vol. V. Boston: Little, Brown, 1881.

Burke, Kenneth. *Attitudes toward History*. Los Altos, Calif.: Hermes, 1959.

Busch, Lawrence, and William B. Lacy. *Science, Agriculture, and the Politics of Research*. Boulder, Colo.: Westview, 1983.

Campbell, Richmond, and Lanning Sowden, eds. *Paradoxes of Rationality and Cooperation*. Vancouver: University of British Columbia Press, 1985.

Cantelon, Philip L., Richard G. Hewlett, and Robert C. Williams. *The American Atom*. Philadelphia: University of Pennsylvania Press, 1984.

Caplan, Arthur L. "Can Applied Ethics Be Effective in Health Care, and Should It Strive to Be?" *Ethics* 93:311–19 (1983).

———. "Ethical Engineers Need Not Apply: The State of Applied Ethics Today." *Science, Technology, and Human Values* 6(33):24–32 (Fall 1980).

Casper, Barry M., "Technology Policy and Democracy," *Science* 194:29–35 (Oct. 1, 1976).

Chalk, Rosemary. "Commentary on the NSA Report." *Science, Technology and Human Values* 8(1):21–24 (Winter 1983).

Chamberlain, N. W. *The Limits of Corporate Responsibility*. New York: Basic, 1973.

Cisler, Walker L. "Electric Power Systems and Nuclear Power." *Bulletin of the Atomic Scientists*. November 1952, pp. 279–82.

Clark, Ian. *Limited Nuclear War*. Princeton, N.J.: Princeton University Press, 1982.

Clifford, W. K. "The Ethics of Belief." *Contemporary Review* (January 1877). Later reprinted in his *Lectures and Essays*. London: Macmillan, 1879.

Coburn, Alexander, and James Ridgeway, eds. *Political Ecology*. New York: Times Books, 1979.

Coburn, R. "Technology Assessment, Human Good, and Freedom." In K. E. Goodpaster and K. M. Sayre, eds. *Ethics & Problems of the 21st Century*. Notre Dame, Ind.: Notre Dame University Press, 1979.

Cohen, Avner, and Steven Lee, eds. *Nuclear Weapons and the Future of Humanity*. Totowa, N.J.: Rowman & Allanheld, 1986.

Cohen, Karl. "A Re-Examination of the McMahon Act." *Bulletin of the Atomic Scientists*. January 1948, pp. 7–10.

Cohen, Marshall, Thomas Nagel, and Thomas Scanlon, eds. *The Rights and Wrongs of Abortion*. Princeton, N.J.: Princeton University Press, 1974.

Coleman, James Samuel. *Foundations of Social Theory*. Cambridge: Harvard University Press, 1990.

Coll, Alberto R., and Anthony C. Arend, eds. *The Falklands War*. Boston: Allen & Unwin, 1985.

Comisión Nacional Sobre la Desaparición de Personas. *Anexos*. Buenos Aires: Editorial Universitaria de Buenos Aires, 1985.

Comisión Nacional Sobre la Desaparición de Personas. *Nunca Màs*. Buenos Aires: Editorial Universitaria de Buenos Aires, 1985.

Comte, Auguste. *System of Positive Polity*. New York: Burt Franklin, 1968.

Connolly, William E. *The Terms of Political Discourse*. 2d ed. Princeton, N.J.: Princeton University Press, 1983.

Cooke, Robert Allan. "Business Ethics at the Crossroads." *Journal of Business Ethics* 5(3):259–63 (June 1986).

Costanza, Robert. "The Nuclear Arms Race and the Theory of Social Traps." *Journal of Peace Research* 21:79–86 (1984).

Coye, Molly Joel. "Health Care for the Uninsured." *Issues in Science and Technology*. Summer 1992, pp. 56–69.

Cropsey, Joseph. *Political Philosophy and the Issues of Politics*. Chicago: University of Chicago Press, 1977.

Cross, J. G., and M. J. Guyer. *Social Traps*. Ann Arbor: University of Michigan Press, 1980.

Dahrendorf, Ralf. "Out of Utopia: Toward a Reorientation of Sociological Analysis." *American Journal of Sociology*. September 1958, pp. 115–27.

Daniels, Norman. *Just Health Care*. Cambridge, England: Cambridge University Press, 1985.

Dawkins, Richard. *The Selfish Gene*. New York and London: Oxford University Press, 1976.

Day, Alan J., ed. *Treatises and Alliances of the World*. 3d ed. Detroit: Gale, 1981.

De George, Richard T. *Business Ethics*. 2d ed. New York: Macmillan, 1986.

DelSesto, Steven L. *Science, Politics, and Controversy: Civilian Nuclear Power in the United States, 1946–1974*. Boulder, Colo.: Westview Press, 1979.

De Magahlães, José Calvet. *The Pure Concept of Diplomacy*. New York; Westport, Conn.; and London: Greenwood Press, 1988.

Dennett, Daniel C. "The Moral First Aid Manual." In Sterling M. McMurrin, ed. *The Tanner Lectures on Human Values, VIII*. Salt Lake City and Cambridge: University of Utah Press, Cambridge University Press, 1988.

Der Derian, James. *On Diplomacy*. Oxford: Basil Blackwell, 1987.

Dewey, John. *The Quest for Certainty*. New York: Putnam, 1960.

———. *Reconstruction in Philosophy*. Boston: Beacon Press, 1957.

Dewey, John, and James H. Tufts. *Ethics*. New York: Henry Holt, 1918.

Dewey, Thomas E. "The Challenge of the Atomic Age." *Bulletin of the Atomic Scientists*. October 1948, pp. 296–98.

Dexter, Lewis Anthony. "Intra-Agency Politics: Conflict and Contravention in Administrative Entities." *Journal of Theoretical Politics* 2:151–72 (1990).

Dexter, Lewis Anthony, and David Manning White. *People, Society, and Mass Communications*. New York: Free Press, 1964.

Didion, Joan. *Slouching towards Bethlehem*. New York: Farrar, Straus and Giroux, 1968.

Dobel, J. Patrick, *Compromise and Political Action: Political Morality in Liberal and Democratic Life*. Totowa, N.J.: Rowman & Littlefield, 1990.

Dolbeare, Kenneth. *Public Policy Evaluation*. Beverly Hills and London: Sage, 1975.

Donaldson, Thomas, and Patricia H. Werhane, eds. *Ethical Issues in Business*. Englewood Cliffs, N.J.: Prentice-Hall, 1983.

Dorf, R. C. *Technology and Society*. San Francisco: Boyd and Fraser, 1974.

Dornbusch, Rudiger. *Open Economy Macro-Economics*. New York: Basic, 1980.

Dorner, Peter, and Mahmoud A. El-Shafie. *Resources and Development: Natural Resource Policies and Economic Development in an Interdependent World*. Madison: University of Wisconsin Press, 1980.

Douglas, Mary, and Aaron Wildavsky. *Risk and Culture*. Berkeley, Los Angeles, and London: University of California Press, 1982.

Drucker, P. F. *Management: Tasks, Responsibilities, Practices*. New York: Harper & Row, 1973.

Dryzek, John S. *Discursive Democracy: Politics, Policy, and Political Science*. New York and Cambridge, England: Cambridge University Press, 1990.

Ducassé, Pierre. *Histoire des techniques*. Paris: Presses Universitaires de France, 1945.

———. *Les Techniques et le philosophe*. Paris, Presses Universitaires de France, 1958.

Dunn, John. *Rethinking Modern Political Theory*. London: Cambridge University Press, 1985.

Dunn, William N. *Public Policy Analysis*. Englewood Cliffs, N.J.: Prentice-Hall, 1981.

Dworkin, Ronald. *A Matter of Principle*. Cambridge: Harvard University Press, 1985.

———. *Taking Rights Seriously*. Cambridge: Harvard University Press, 1977.

Dye, Thomas R. *Understanding Public Policy*. Englewood Cliffs, N.J.: Prentice-Hall, 1972.

Dye, T. R., and V. Gray. *The Determinants of Public Policy*. Lexington, MA: Lexington Books, 1980.

Edelman, R. J. *The Psychology of Embarrassment*. New York: Wiley, 1987.

Editorial Staff. "Atoms for Peace in the U.N." *Bulletin of the Atomic Scientists*. January 1955, pp. 24–25.

Eisenhower, Dwight D. "The President's Proposal." *Bulletin of the Atomic Scientists*. December 1953, pp. 2–4.

Ellul, Jacques. *The Technological Society*. New York: Random House, 1964.

Elster, Jon. *The Cement of Society*. Cambridge, England, and New York: Cambridge University Press, 1989.

———. *Explaining Technical Change*. Cambridge, England: Cambridge University Press, 1983.

———, ed. *Rational Choice*. New York: New York University Press, 1986.

Elster, Jon, and Aanund Hylland, eds. *Foundations of Social Choice Theory*. Cambridge, England: Cambridge University Press, 1989.

Enos, Darryl D., and Paul Sultan. *The Sociology of Health Care*. New York: Praeger, 1977.

Enthoven, Alain C., and K. Wayne Smith. *How Much Is Enough?* New York: Harper & Row, 1971.

Etzioni, Amitai. *The Moral Dimension: Toward a New Economics*. New York: Free Press, 1988.

Fain, Haskell. *Normative Politics and the Community of Nations*. Philadelphia: Temple University Press, 1987.

Faris, Ralph M. *Crisis and Consciousness*. Amsterdam: B. R. Grüner, 1977.

Feinberg, Joel, ed. *The Problems of Abortion*. Belmont, Calif.: Wadsworth, 1973.

Fink, Conrad C. *Media Ethics*. New York: McGraw-Hill, 1988.

Fischer, Frank. *Politics, Values, and Public Policy. The Problem of Methodology*. Boulder, Colo.: Westview Press, 1980.

Fishkin, James S. *Tyranny and Legitimacy: A Critique of Political Theories*. Baltimore and London: Johns Hopkins University Press, 1979.

Flint, Dana R. "Review of Contemporary Moral Controversies in Technology." *Ethics* 99(1):215 (October 1988).

Florman, Samuel, "Science for Public Consumption: More than We Can Chew?" *Technology Review*. April 1983, pp. 1–13.

Foley, Gerald, and Charlotte Nassim. *The Energy Question*. New York: Penguin Books, 1976.

Foot, Philippa. "Hypothetical Imperatives." *Philosophical Review* 81:305–16 (1972).

Freedman, J. O. *Crisis and Legitimacy*. Cambridge, England: Cambridge University Press, 1978.

Freedman, Lawrence. "The War of the Falkland Islands, 1982." *Foreign Affairs*. Fall 1982, pp. 196–210.

Freeman, A., R. Haveman, and A. Kneese. *The Economics of Environmental Policy*. Baltimore: Resources for the Future and Johns Hopkins University Press, 1973.

French, Peter A., Theodore E. Uehling, Jr., and Howard K. Wettstein, eds. *Midwest Studies in Philosophy*. Minneapolis: University of Minnesota Press, 1982.

Friedman, Milton. *Essays in Positive Economics*. Chicago: University of Chicago Press, 1953.

Friedrich, Carl J. *Authority*. Cambridge: Harvard University Press, 1958.

———. *Community*. New York: Liberal Arts Press, 1959.

———. *Liberty*. New York: Atherton Press, 1962.

———. *The Public Interest*. New York: Atherton Press, 1962.

———. *Justice*. New York: Atherton Press, 1963.

———. *Rational Decision*. New York: Atherton Press, 1964.

Fries, Sylvia Doughty. "Expertise against Politics: Technology as Ideology on Capitol Hill, 1966–1972." *Science, Technology, and Human Values* 8(2):6–15 (Spring 1983).

Frisch, O. R. "On the Feasibility of Coal-Driven Power Stations." *Bulletin of the Atomic Scientists*. June 1954, p. 224.

Frohock, Fred M. *Public Policy: Scope and Logic*. Englewood Cliffs, N.J.: Prentice-Hall, 1979.

Gamba, Virginia. *The Falklands/Malvinas War*. Boston: Allen & Unwin, 1987.

Gardels, Nathan. "Two Concepts of Nationalism: An Interview with Isaiah Berlin." *The New York Review of Books* 38(19):19–23 (November 21, 1991).

Gendron, Bernard. *Technology and the Human Condition*. New York: St. Martin's Press, 1977.

Gibbons, John H., et al. *Automation and the Workplace*. Washington, D.C.: Congress of the United States Office of Technology Assessment, 1983.

———. *Computer-Based National Information Systems*. Washington, D.C.: Congress of the United States Office of Technology Assessment, 1981.

———. *Computerized Manufacturing Automation*. Washington, D.C.: Congress of the United States Office of Technology Assessment, 1984.

———. *Space Science Research in the United States*. Washington, D.C.: Congress of the United States Office of Technology Assessment, 1982.

Gillespie, Norman C. "The Business of Ethics." *University of Michigan Business Review* 26(6):1–4 (November 1975).

Goldman, Alan H. *Justice and Reverse Discrimination*. Princeton, N.J.: Princeton University Press, 1979.

Goldschmidt, Bertrand, *The Atomic Complex*. La Grange Park, Ill.: American Nuclear Society, 1982.

Goodin, Robert E. *Manipulatory Politics*. New Haven and London: Yale University Press, 1980.

Goodpaster, K. E., and K. M. Sayre, eds. *Ethics & Problems of the 21st Century*. Notre Dame, Ind.: Notre Dame University Press, 1979.

Gottlieb, Gidon. *The Logic of Choice*. New York: Macmillan, 1968.

Gray, Colin S. "Nuclear Strategy: The Case for a Theory of Victory." *International Security* 4(1):54–87 (1979).

Gray, Colin S., and Keith Payne. "Victory Is Possible." *Foreign Policy* 59:14–27 (1980).

Gregg, Phillip M. *Problems of Theory in Policy Analysis*. Lexington, MA: Lexington Books, 1976.

Groussard, Serge. *The Blood of Israel*. New York: William Morrow, 1975.

Grubel, Herbert C. *International Economics*. Homewood, Ill.: Irwin, 1981.

Grumm, John G., and Stephen L. Wasby, eds. *The Analysis of Policy Impact*. Lexington, MA: Lexington Books, 1981.

Habermas, Jürgen. *Knowledge and Human Interests*. Boston: Beacon Press, 1968.

———. *Legitimation Crisis*. Boston: Beacon Press, 1975.

———. "Morality and the Law." In Sterling M. McMurrin, ed. *The Tanner Lectures on Human Values, VIII*. Salt Lake City and Cambridge, England: University of Utah Press, Cambridge University Press, 1988.

———. *Theory and Practice*. Boston: Beacon Press, 1973.

Hahn, Frank, and Martin Hollis, eds. *Philosophy and Economic Theory*. Oxford, New York: Oxford University Press, 1979.

Hallin, Daniel C. *The Uncensored Press: The Media and Vietnam*. New York: Oxford University Press, 1987.

Halperin Donghi, Tulio. "Argentina's Unmastered Past." *Latin American Research Review* 23(2):3–24 (1988).

Hamlett, Patrick W. "Science, Technology, and Liberal Democratic Theory." *Technology in Society* 6:249–62 (1984).

———. "A Typology of Technological Policymaking in the U.S. Congress." *Technology and Human Values* 8(2):33–40 (Spring 1983).

Hampshire, Stuart. *Morality and Conflict*. Cambridge: Harvard University Press, 1983.

Hardt, J. P., and G. D. Holliday. "U.S.-Soviet Commercial Relations: The Interplay of Economics, Technology Transfer and Diplomacy." Washington, D.C.: U.S. Government Printing Office, 1973.

Hare, R. M. *Freedom and Reason*. New York: Oxford University Press, 1963.

Harrington, Michael. *The Next Left*. New York: Holt, 1986.

Hausman, Daniel M., ed. *The Philosophy of Economics*. Cambridge, England, New York: Cambridge University Press, 1984.

Hawkes, Jacquetta, Sir Leonard Wooley, et al., eds. *Historia de La Humanidad*. Buenos Aires: Editorial Sudamericana, 1963.

Haynes, Richard, and Ray Lanier, eds. *Agriculture, Change, and Human Values*. Vols. 1 and 2. Gainesville, Fla.: University of Florida Humanities and Agriculture Program, 1983.

Heath, Anthony. *Rational Choice and Social Exchange*. Cambridge, England: Cambridge University Press, 1976.

Heidegger, Martin. *Basic Writings*. New York: Harper & Row, 1977.

Heilbroner, Robert L. *Between Capitalism and Socialism*. New York: Vintage, 1970.

————. *The Making of Economic Society.* Englewood Cliffs, N.J.: Prentice-Hall, 1962.

Held, Virginia. "The Political 'Testing' of Moral Theories." In Peter A. French, Theodore E. Uehling, Jr., and Howard K. Wettstein, eds. *Midwest Studies in Philosophy* 7:343–63 (1982).

————. *The Public Interest and Individual Interest.* New York: Basic, 1970.

Held, Virginia, Sidney Morgenbesser, and Thomas Nagel, eds. *Philosophy, Morality, and International Affairs.* New York and London: Oxford University Press, 1974.

Hellerstein, David. "Overdosing on Medical Technology." *Technology Review.* August-September 1983, pp. 13–17.

Herrick, Charles N. "Science and Climate Policy: A History Lesson." *Issues in Science and Technology.* Winter 1991–92, pp. 56–57.

Hill, Philip G. *Power Generation.* Cambridge, Mass., and London: MIT Press, 1977.

Hitch, Charles J., and Roland McKean. *The Economics of Defense in the Nuclear Age.* Cambridge: Harvard University Press, 1962.

Hobbes, Thomas. "Leviathan." In D. D. Raphael, ed. *British Moralists 1650–1880.* Oxford: Clarendon Press, 1969.

Hoffman, Ross J. S., and Paul Levack, eds. *Burke's Politics.* New York: Knopf, 1949.

Hoffman, W. Michael, and Jennifer Mills Moore, eds. *Ethics and the Management of Computer Technology.* Cambridge: Oelgeschlager, Gunn and Hain, 1982.

Honderich, Ted. *Political Violence.* Ithaca, N.Y.: Cornell, 1976.

Hook, Sidney, ed. *Human Values and Economic Policy.* New York: New York University Press, 1967.

————. *Philosophy and Public Policy.* Carbondale, Edwardsville: Southern Illinois University Press, 1980.

Hooker, C. A., J. J. Leach, and E. F. McClennen, eds. *Foundations and Applications of Decision Theory.* Dordrecht, Holland: Reidel, 1978.

Hopkins, Raymond F., and Donald J. Puchala, eds. *The Global Economy of Food.* Madison: University of Wisconsin Press, 1978.

Horowitz, I. L., and J. E. Katz. *Social Science and Public Policy in the U.S.* New York: Praeger, 1975.

Hume, David. *A Treatise of Human Nature.* Oxford: Oxford University Press, 1967 (1888).

Hysom, John L., and William J. Bolce. *Business and Its Environment.* St. Paul, Minn.: West, 1983.

Iannone, A. Pablo. "Character Traits." Ph.D. thesis, University of Wisconsin-Madison, 1975.

————, ed. *Contemporary Moral Controversies in Business.* New York and London: Oxford University Press, 1989.

————, ed. *Contemporary Moral Controversies in Technology.* New York and London: Oxford University Press, 1987.

————. "Critical Interaction: Judgment, Decision, and the Social Testing of Moral Hypotheses." *International Journal of Social and Moral Studies* 6(2):135–48 (Summer 1991).

————. "Informing the Public: Ethics, Policy Making, and Objectivity in News Reporting." *Philosophy in Context* 20:1–21 (1990).

————. "Review of Sterling M. McMurrin's *The Tanner Lectures on Human Values, VIII.*" *History of European Ideas* 10(4):484–85 (1989).

————. "Social Choice Theory: Formalism Infatuation and Policy Making Realities." *Epistemologia: Italian Journal for the Philosophy of Science* (1992).

————. "Social Traps: High-Tech Weapons, Rarefied Theories, and the World of Politics." *Epistemologia: Italian Journal for the Philosophy of Science* 1991: 219–37.

————. *Through Time and Culture.* Englewood Cliffs, N.J.: Prentice-Hall, 1993.

Inglis, David R. "Atomic Profits and the Question of Survival." *Bulletin of the Atomic Scientists.* May 1953, pp. 114–18.

Jackson, David A., and Stephen P. Stich, eds. *The Recombinant DNA Debate.* Englewood Cliffs, N.J.: Prentice-Hall, 1979.

Jaeger, W. *Paideia. The Ideals of Greek Culture.* New York: 1939.

James, William. *The Will to Believe and Other Essays in Popular Philosophy.* New York: Dover, 1956.

Jenkins, W. I. *Policy Analysis.* New York: St. Martin's Press, 1978.

Jones, Charles O. *An Introduction to the Study of Public Policy.* Belmont, Calif.: Duxbury/Wadsworth, 1970.

Kahneman, Daniel, Paul Slovic, and Amos Tversky, eds. *Judgment Under Uncertainty: Heuristics and Biases.* Cambridge, England: Cambridge University Press, 1982.

Kammeyer, Kenneth C. W., ed. *Population Studies: Selected Essays and Research.* Chicago: Rand McNally, 1975.

Kanel, Don. "The Human Predicament: Society, Institutions, and Individuals." *Journal of Economic Issues* 22(2):427–34 (1988).

————. "Institutional Economics: Perspectives on Economy and Society." *Journal of Economic Issues* 19(3):815–28 (1985).

Kant, Immanuel. *Foundations of the Metaphysics of Morals.* Robert Paul Wolff, ed. Indianapolis and New York: Bobbs-Merrill, 1969.

Kavanagh, John P. "Ethical Issues in Plant Relocation." *Business and Professional Ethics Journal.* Winter 1982, pp. 21–33.

Keeny, Spurgeon M. Jr., et al. *Nuclear Power Issues and Choices.* Cambridge: Ballinger, 1977.

Keeny, Spurgeon M. Jr. "Proposed Modifications to Nonproliferation Legislation." *United States Department of State Bulletin.* November 14, 1977, pp. 671–73.

Kennedy, Duncan. "Cost-Benefit Analysis of Entitlement Problems: A Critique." *Stanford Law Review* 33 (1981).

Keynes, John Maynard. *The General Theory of Employment, Interest, and Money.* New York: Harcourt, Brace & World, 1964.

Klemke, E. D., A. David Kline, and Robert Hollinger. *Philosophy: The Basic Issues.* New York: St. Martin's Press, 1986.

Kohlberg, L. *The Philosophy of Moral Development.* San Francisco: Harper & Row, 1981.

Krushwitz, Robert B., and Robert C. Roberts. *The Virtues.* Belmont, Calif.: Wadsworth, 1987.

Kruytbosch, C. E. *Academic-Corporate Research Relationships: Forms, Functions, and Fantasies.* Washington, D.C.: National Science Foundation, 1981.

Kuehn, Thomas J., and Alan L. Porter, eds. *Science, Technology, and National Policy.* Ithaca and London: Cornell University Press, 1981.

Kuhn, Thomas S. *The Structure of Scientific Revolutions.* 2d ed. Chicago: University of Chicago Press, 1970.

Kuyper, Adrian. "A Look at the New Atomic Energy Act." *Bulletin of the Atomic Scientists.* December 1954, pp. 389–92.

Lacey, A. R. *A Dictionary of Philosophy.* New York: Scribner's Sons, 1976.

Lackey, Douglas P. *Ethics and Strategic Defense.* Belmont, Calif.: Wadsworth, 1989.

———. "A Modern Theory of Just War." *Ethics* 92:533–46 (April 1982).

———. *Moral Principles and Nuclear Weapons.* Totowa, N.J.: Rowman & Allanheld, 1984.

Lakatos, Imre, and Alan Musgrave, eds. *Criticism and the Growth of Knowledge.* Cambridge, England: Cambridge University Press, 1970.

Lamont, W. D. *The Value Judgement.* Edinburgh: Edinburgh University Press, 1955.

Lanys, G. A., and W. C. McWilliams. *Crisis and Continuity in World Politics.* New York: Random House, 1966.

Lapp, R. E. "The Nuclear Power Controversy-Safety." *The New Republic.* January 23, 1971, p. 18.

Lappé, F. M., et al. *Aid as Obstacle.* San Francisco: Institute for Food and Development Policy, 1980.

Lecky, William Edward Hartpole. *The Map of Life.* London: Longmans, Green, and Co., 1921.

Ledogar, Robert J. *U.S. Food and Drug Multinationals in Latin America.* New York: IDOC, North America, Inc., 1975.

Lekachman, Robert. *Economists at Bay.* New York: McGraw-Hill, 1976.

Lerner, Abba P. "Should We Break Our Biggest Monopoly?" *Bulletin of the Atomic Scientists.* May 1953, pp. 110–14, 150.

Levi, Isaac. *Hard Choices.* Cambridge, England: Cambridge University Press, 1986.

Levidow, Les, and Bob Young, eds. *Science, Technology, and the Labour Process.* Vol. I. Atlantic Highlands, N.J.: Humanities Press, 1981.

―――. *Science, Technology, and the Labour Process.* Vol. II. Atlantic Highlands, N.J.: Humanities Press, 1985.

Levitan, Sar A., and Clifford M. Johnson. "The Future of Work: Does It Belong to Us or to the Robots?" *Monthly Labor Review* 105:10–14 (September 1982).

Lieberman, Jethro K. *The Litigious Society.* New York: Basic, 1981.

Limerick, Patricia Nelson. "Information Overload Is a Prime Factor in Our Culture Wars." *The Chronicle of Higher Education.* July 29, 1992, p. A32.

Lindblom, Charles E., and David K. Cohen. *Usable Knowledge: Social Science and Social Problem Solving.* New Haven, Conn.: Yale University Press, 1979.

Lineberry, Robert L. *American Public Policy.* New York: Harper & Row, 1977.

Lloyd, Dennis. *Public Policy.* London: Athlone Press, 1953.

Louthan, William C. *The Politics of Justice. A Study of Law, Social Science, and Public Policy.* New York: Kenikat, 1979.

MacIntyre, Alasdair. *After Virtue.* Notre Dame, Ind.: Notre Dame University Press, 1981.

―――. "Relativism, Power, and Philosophy." Kenneth Baynes, James Bohman, and Thomas McCarthy, eds. *After Philosophy.* Cambridge: MIT Press, 1987.

―――. "Utilitarianism and Cost-Benefit Analysis: An Essay on the Relevance of Moral Philosophy and Bureaucratic Theory." In D. Scherer and T. Attig, eds. *Ethics and the Environment.* Englewood Cliffs, N.J.: Prentice-Hall, 1983.

―――. *Whose Justice? Which Rationality?* Notre Dame, Ind.: University of Notre Dame Press, 1988.

Mackie, J. L. *Inventing Right and Wrong.* New York: Penguin Books, 1977.

Majone, Giandomenico. *Evidence, Argument, and Persuasion in the Policy Process.* New Haven, Conn.: Yale University Press, 1989.

Mandelbrot, Benoit B. *The Fractal Geometry of Nature.* New York and San Francisco: W. H. Freeman, 1983.

Margolis, Joseph. "The Peculiarities of Nuclear Thinking." In Avner Cohen and Steven Lee, eds. *Nuclear Weapons and the Future of Humanity.* Totowa, N.J.: Rowman & Allanheld, 1986.

Marx, Karl, and Friedrich Engels. "The German Ideology." In Lewis S. Feuer, ed. *Marx & Engels*. Garden City, N.Y.: Anchor, 1959.

Materials Policy Commission. *Resources for Freedom*. Washington, D.C.: 1952.

Mauss, Marcel. *Sociologie et anthropologie*. Paris: Presses Universitaires de France, 1949–50.

Maxwell, W., ed. *Thinking: The New Frontier*. Pittsburgh: Franklin Press, 1983.

May, Judith, and Aaron B. Wildavsky. *The Policy Cycle*. Beverly Hills and London: Sage, 1978.

Mazmanian, D. A., and P. A. Sabatier. *Effective Policy Implementation*. Lexington, MA: Lexington Books, 1981.

Mazuzan, George T., and J. Samuel Walker. *Controlling the Atom: The Beginnings of Nuclear Regulation, 1946–1962*. Berkeley: University of California Press, 1985.

McCloskey, H. J. *Ecological Ethics and Politics*. Totowa, N.J.: Rowman and Littlefield, 1983.

McMurrin, Sterling M., ed. *The Tanner Lectures on Human Values, VIII*. Salt Lake City, Cambridge, England: University of Utah Press, Cambridge University Press, 1988.

Menke, John R. "Why the Dual Purpose Breeder Reactor?" *Bulletin of the Atomic Scientists*. June 1953, pp. 162–64.

Merton, Robert K. *Social Theory and Social Structure*. New York: Free Press, 1968.

Mesthene, Emmanuel G. *Technological Change*. Cambridge: Harvard University Press, 1970.

Metzner, Charles A., and Julia B. Kessler. "What Are the People Thinking?" *Bulletin of the Atomic Scientists*. November 1951, pp. 341, 352.

Meyer, Laurence H. *Macroeconomics*. Cincinnati: South–Western Publishing Co., 1980.

Michalos, Alex C. "A Reconsideration of the Idea of a Science Court." In P. T. Durbin, ed. *Research in Philosophy and Technology*. Vol. 3. Greenwich, Conn.: JAI Press, 1980.

Mikula, G. *Justice and Social Interaction*. New York: Springer-Verlag, 1980.

Mill, John Stuart. "On Liberty." In Mary Warnock, ed. *Utilitarianism, On Liberty, Essay on Bentham, Together With Selected Writings of Jeremy Bentham and John Austin*. Cleveland and New York: Meridian, 1968. Also in Max Lerner, ed. *Essential Works of John Stuart Mill*. New York and London: Bantam Books, 1965.

———. *Principles of Political Economy*. London: Parker, 1848.

———. "Utilitarianism." In Max Lerner, ed. *Essential Works of John Stuart Mill*. New York and London: Bantam Books, 1965.

Miller, Byron S. "Atomic Energy Act: Second Stage." *Bulletin of the Atomic Scientists*. January 1952, pp. 14–16.

Milo, Ronald D. *Immorality*. Princeton, N.J.: Princeton University Press, 1984.

Mintzberg, H. *Power in and around Organizations*. Englewood Cliffs, N.J.: Prentice-Hall, 1983.

Mitcham, Carl. "Review of *Contemporary Moral Controversies in Technology*." In *Canadian Philosophical Reviews* 7(8):312 (August 1987).

Moessinger, Pierre. *La psychologie morale*. Paris: Presses Universitaires de France, 1989.

———. "La théorie du choix rationnel: critique d'une explication." *Information sur les sciences sociales* 31(1):87–111 (1992).

Molander, E. *Responsive Capitalism: Case Studies in Corporate Social Conduct*. New York: McGraw-Hill, 1980.

Morley, John, *On Compromise*. London: Macmillan, 1923.

Moser, Paul K. *Rationality in Action*. New York and Cambridge, England: Cambridge University Press, 1990.

Murphy, Arthur Edward. *The Theory of Practical Reason*. La Salle, Ill.: Open Court, 1965.

Murray, Thomas E. "Don't Leave Atomic Energy to the Experts." *Bulletin of the Atomic Scientists*. February 1954, pp. 48–50.

Nader, Ralph, and John Abbotts. *The Menace of Atomic Energy*. New York and London: W. W. Norton, 1979.

Nagel, Stuart S. *Improving Policy Analysis*. Beverly Hills and London: Sage, 1980.

Nagel, Thomas. "Moral Conflict and Political Legitimacy." *Philosophy and Public Affairs* 16(3):215–40 (Summer 1987).

———. *Mortal Questions*. Cambridge, England, New York: Cambridge University Press, 1979.

———. *The View from Nowhere*. New York: Oxford University Press, 1986.

Nash, Hugh, ed. *The Energy Controversy*. San Francisco: Friends of the Earth, 1979.

National Academy of Sciences. *Scientific Communication and National Security*. Washington, D.C.: National Academy of Sciences, 1982.

Navarro, Vicente. "Class and Race: Life and Death Situations." *Monthly Review*. September 1991, pp. 1–13.

Nelkin, Dorothy, ed. *Controversy. Politics of Technical Decisions*. Beverly Hills: Sage, 1979.

Nelkin, Dorothy. *The Languages of Risk*. Beverly Hills and London: Sage, 1985.

Nelkin, Dorothy, and Michael Pollak. *The Atom Besieged*. Cambridge, Mass., and London: MIT Press, 1982.

Nicolson, Sir Harold. *Diplomacy*. 3d. ed. London, Oxford, and New York: Oxford University Press, 1963.

Nielsen, Kai. "Philosophy as Critical Theory." *Proceedings and Addresses of the American Philosophical Association* 61(Suppl.):89–108 (September 1987).

Nye, Joseph S. Jr. "Nuclear Power without Nuclear Proliferation." *United States Department of State Bulletin.* November 14, 1977, pp. 666–71.

———. "United States Policy on Nuclear Technology: Combining Energy and Security." *United States Department of State Bulletin.* May 30, 1977, pp. 550–54.

Oppenheim, Felix E. *Political Concepts. A Reconstruction.* Chicago: University of Chicago Press, 1981.

Oser, Jacob. *The Evolution of Economic Thought.* New York: Harcourt, Brace & World, 1963.

Palumbo, D. J., and M. A. Harder. *Implementing Public Policy.* Lexington, MA: Lexington Books, 1981.

Papathanasis, Anastasios, and Christopher Vasillopulos. "Task and Job: The Promise of Transactional Analysis." *The American Journal of Economics and Sociology* 50(2):169–82 (April 1991).

Parker, Donn B. *Ethical Conflicts in Computer Science and Technology.* Arlington: AFIPS, 1977.

Parsons, Talcott, Edward Shils, Kaspar D. Naegele, and Jesse R. Pitts, eds. *Theories of Society.* New York: Free Press, 1965.

Passmore, John. *Man's Responsibility for Nature.* New York: Charles Scribner's Sons, 1974.

Patterson, Walter C. *Nuclear Power.* New York: Penguin Books, 1976.

Paul, Ellen Frankel, Fred D. Miller, Jr., and Jeffrey Paul, eds. *Ethics and Economics.* Oxford: Basil Blackwell, 1985.

Peirce, Charles Sanders. "Abduction and Induction." In Justus Buchler, ed. *Philosophical Writings of Peirce.* New York: Dover Publications, 1940, 1955.

———. "The Fixation of Belief." *Popular Science Monthly.* November 1877, pp. 1–15.

Pennock, J. Roland, and John W. Chapman. *Privacy.* New York: Atherton, 1971.

Perelman, M. *Farming for Profit in a Hungry World: Capital and the Crisis in Agriculture.* Montclair, N.J.: Allanheld, Osmun and Co., 1977.

Perry, Thomas D. *Moral Reasoning and Truth.* Oxford: Clarendon Press, 1976.

Peterson, Ivars. "Send This Computer to Kindergarten." *Science News.* July 7, 1984, pp. 10–11.

Pierce, Christine, and Donald VanDeVeer, eds. *AIDS: Ethics and Public Policy.* Belmont, Calif.: Wadsworth, 1988.

Piven, F. F., and R. A. Cloward. *Poor People's Movements.* New York: Vintage Books, 1979.

Plall, J. "Social Traps." *American Psychologist* 28:642–51 (1973).

Potter, Nelson T., and Mark Timmons, eds. *Morality and Universality*. Dordrecht and Boston: Reidel, 1986.

Press, Frank, Leon T. Silver, et al. *New Pathways in Science and Technology*. New York: Vintage, 1985.

Putzell, Edwin J. Jr. "The Prospects for Industry." *Bulletin of the Atomic Scientists*. November 1952, pp. 275–77.

Pytlik, E. C., D. P. Lauda, and D. L. Johnson. *Technology, Change, and Society*. Worcester, Mass.: Davis, 1978.

Quade, E. S. *Analysis for Public Decision*. Amsterdam: North Holland, 1982.

Raleigh, Walter, ed. *The Complete Works of George Savile, First Marquess of Halifax*. Oxford: Clarendon Press, 1912.

Raloff, Janet. "Approaching the Age of Reason." *Science News*. May 26, 1984, pp. 330–32.

———. "Computing for Art's Sake." *Science News*. November 20, 1982, pp. 328–31.

———. "In Search of Gigalips Architectures." *Science News*. June 16, 1984, pp. 378–81.

———. "Swift Mechanical Logic." *Science News*. June 2, 1984, pp. 346–47.

Rawls, John. *A Theory of Justice*. Cambridge: Harvard University Press, 1971.

Regan, Richard J. *The Moral Dimensions of Politics*. New York and Oxford: Oxford University Press, 1986.

———. *Matters of Life and Death*. New York: Random House, 1980.

Regan, Tom, ed. *Earthbound*. New York: Random House, 1984.

Regan, Tom, and Peter Singer, eds. *Animal Rights and Human Obligations*. Englewood Cliffs, N.J.: Prentice-Hall, 1976.

Rescher, Nicholas. *Unpopular Essays on Technological Progress*. Pittsburgh: University of Pittsburgh Press, 1980.

Rhoads, Steven E. *The Economists' View of the World*. Cambridge, England, New York: Cambridge University Press, 1985.

Rich, Robert F. *Translating Evaluation into Policy*. Beverly Hills and London: Sage, 1979.

Roberts, K. H., and L. Burstein. *Issues in Aggregation*. San Francisco: Josey Bass, 1980.

Roberts, Leslie. "NIH Gene Patents, Round Two.' *Science* 255:912–13 (February 21, 1992).

Robin, Dorothy, W. Wendell Fletcher, and John A. Alic. "Bringing Superconductivity to Market." *Issues in Science and Technology*. Winter 1988–89, pp. 38–45.

Rohr, John. *Ethics for Bureaucrats: An Essay on Law and Values*. New York: Dekkar, 1978.

Rosas, Allan. "The Militarization of Space and International Law." *Journal of Peace Research* 20(4):357–64 (1983).

Rose, Arthur Edward. *Slanted News*. Boston: Beacon Press, 1957.

Rose, Richard. *The Dynamic of Public Policy*. Beverly Hills and London: Sage, 1976.

Rosen, Cory. *Employee Ownership: An Alternative to Plant Closings*. Arlington, Va.: National Center for Employee Ownership, 1982.

Rosen, Stanley. "Philosophy and Revolution." *The Independent Journal of Philosophy* 3:71–78 (1979).

Rosenfeld, Alvin. "The Jewish Reporter and the Code of Objectivity." *The National Jewish Monthly*. June 1975, pp. 22–25.

Roy, Rustum. "Technological Literacy: An Uphill Battle." *Technology Review*. November-December 1983, pp. 18–19.

Sábato, Jorge, and Raúl J. Frydman. "Latin America Goes Nuclear." *Atlas World Press Review*, June 1977, pp. 26–27.

Sagoff, Mark. *The Economy of the Earth*. Cambridge, England: Cambridge University Press, 1988.

Sandel, Michael J. *Liberalism and the Limits of Justice*. New York and Cambridge, England: Cambridge University Press, 1982.

Sayre, Kenneth M., et al. *Regulation, Values and the Public Interest*. Notre Dame, Ind.: University of Notre Dame Press, 1980.

Scanlon, T. M. "The Significance of Choice." In Sterling M. McMurrin, ed. *The Tanner Lectures on Human Values, VIII*. Salt Lake City, Cambridge, England: University of Utah Press, Cambridge University Press, 1988.

Scheingold, Stuart A. *The Politics of Rights*. New Haven and London: Yale University Press, 1974.

Schelling, T. C. *Micromotives and Macrobehaviour*. New York: W. W. Norton, 1978.

Schneider, Claudine. "Preventing Climate Change." *Issues in Science and Technology*. Summer 1989, pp. 55–62.

Schroeder D. A., and D. E. Johnson. "Utilization of Information in a Social Trap." *Psychological Reports* 50:107–13 (1982).

Schulman, Paul R. *Large-Scale Policy Making*. New York: Elsevier, 1980.

Schumacher, E. F. *Small Is Beautiful: Economics as If People Mattered*. New York: Harper & Row, 1973.

Schumpeter, Joseph A. *Capitalism, Socialism and Democracy*, 3d. ed. New York: Harper & Row, 1950.

Schuurman, Egbert. *Technology and the Future*. Toronto: Wedge Publishing Foundation, 1980.

Schwartz, Thomas. *The Logic of Collective Choice*. New York: Columbia University Press, 1986.

Schweitzer, Glenn E. *Techno-Diplomacy*. New York and London: Plenum Press, 1989.

Scioli, F. P. Jr., and Thomas J. Cook. *Methodologies for Analyzing Public Policies*. Lexington, MA: Lexington Books, 1975.

Seaborg, G. T. "Science, Technology and Development: A New World Outlook." *Science* 181:13–19 (1973).

Self, Peter. *Econocrats and Policy Process: The Politics and Philosophy of Cost-Benefit Analysis*. London: Macmillan, 1975.

Sellers, Leonard L., and William L. Rivers, eds. *Mass Media Issues*. Englewood Cliffs, N.J.: Prentice-Hall, 1977.

Sen, Amartya K. "Rational Fools: A Critique of the Behavioral Foundations of Economic Theory." *Philosophy and Public Affairs* 6:317–44 (Summer 1977).

Sen, Amartya K., and Bernard Williams, eds. *Utilitarianism and Beyond*. Cambridge, England, New York: Cambridge University Press, 1982.

Shackle, G. L. S. *Time and Economics*. Amsterdam: North Holland, 1958.

Shapiro, Michael. *Language and Politics*. New York: New York University Press, 1984.

Shklar, Judith. "Decisionism." In C. J. Friedrich, ed. *Nomos*. Vol. 7: *Rational Decision*. New York: Atherton, 1964.

Shrader-Frechette, K. S. *Nuclear Power and Public Policy*. Dordrecht and Boston: Reidel, 1980.

———. *Risk Analysis and Scientific Method*. Dordrecht, Boston: Reidel, 1985.

———. *Science Policy, Ethics, and Economic Methodology*. Dordrecht, Boston: Reidel, 1985.

Shurkin, Joel. "Can Computers Speak and Understand Natural Languages?" *The Stanford Observer*. January 1986, pp. 1, 9.

Sidgwick, Henry. *The Elements of Politics*. London: Macmillan, 1891.

———. *The Methods of Ethics*. London: Macmillan, 1874.

———. *Practical Ethics*. London: Macmillan, 1898.

Sikora, R., and B. Barry, eds. *Obligations to Future Generations*. Philadelphia: Temple University Press, 1978.

Simon, Herbert. *Models of Man*. New York: Wiley, 1961.

Simon, Yves R. *The Definition of Moral Virtue*. New York: Fordham University Press, 1986.

Singer, Marcus G. "Freedom from Reason." *Philosophical Review* 89:253–61 (April 1970).

———. *Generalization in Ethics*. New York: Atheneum, 1961.

———. "The Ideal of a Rational Morality." American Philosophical Association's *Proceedings and Addresses* 60(1):15–38 (September 1986).

———. "Is Ethics a Science? Ought It to Be?" *Zygon* 15(1):37–38 (March 1980).

———. "Moral Issues and Social Problems: The Moral Relevance of Moral Philosophy." *Philosophy* 60:10–16 (1985).

———, ed. *Morals and Values*. New York: Charles Scribner's Sons, 1977.

———. "Some Preliminary Observations on Truth in Ethics." *Philosophy in Context* 16 (1986), *Moral Truth*, pp. 11–16.

Singer, Marcus G., and Robert R. Ammerman, eds. *Introductory Readings in Philosophy*. New York: Scribner's, 1974.

Sivard, Ruth Leger. *World Military and Social Expenditures*. Washington, D.C.: World Priorities, Inc., 1985 through 1992.

Slaughter, John B., et al. *Emerging Issues in Science and Technology, 1981*. Washington, D.C.: National Science Foundation, 1982.

Smart, C. E., and W. T. Stanbury. *Studies on Crisis Management*. Toronto: Institute for Research on Public Policy, 1978.

Smart, J. J. C., and Bernard Williams. *Utilitarianism: For and against*. Cambridge, England, New York: 1973.

Socolow, Robert H. "Failures of Discourse: Obstacles to Integration of Environmental Values into Natural Resource Policy." In D. Scherer and T. Attig, eds. *Ethics and the Environment*. Englewood Cliffs, N.J.: Prentice-Hall, 1983.

Spencer, Herbert. *Social Statics or Order Abridged and Revised*. New York: Appleton, 1915.

Sporn, Philip. "How Can Private Industry Best Participate in the Development of Atomic Energy?" *Bulletin of the Atomic Scientists*. February 1951, pp. 48–50.

———. "Prospects for Nuclear Power." *Bulletin of the Atomic Scientists*. May 1953, pp. 129–34.

Stanlis, Peter J. *Edmund Burke and the Natural Law*. Ann Arbor: University of Michigan Press, 1958.

Starling, Grover. *The Changing Environment of Business*. Boston: Kent, 1980.

Starling, G., and O. W. Bashkin. *Issues in Business and Society: Capitalism and Public Purpose*. Boston: Kent, 1985.

Steiner, George A., and John F. Steiner. *Business, Government, and Society*. 3d ed. New York: Random House, 1980.

Stephen, James Fitzjames. *Liberty, Equality, Fraternity*. Cambridge, England: Cambridge University Press, 1967.

Stokey, Edith, and Richard Zeckhauser. *A Primer for Policy Analysis*. New York: W. W. Norton, 1978.

Stover, Carl F., ed. *The Technological Order*. Detroit: Wayne University Press, 1963.

Sullivan, William M. *Reconstructing Public Philosophy*. Berkeley, Los Angeles, and London: University of California Press, 1986.

Task Force of the Presidential Advisory Group on Anticipated Advances in Science and Technology. "The Science Court Experiment: An Interim Report." *Science* 193:653–56 (August 20, 1976).

Tawney, R. H. *The Acquisitive Society*. New York: Harcourt, Brace & World, 1920.

———. *Equality*. New York: Harcourt, circa 1931.

Teich, J. L. *Inventory of University-Industry Research Support Agreements in Biomedical Science and Technology*. Bethesda: National Institutes of Health, 1982.

Telkes, Maria. "Future Uses of Solar Energy." *Bulletin of the Atomic Scientists*. August 1951, pp. 217–19.

Thirring, Hans. *Energy for Man, Windmills to Nuclear Power*. Bloomington Ind: Indiana University Press, 1958.

———. "Is It Wise to Use Uranium for Power?" *Bulletin of the Atomic Scientists*. August 1952, pp. 171, 205–6.

———. *Power Production, the Practical Application of World Energy*. London: Harrp, 1956.

Thomson, Dietrick E. "Making Music-Fractally." *Science News*. March 22, 1980, pp. 187, 190.

Tribe, Lawrence. *Where Values Conflict: Essays on Environmental Analysis, Discourse, and Decision*. Cambridge, Mass.: Ballinger, 1976.

Trivers, Robert L. "The Evolution of Reciprocal Altruism." *The Quarterly Review of Biology*. March 1971, pp. 35–56.

Truman, Harry. "President Truman Answers Dewey." *Bulletin of the Atomic Scientists*. November 1948, p. 336.

Tulchin, Joseph S. "The Malvinas War of 1982: An Inevitable Conflict that Never Should Have Occurred." *Latin American Research Review* 22(3):123–41 (1987).

Tyllock, G., and R. E. Wagner. *Policy Analysis and Deductive Reasoning*. Lexington: Lexington Books, MA, 1978.

U.S. Congress. *Congressional Record, House*. May 4, 1982, pp. H1739–46.

U.S. Congress, House Subcommittee on Science, Research and Development of the Committee on Science and Astronautics. *National Science Policy*. 91st Congress, 2d session, 1970 (Washington, D.C.: U.S. Government Printing Office, 1970.

U.S. Congress, House Subcommittee on Science, Research and Development of the Committee on Science and Astronautics. *Teaching and Research in the Field of*

Science Policy—A Survey. 92d Congress, 2d session, 1972 (Washington, D.C.: U.S. Government Printing Office, 1972.

U.S. Congress, Joint Committee. "A Summary of the Joint Committee Report." *Bulletin of the Atomic Scientists.* May 1953, pp. 135–40, 144.

VanDeVeer, Donald, and Christine Pierce, eds. *People, Penguins, and Plastic Trees.* Belmont, Calif.: Wadsworth, 1986.

Volti, Rudi. *Society and Technological Change.* New York: St. Martin's Press, 1988.

Wallace, James D. *Moral Relevance and Moral Conflict.* Ithaca and London: Cornell University Press, 1988.

Wallerstein, Mitchel B. "Controlling Dual-Use Technologies in the New World Order." *Issues in Science and Technology.* Summer 1991, pp. 70–84.

Walton, C. C., ed. *The Ethics of Corporate Conduct.* Englewood Cliffs, N.J.: Prectice-Hall, 1977.

Walton, Richard E. "Social Choice in the Development of Advanced Information Technology." *Technology in Society* 1982: 41–49.

Walzer, Michael. "Response to Lackey." *Ethics* 92: 547–48 (April 1982).

Warnock, J. G. *The Object of Morality.* London: Methuen, 1971.

Warnock, Mary. *A Question of Life.* Oxford: Basil Blackwell, 1985.

Weekley, Thomas L. "Workers, Unions, and Industrial Robotics." *Annals of the American Academy of Political and Social Science* 470: 146–51 (November 1983).

Weinberg, Alvin M. "How Shall We Establish a Nuclear Power Industry in the United States?" *Bulletin of the Atomic Scientists.* May 1953, pp. 120–24.

Wells, Donald A. "How Much Can 'The Just War' Justify?" *The Journal of Philosophy* 66 (23): 819–29 (December 4, 1969).

Westin, Alan F. *Privacy and Freedom.* New York: Atheneum, 1967.

Wiener, Philip P., ed. *Charles Sanders Peirce: Selected Writings.* New York: Dover, 1958.

Wiesel, Elie. "Review of *The Blood of Israel.*" *The New York Times Book Review.* July 8, 1975, p. 5.

Wildavsky, Aaron. *Searching for Safety.* New Brunswick, N.J.: Transaction Press, 1988.

Williams, Bernard. *Ethics and the Limits of Philosophy.* Cambridge: Harvard University Press, 1985.

———. *Moral Luck.* Cambridge, England: Cambridge University Press, 1981.

Williams, Robin. "Some Further Comments on Chronic Controversy." *American Journal of Sociology.* May 1966, pp. 717–21.

Winner, Langdon. *Autonomous Technology*. Cambridge: MIT Press, 1977.

Woodgate, H. S. *Planning by Network*. London: Business Books, 1977.

York, Carl M. "Steps toward a National Policy for Academic Science." *Science* 172: 29–35 (1971).

Zinn, Walter H. "The Case for Breeding." *Bulletin of the Atomic Scientists*. June 1953, pp. 169–75.

Zuckert, Eugene M. "Policy Problems in the Development of Civilian Nuclear Power." *Bulletin of Atomic Scientists*. November 1952, pp. 277–79.

Index